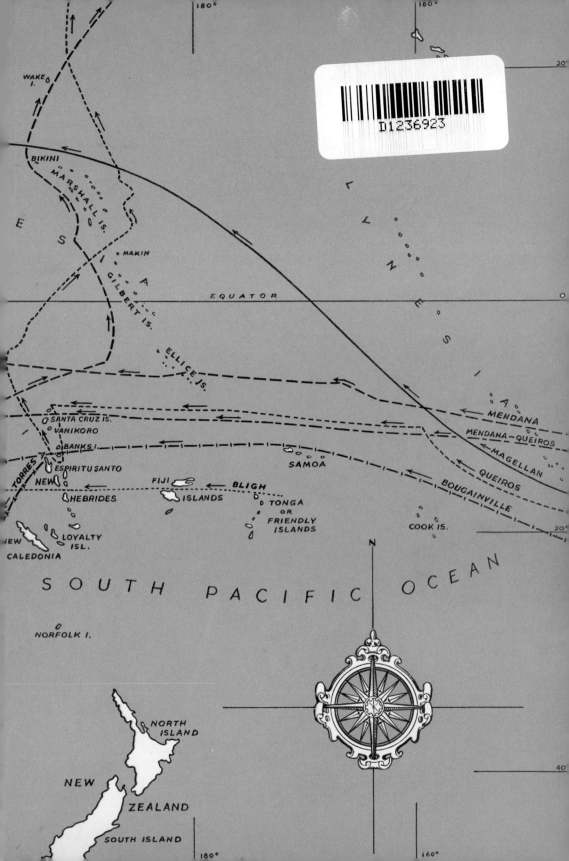

180°

160°

20°

WAKE I.

BIKINI

MARSHALL IS.

E

S

MAKIN

GILBERT IS.

A

EQUATOR

0°

L

L

N

E

S

I

ELLICE IS.

SANTA CRUZ IS.

VANIKORO

BANKS I.

MENDANA

MENDANA–QUEIROS

MAGELLAN

QUEIROS

SAMOA

TORRES

NEW

ESPIRITU SANTO

FIJI

BLIGH

HEBRIDES

ISLANDS

TONGA
OR
FRIENDLY
ISLANDS

BOUGAINVILLE

20°

NEW
CALEDONIA

LOYALTY
ISL.

COOK IS.

SOUTH   PACIFIC   OCEAN

NORFOLK I.

N

NORTH
ISLAND

NEW

ZEALAND

SOUTH ISLAND

40°

180°

160°

THE CORAL SEA

OCEANS OF THE WORLD

The Pacific Ocean   FELIX RIESENBERG

The Mediterranean   EMIL LUDWIG

The Antarctic Ocean RUSSELL OWEN

The Coral Sea   ALAN VILLIERS

BOOKS BY ALAN VILLIERS

Falmouth for Orders

By Way of Cape Horn

Cruise of the *Conrad*

Grain Race

Sons of Sinbad

Whaling in the Frozen South

Last of the Windships

The Making of a Sailor

The Set of the Sails

THE CORAL SEA

ALAN VILLIERS

WHITTLESEY HOUSE

McGRAW-HILL BOOK COMPANY, INC. New York & Toronto

THE CORAL SEA

Copyright, 1949, by Alan Villiers

Illustrations by James Fuller

Maps by Stephen J. Voorhies

PUBLISHED BY WHITTLESEY HOUSE

A division of the McGraw-Hill Book Company, Inc.

Printed in the United States of America

CONTENTS

CHAPTER ONE

THE CORAL SEA

THE DAWN that day was wild with a sickly green hue and the flung clouds flying. I had no room to heave to, for the reefs pressed all around me. The barometer fell and kept on falling. The sea rose and kept on rising, and the tumult of the wind rose with it. I could only run, and I ran on before such press of sail as I dared show. I was caught between the fanged teeth of two hundred miles of reef and the gigantic strength of the tropical cyclone.

If I could run across the face of this vast whirlpool of the air, I would be all right. All that day and night I ran. Only the best hands went to the wheel, for our little full-rigged ship was hardmouthed and inclined to yaw as she staggered in the mountainous seas. It was not her fault. The sea was not true;

it raged and threw itself in all directions, so that we constantly put out oil to keep the worst of it from smashing aboard and staving in the skylights. My ship had high bulwarks and many companionways and skylights, for the 'tween decks were lived in. So she was vulnerable. She buckjumped like a mule, and the spume filled the heated air until the dome of the heavy sky seemed close above the mastheads, and the face of the cyclone roared in the rigging.

I ran on, and by the grace of God and the excellence of my ship, got out of it. But that Coral Sea cyclone scarred the little ship and all hands—and ever since, I have found it difficult to think of that tropical area with any affection. Grim, dangerous seas! It is no cause for wonder that you daunted the ancient Polynesian navigators, kept European man from the discovery of *Terra Australis* for several hundred years, and in our own mechanized century your tremendous distances staged a grandiose struggle.

Another time, on that same voyage, in the loveliness of early morning, the mountains of Misima to the northeast and of Sudest in the east were bluish on the horizon, like sharp-edged clouds which the haze of day would soon disperse. The rollers of the South Pacific thundered on the outer edges of the reefs, though there was as yet not wind enough to set the palms in motion along the fringe of land by Duperré's beaches. In the lagoon of Bramble Haven my ship lay anchored, for I had been forced in there by a hard rain squall on the previous evening. Night navigation among the reefs and islands of the Louisiade group is unsafe for sailing-ships, without the added hazard of black rain squalls. The place is reef-littered, treacherous, ill charted, and unlit. I was being cautious, as behooves a mariner in the Coral Sea no matter what he may command, and my ship drew thirteen feet of water. But here in the sunrise we were safe; on this day the sea was friendly.

These were two moods of the huge Coral Sea, an area

bounded on the west by the Australian mainland and the tail end of that enormous reptilian-looking island called New Guinea, and on the east by the chain of islands that comprise the Solomons, the New Hebrides, New Caledonia, and the Loyalties. Ordinary maps give little impression of the extent of this sea, which is but a small segment of the western areas of the Pacific Ocean. But the northern boundaries of the Coral Sea would, if superimposed upon a map of the United States, extend from New York City to the Rocky Mountains in Wyoming, and its southern boundaries would reach to the mouth of the Rio Grande, while its eastern islands would extend roughly from Miami to the coast of southern New England. In all, its area of a million and a half square miles is almost half that of the United States. On that superimposed map the Louisiade Archipelago would lie south of Lake Superior.

Even when you have crossed down the gray Atlantic from England to Patagonia, fought around the Horn, and beaten through the emptiness of the South Pacific to the first string of islands, the distances of the Coral Sea are unbelievable if you have been reared on the flat school maps of Mercator's projection. Each time I sail this sea I am impressed anew. Here at Bramble Haven, on an island too small to appear on ordinary maps, was a lagoon forty miles square, but even the collection of islets around it seldom appears.

I had landed on the cays of the Duperré, for we were short of firewood. In the trees, pigeons were cooing but we saw none of them. Over the middle of the woods two large eagles were hovering. The golden beach was full of crabs of every size and variety; in the translucent water close by, three young tiger sharks swam, looking for prey. Once we saw the tracks of a small animal which might have been a cat, and might not. There were many marks of turtle which had come up from the sea to lay their eggs, and here and there an upturned calabash on the sand, with the remains of a fire beside it, showed where there had been a native feast. There were no natives about just then. The islets were quiet except for the surf breaking on their weather sides: the huge lagoon was silent, like the slow-growing protoplasm of a great atoll, which had been countless thousands of years in the forming and which for countless thousands would continue its patient growth.

The Duperré islets were raised only a few feet above the surface of the sea. They were no more than sand cays, to which some coconuts and a little undergrowth clung precariously, and in the interiors were tracts of marsh. On the reef there was another islet, a more livable place, called Punawan, where birds and lizards were abundant. As we walked across the beach, geckos and skinks crawled into the undergrowth, for these small lizards do not care for man. In a clearing was a grass hut, and the geckos scurried on the inside of the sloping roof. The approaches to the hut were barred by the *tabus* of one of the secret societies with which all the New Guinea islands abound—perhaps the DUK-DUKS, racketeers who "protect" the gardens of those who contribute to their funds, or the Bull-roarers, whose only roaring is done with a stick whirled on the end of a string, but whose power is great. On Punawan the principal *tabu* was a string of the dried skins of turtle eggs, stretched between the trees. No native would dare to pass the mark of any *tabu*, which in the guarding of property at least serves some purpose. The grass hut was obviously the rendezvous of turtle hunters and copra collectors from nearby larger islands. A dugout canoe belonging to them lay in the undergrowth, carefully screened against the great heat of the sun. The hut was comfortable enough inside, though simply constructed of a few boughs and some thatching of the coconut palm. The floors were covered with mats, and there were some sleeping mats besides. There was a small, rough table, made of twigs, and a much-used signal drum stood in one corner. On the trunk of a large tree nearby, many natives had cut their names in rough English characters, which looked strange with the lengthy outlandishness of the primitive names.

On the way to the beach going back, the youngest cadet came upon a skull lying bleached in the sand. It was small, perhaps a woman's or a child's. But how had it come there? Cannibalism, perhaps? It is not long since the islanders of the Louisiades were ferocious man-eaters. I remembered that on nearby Rossel Island the ship *St. Paul* had gone ashore in just such a black squall as forced me into Bramble Haven. She was carrying three hundred coolies from China to Queensland. They survived the wreck, and the master set off by lifeboat to bring them aid. By the time he returned, every Chinese had been killed and eaten by the wild men of Rossel, to whom the sea had never brought a more abundant meal.

I picked up the skull and took it aboard; and when the breeze rose with the morning sun, weighed anchor, and stood on toward Samarai, the port of entry in those parts. I was bound for the Louisiades in general and the island of Sudest in particular, to land some prospectors there to look for gold: but the law required me first to go to Samarai, which was to leeward. It was not my wish that I was sailing in those waters, which are hazardous to a full-rigged ship and wearying to the navigator. I conned carefully from the topgallant masthead, observing the precaution of keeping the sun behind me, and the niggerheads of coral that rose everywhere in the lagoon had my heart in my mouth more than once, for there seemed no way past them. From aloft, the water was lovely with shades of green and a profusion of colors from the growing coral; but I was looking for blue water, for the dark shades which would tell of deeper water and a safe way out to sea. Off a mangrove swamp the sea darkened, but this was only the treacherous discoloration of mangrove mud. Below me, sharks swam with all the accustomed languor of those hateful fish;

once a giant ray scuttled off when the shadow of the ship fell
upon him. I sailed out through the northwest entrance of the
lagoon, and all day, sounding from the chains, ceaselessly
alert, sailed through a sea of mirage and treachery, seeking
safe passage toward Samarai.

I had the latest Admiralty charts, but that for the area of
Bramble Haven and the Conflict group nearby bore a large
label "No Survey of These Waters." In smaller type, and by
no means so certain, was the phrase "Trading Vessels Report
Clear Passage Along This Line." This indicated a pecked line
on the chart somewhere between the Conflicts and Long Reef.
But how convert a pecked line on a chart into the track of a
ship in the sea? And, like as not, the trading vessels drew five
feet. The mirage of the noon sun set the mangroves and the
coconut palms of all the cays ashimmer; shoals of fish gambol-
ing in the water looked for all the world like coral reefs where
no reefs should be; the haze had robbed the horizon of the
mountains of the volcanic islands, just when bearings from
them would have been of use. The wind came in cat's-paws or
in heavy squalls, accompanied by blinding rain. The lead was
useless, though I had good men sounding in the chains. A
hundred-fathom line would show no bottom there within
half a cable of a wretched reef. I cursed the waters of the Coral
Sea and all its islands—not for the first time nor the last!

All this, as the reader has probably suspected, took place
before the Coral Sea became a familiar name to millions of
Americans, before the sea and air armadas of the United States
and Australia fought it out with the Japanese over a wild and
hitherto little-known area of the earth's surface. Half a decade
later the Coral Sea sprang into prominence as the place where
the encroaching Nipponese had their first setback, when their
ships were blasted from the air in an action which will go
down in history as the Battle of the Coral Sea.

After that, for a few brief years, these remote and dangerous waters, lying under the sun and the squalls of the tropics, carried more ships than in all their previous history. Invasion fleets moved through them. Vital supply lines were established across them and around their fringes. Homeric battles were fought on the beaches and in the hot, malarial swamps of their islands. In two years, more was learned of the region than had been learned in the previous two hundred.

But the war of 1941–1945 passed on, and with its passing the Coral Sea was left once more a backwash in the affairs of men. Its reefs, its atolls, its cyclones, and its humid heat remained. In the war with Japan all vessels were powered; their navigation was a matter of plotting a safe course and keeping to that. The result was that, away from the few used lanes, much of the area was as undisturbed by the keels of ships as it had been in the days of sail or in the previous aeons of outrigger canoes.

In this prewar voyage, when at last I reached Samarai I had to beat back again and then fight my way out of the length of the Coral Sea. My next port of call, after the Louisiades, was to be Tahiti, which lay 4,000 miles to windward, through the trades. I beat for six dreadful weeks, fighting always against the southeast trade wind, which was forcing me against the Barrier Reef; and against the sets and the currents, which were driving the ship the same way. For forty days and more the Coral Sea was a nightmare, a reef-filled backwash of the misnamed Pacific Sea, where all things were adverse and a full-rigged ship had no right to be sailing. The year was 1936; it might have been 1836 for all the use most of the charts were. Even the Admiralty sailing directions abounded in such vague information as that such and such a reef "was seen from the ships *Claudine* and *Mary* in 1818, and appeared to be a southerly continuation of the reefs seen by Mr Ashmore, commander of the ship *Hibernia,* in 1811." Good Lord, I thought, as I thrashed my poor ship to wind'ard under a press of sail and

wore her round in rising wind at the end of every watch, often
twice a watch, has no one been here since? Those ships were
vessels of the Honourable East India Company, engaged to lift
convicts and troops to Sydney from the United Kingdom and
forced into the Coral Sea later while on passage toward China
for homeward freight. I kept a good lookout for the reefs
seen by "Mr Ashmore, commander of the ship *Hibernia*," and
wondered which of us spent more sleepless nights, for at any
rate he had a fair wind of the southeast trade, being bound
north, and was not bothered by charts full of *vigias* and other
rumors. A *vigia* is a reported reef, or shallow patch, or a mere
discoloration of the water, which there has not been a chance
to survey. There are more *vigias* in the Coral Sea than in all the
rest of the navigable waters of the globe.

"A great number of these doubtful dangers is reported from
whaling vessels," states the Admiralty volume of sailing directions for the area, and it is too polite to mention that, if there
was a spout in sight, the whalemen had only the vaguest idea
of where it was. As though there were not enough real reefs—
most of them nightmares rising steeply from the ocean bed
with no possible warning of their proximity—no part of the
ocean produces more mirages of reefs, and queer phenomena
which give the appearance of breaking water or of shallows
where no shoaling exists. The reflections of unusually white
clouds; discoloration caused by drifting fields of the curious
confervoid algae which seamen call sea sawdust (actually a sort
of dust often lying thickly upon the sea); the white scum
from the queer Fijian *balolo* which appears upon the reefs of
those islands precisely between the hours of 0300 and sunrise
for two days in November of each year, and drifts away before
the trade wind and its currents, to spread far into the corners
of the Coral Sea—all these have alarming reeflike characteris-
tics, seen from a wandering ship. Each of them, probably, has

added half a hundred *vigias* to the charts, and many years of laborious research will be required to remove them.

My track out of the Coral Sea upon that memorable voyage is before me now, as I write in a quiet corner of the firm land ten eventful years afterward. It is a twisting, writhing track, like the escape of a tormented thing. For four days there are pecked lines, while I fought a cyclone which was trying to hurl me toward the Great Barrier of Australia, and lack of sun and stars gave no chance of establishing accurately where the ship might be. Again and again the track comes within a mile or two of some dangerous reef or series of reefs and turns away again, always seeking the open sea. At one spot I got upon the reef, and it was touch and go whether the ship would ever get off again. But we carried out anchors and, by prodigious labor, managed to refloat her. She was well bulkheaded, with plenty of watertight compartments. She was built of Swedish iron, and by the grace of God, and her own strength, suffered no grave damage on that occasion, though the savage winds of the cyclone had badly strained the rigging and my boy crew was almost worn out. I beat at length down to Sandy Cape, on the coast of Queensland south of the tropic's edge. By that time the weight of the trade wind had gone, and I could sail in variables toward Lord Howe Island, to refresh my crew.

Among seamen and geographers, the limits of the Coral Sea are not sharply defined, though they are laid down with fair precision in the Admiralty sailing directions. The *Australia Pilot*, Volume III, describes the Coral Sea as "that part of the Pacific Ocean off the east coast of Australia between the parallels of Sandy Cape and Torres Strait. It may be considered as bounded north-eastward by part of New Caledonia, a line thence to the Louisiade Archipelago, and part of the southern coast of New Guinea. The western boundary is formed by the Swain reefs on the Great Barrier Reef." This narrow definition would omit much of the area generally included, for usage has embraced, in the term Coral Sea, most of the waters of Melanesia.

Melanesia—the "black islands"—is the inner line of islands, many of them very large, spreading round the continent of Australia. There is an outer line which is formed of the atoll groups of Micronesia—the small islands—and western Polynesia. When I was a child at school in Australia, this area used to be known as Oceania: with New Zealand, as well, it was called Australasia, until the New Zealanders objected. They were not, they said, Australasians. They were New Zealanders. I don't recall that anyone ever asked the Melanesians how they wished to be described. The few I ever saw in mainland ports were generally called Kanakas.

The islands of Melanesia begin at New Guinea and make a wide, imperfect arc toward the north end of New Zealand. They include the Bismarck Archipelago (of which the chief islands are the volcanic New Britain and New Ireland), the Solomons, Santa Cruz, the New Hebrides, and New Caledonia with its neighboring group, the Loyalties. To the east of the New Hebrides lies the Fiji group, larger than the Hawaiian Islands and just as interesting. Half the colored inhabitants of the eighty inhabited islands of the Fijis today are Indian; but the original inhabitants are Melanesians. Until the Japanese war the islands of Melanesia were of comparatively minor importance in world affairs, and few persons outside Oceania had ever heard of Guadalcanal or Vella Lavella, Savo or Santa Cruz. In Melanesia the sea was rich and the land was comparatively poor: other tropic areas lent themselves more readily to development and exploitation. Atolls look beautiful and produce remarkably little. Less than a fourth of the land in the volcanic islands was of any use. Melanesia had no history, properly speaking. We know merely the story of its discovery

The Coral Sea

by the European and the treatment which the inhabitants received from foreigners. The Melanesian was fierce and often also a cannibal. He fought back furiously, when he could, against the white marauders. His corner of the Pacific remained in isolation longer than most of the rest of that ocean, and he himself had a bad deal from most Europeans for at least two centuries.

Yet there are islands in Melanesia as interesting, and in their own way as colorful and adventurous, as any in the world. Consider, for a moment, the great darkness which is New Guinea, which after Greenland is the largest island on the globe. When I was a child, not far from New Guinea, the figure of the wild man from Borneo was one to stir the imagination, to conjure up visions of an exciting land full of mystery and strange romance. Wild men from New Guinea were too numerous to be considered, and wilder men in Malaita and elsewhere in the Solomons were still hitting Europeans on the head and eating them when opportunity offered. Yet no one told me the stirring stories of these islands. The whole area of Melanesia was referred to vaguely as the "Islands," where ne'er-do-wells went off beachcombing (whatever that was; it sounded a pleasant occupation to me at the age of ten) or perhaps to fossick in mountain streams for gold and die of fever. Relations who went to the "Islands" were written off. More Australians wanted to go to Europe, 14,000 miles away, than ever dreamt of visiting New Guinea and the island groups outside their own front door. Bananas came from the Fiji Islands (until a prohibitive tariff stopped them); copra came down from the Solomons and New Hebrides for the soap works in Sydney; chrome ore and the like dull stuff came in from New Caledonia, and phosphate rock for the farmers was unloaded from remote places called Nauru and Ocean Island. We were asked for our pennies for the missions, in

Sunday school, and I wondered vaguely what good the money would do the queer Kanakas.

New Guinea is a world unto itself. Great mountains, some of them more than thirteen thousand feet in height; huge areas of impenetrable swamp, especially in the west, and enormous rivers are all to be found there. Gloomy mountains hiding gold and strange tribes, some of them pygmies; tremendous forests in which the lovely bird of paradise flaunts its gorgeous hues (so sought after that now it is a forbidden article of trade to Europeans, lest the species die); much of its three hundred and twenty thousand square miles consists of exceptionally difficult mountain terrain, swamp, and the odd fertile plateau. The climate near sea level is hot and moist always, with a mean temperature of about 80 degrees Fahrenheit. Much of it knows no cool season, and rain may fall the year around. The annual rainfall on the northeast coast is anything from eight to thirteen *feet*, not inches.

No one used to go up in the mountains, save the savage hill tribesmen who lived there; but the Japanese changed that when they sought to cross the Owen-Stanley range of mountains and to attack the administrative town of Port Moresby, on the Gulf of Papua, from the north. More Australians and Americans now have trekked the wild New Guinea hills than otherwise would have gone that way throughout the next century; it would be difficult to find one who recalls the experience with pleasure. New Guinea was a hellish place to fight in, to Japanese, American, and Australian alike. The farther west the fighting, the worse it was. In much of Dutch New Guinea, which is the whole western part of the great island, the climate is most unhealthful for Europeans. Skin diseases are rife; the malarial mosquito is found even as high as 2,000 feet; the natives suffer from beriberi, elephantiasis, horrible skin diseases, syphilis, and pneumonia. In the dank grass, leeches

abound, and the deserted and overgrown plantations, relics of
the war, teem with the mite which spreads scrub typhus. "The
country," states the official guide, without undue candor, "is
not at all suited for the residence of Europeans." Dutch New
Guinea, to this day, is probably, in its interior, one of the least-
known areas of the globe.

That part of New Guinea which fronts the Coral Sea is
somewhat better, though here also there are great mountains
and immense marshes, and the network of creeks and swamps
about the mighty Fly River is a humid and unhealthful maze.
The whole area of Torres Straits, which separates New Guinea
from the north of Australia, is a labyrinth of reefs and shallows which the silt from the Fly, flowing into the Gulf of
Papua, does much to discolor. The island groups to the east
of this part of New Guinea are interesting and important,
though navigation among them, because of poor charts, strong
tidal streams, uncertain winds, and frequent poor visibility, is
inordinately difficult even for large powered vessels. Here lie
the great groups of the Louisiades, the D'Entrecasteaux, the
Trobriands (famous for their canoe seamen and their gardens), Misima, and Sudest, where much gold has been found.
With the exception of a few low coral islands, most of these
groups are rugged and high. Some are partly volcanic. In New
Britain, to the north, a sudden outburst of the volcano by
Rabaul harbor killed 600 persons and all but ruined the port
in 1937. Much of New Britain and New Ireland have the
luscious beauty of the romantic South Seas; but on the whole,
Melanesia is no place to look for a tropic paradise. If the appearance of any such is found, residence will quickly dispel
the illusion.

Pointing southeast, the two lines of the Solomon Islands
head away from New Ireland 900 miles into the Pacific; it
would take a native canoe the best part of a month to make the
passage of the islands, if any islanders felt brave enough to

undertake the voyage. The sea about them is properly called the Solomon Sea, though I have never heard the term in use. The northernmost of the Solomon Islands is Buka, which can be seen forty miles away on a clear day. On my circumnavigation with the *Joseph Conrad* from 1934 to 1936, I spent some time in the lagoon at Nissan between New Ireland and Buka, and natives from both places came across in big canoes to visit the ship and exchange produce for stick tobacco. On a clear morning in Nissan, which is a low atoll, I could see the mountains of both New Ireland and Buka, and, on an exceptional day, of Bougainville besides. I did not go to Buka, for the island had a bad name, both for its reefs and the alleged treachery of its inhabitants.

Bougainville, named for the famous French discoverer, is the largest of the Solomons. Its mountains rise to 10,000 feet and more, and much of it is covered with dense jungle. There are several active volcanoes. "The natives are strong and vigorous and tribal fighting still occurs," says the sober *Admiralty Pilot*. Some of the terrain on Bougainville defied even the efficiency of American construction men during the war, and the hot and steamy coastal jungle was extremely trying. From Bougainville the rest of the main islands in the group extend in a double line, the northerly including the large islands of Choiseul, Ysabel, and wild Malaita, which to this day is one of the toughest places in the world. The southerly group includes Vella Lavella, Gizo, New Georgia, Pavuvu, Guadalcanal, and San Cristoval, with the unspoiled Bellona and Rennell islands well to the south.

Between these two lines, and beyond them to the north, lie other islands, most of which are high and rugged, and surrounded by fringing reef. There is an outer arc of atolls reaching up toward the Line. Here the Carterets and Ontong Java are especially interesting, and not alone because these are Polynesian outposts in a Melanesian sea. The Polynesians of

Ontong Java are excellent seamen, as they would have to be to find such a place on their canoe voyages. Like most atolls, Ontong Java produces little save the coconut. There is much intercourse between the atoll and the Solomons ports, though the nearest is several hundred miles away.

Rennell Island, a hundred miles south of Guadalcanal, is one of the finest examples of the raised atoll to be found in the Pacific. The whole island is composed of coral limestone. Owing to its remoteness and lack of trade, Rennell is one of the least visited of the Pacific islands, and native life here has gone on even into the late 1940's almost undisturbed. An enlightened administration bars the island to the odd wanderer (though Irving Johnson, with the schooner *Yankee*, paid a brief visit in 1938). As recently as the 1930's the Rennell Islanders killed some missionaries sent to "convert" them; since that time their chief visitors were probably Japanese luggers, making clandestine calls on the way to the *bêche-de-mer* fisheries of Indispensable Reef. The Japanese were indefatigable and unwelcome exploiters of the sea wealth of the southwest Pacific long before their country went to war; their charts of the area were the best, and their knowledge most extensive. But except for some interesting clubs and spears, it is doubtful if they got much out of the Rennell Islanders.

One of the strange things about this unusual island is the fact that the inhabitants, with their great mops of fuzzy hair, look like Melanesians, speak a sort of Polynesian dialect, are light copper in color, and have only recently emerged from the Stone Age. In the interior is a lake 20 miles long by 6 miles wide, on which are many canoes with sails made from the pandanus leaf. The islanders live on the produce of their gardens (mostly yams and taro), some fruit, and fish out of the sea. Rennell is only 1,500 miles from the great port of Sydney, in Australia; yet in 1948 it remains much as it must have been in the time of Cook, Bligh, and Bougainville.

Beyond the Solomons, past Santa Cruz and Vanikoro, are the New Hebrides to the south. Here again the principal islands extend in two lines, though much shorter than the Solomons. The best known are perhaps Espiritu Santo and Malekula. Santo, as the first is familiarly known, was mistaken by the Portuguese Queiros in 1606 for the mainland of the great new continent of the South Seas, the fabulous *Terra Australis,* and Queiros sailed off believing firmly he had found a mainland. Malekula rivals Malaita, in the Solomons, as an abode of fierce, intractable savages. The island is large and mountainous, hot, humid, and unhealthful, rich in tropic forests and in fields of study for the hardy anthropologist, who, indeed, can still find much of value and great interest throughout Melanesia. In parts of the New Hebrides pigs are as important as most humans—more important than many.

All the New Hebrides are under an Anglo-French condominium, which is sometimes referred to as a "pandemonium" by the less kindly of the white inhabitants. There are in all some eighty islands and countless islets and small reefs. There are three large volcanoes and several excellent harbors. Though New Hebrideans formerly supplied the recruiters of the South Seas with much of their labor, for many years labor supplies have been inadequate in the group, and many Tonkinese have been imported—just as Indian coolies were brought to Fiji, and Chinese to the guano islands.

The sort of thing which adds to the navigational difficulties of the Coral Sea area was an eruption at the lovely island of Tanna, in the New Hebrides, where what had been an excellent harbor was suddenly raised sixty feet, so that ships could no longer use it. The place was Port Resolution, so named by Captain Cook, who thought highly of it. The eruption lifted the whole southeastern end of the island.

Northeast of the New Hebrides are the Banks Islands, a volcanic and exceedingly fertile small group populated by

Polynesian sailors who roamed the Pacific far and wide, long
before any European sailed there. Southwest of the New
Hebrides are the Loyalty Islands, and New Caledonia, where
for many years the French had another Devil's Island. The
Loyalties, a chain of lovely upraised reefs, are noted for the
bitter religious war waged there in the 1880's between natives
of different sects: the islander found it impossible to accept
two versions of worship of the new God. Two sorts of new
Christians, therefore, set about each other with a far from
godly spirit, to such purpose that many were killed, both
Protestant and Catholic. The trouble arose because the islanders
were first "converted" by one church, and then, under French
influence, espoused by another. A war seemed the only way out
of their confusion, and a war they had.

New Caledonia is 700 miles east of the Queensland coast,
almost at the tropic's edge. Its inhabitants were truculent cannibals who waged guerrilla war against the occupying French
for many years. The French used part of the big island as a
penal colony. Many who were sent there were guilty of no
"crime" other than that of being socialists. Transportation
was stopped in 1894, but to this day there are still some former
convicts and many of their descendants, who are excellent
citizens of New Caledonia. The island is mountainous, rising
to over five thousand feet. The climate is among the most
pleasant of the South Seas, though the island is in the cyclone
belt. It is rich in timber and in chrome and nickel ore. Its port
of Nouméa is one of the most pleasant places in the western
Pacific. Here, French businessmen and officials mingle with the
Javanese and Tonkinese descendants of imported labor, and
some of the half-caste island girls are lovely.

All these islands of Melanesia lie south of the equator, between the Line and the Tropic of Capricorn. This is within the
area of the southeast trade wind, which blows more or less
steadily there for most of the year. Nearer the Queensland

coast the trade is interrupted in the summer months by the northwest monsoon. In Torres Strait and the Gulf of Papua— in the northwestern corner of the Coral Sea—the southeast trade blows from April until the beginning of November, after which there are variables and calms until the northwest monsoon sets in during December, lasting until March. Then there is another period of variables and doldrum conditions— rain squalls and light, fluky airs—until April. A monsoon is a season, not necessarily a wind. During the northwest season the wind might blow from any point of the compass, but the weather comes from the northwest.

If the monsoon is a season, the cyclone of the Coral Sea is a tropic hurricane, a savage, whirling storm of the kind familiar in the tropical and subtropical parts of the western sides of all the great oceans, save the fortunate South Atlantic, where they are unknown. A Coral Sea cyclone is a West Indies hurricane by another name, and it is a disturbance to be avoided, a whirlpool of violent wind moving along a well-defined arc toward the coast of Australia. So numerous are these damaging onslaughts that the Australian government maintains a station on the lonely Willis group, in the heart of the Coral Sea, to give warning.

If, in this age of steam, the cyclones can do great damage, drive ships onto reefs, or send them to the depths, it is no wonder they were a constant threat to the primitive but uniquely skilled Polynesians, who for so many years skimmed the seas there in their curious craft.

CHAPTER TWO

THE INDUSTRIOUS POLYP

OF ALL the astonishing creatures in the teeming marine life of the Coral Sea, the industrious polyp is surely the most amazing. Alongside the friendly humpback whale and the squid-eating sperm, which also thrive there, he is nothing but a pinhead; but in one place alone the remains of quadrillions of his kind have left a reef zone 80,000 square miles in extent and nearly 1,300 miles long. This is the Great Barrier Reef of Queensland, the largest and most interesting of its kind in the world. This vast maze of coral is formed from calcium carbonate, or lime, which the anthozoan polyp has drawn out of the sea. All ocean sea abounds with lime, and the coral polyp thrives elsewhere, notably in the Red Sea, the East and West Indies, and in the warm waters of the South China Sea.

He has been dredged from 700 fathoms down, 30 miles off-shore, in the East Indies. He built Zanzibar Island, and Pemba, off the east coast of Africa; he raised a thousand atolls up and down the tropic lengths of the Pacific and the Indian oceans. But in the Coral Sea he is the first citizen. There he has his kingdom, and the results of his industry lighten the ocean, and darken the charts.

A polyp is a sea animal of low development, a sort of sea anemone, related to the jellyfish. Unlike many jellyfish, the polyp ordinarily does not move. It likes to live in colonies, clinging to the whited skeletons of trillions of its kind. It has no means of locomotion. It cannot see or hear; it has no heart or veins, no lungs or gills, and nothing of a brain. It is, indeed, nothing but a simple sac, open at one end and squatting on the skeletons of its kind at the other. Round its mouth wave a band of minute tentacles which seize upon such tiny things as have the misfortune to drift against them. These tentacles can draw in its food to the mouth and so to the digestive space inside. This one space serves for everything; it is stomach and all other organs; and the indigestible remains of food are voided through the opening by which they came in. The lowly polyp thrives on mutilation, like Hydra, the multi-headed snake. Any part which is cut off becomes another polyp, ad infinitum, and anchors itself to set forthwith about its lifework of leaving more limestone to help build a reef.

Though the limestone which remains when the polyp dies is usually described as its skeleton, it is actually a sort of cup or seat in which the little animal lives. Examine any fragment of coral which has not been destroyed, and you will see that it is full of these distinctive cups. The limestone is not bone, in the sense that more highly developed organisms produce or need such solid framework. It is a secretion outside the body of the animal; from first to last the polyp does very well without a skeleton, in the real sense of that word. Just why he should produce limestone at all, it would be difficult to say, except that perhaps he requires a place to live. Many other sea animals have the power to take calcium carbonate out of the sea and make use of it. The oyster and the clam use it for their shells, and without it the lobster and the crab would be defenseless, for it forms the reinforcement of their hard outer shells. The Coral Sea is one vast factory for the recovery of lime from the ocean, and its conversion into reefs and, subsequently, islands. Though many of the islands there—all the larger ones—are lush, exuberant masses of mountain and jungle, none is without its barrier or its fringing reef. On many of them, coral limestone is found upon the hills, a thousand feet and more high, where obviously the earth's crust has moved and thrown what once was well below the surface high into the light of day.

Your scientist will tell you that the coral polyp dies when he reaches the surface, or even before. But how do so many reefs break surface? How are so many islands—not only atolls and atollons—formed of coral limestone? The explanation sometimes given—that the polyps have built upon the lips of extinct craters beneath the sea which have subsequently been raised—will not do, for even in the waters of New Ireland, New Britain, and the northern Solomons there could scarcely be so many craters without the earth blowing itself to pieces. (There is, of course, the old yarn to the effect that the moon is the earth of the Pacific bed, flung out in some ancient, great eruption— an obvious misconception, for even the vast area of the Pacific could not provide a moon.) Certainly in the area of the Coral Sea there has been much raising and lowering of the ocean bed, for much of the earth's crust there is faulty. Many reefs have doubtless risen upon old craters and sunken hills, and many more thrive upon the submerged continental shelf of northeast Australia. The coral-producing animals require warm, comparatively shallow waters; yet they have also been found at great depths, and many reefs—far too many—rise suddenly on the ocean bed from enormous depths. The layman is left to conclude that there must have been a tremendous raising and general changing of earth-crust levels, and not only in the region of the Coral Sea.

An elevated coral reef of itself will not form land, in the useful sense of earth in which plants and trees may grow, but when once the surface of the sea is broken, the obstruction which emerges will act as a trap for all drifting things, fragments of coral broken by the sea's action from other reefs, seeds, driftwood, coconuts, trees. The quantity of drifting material loose in the sea in some tropic waters is almost incredible, especially in the neighborhoods of great rivers like the Fly in New Guinea and the Barito in Borneo, after the rains. Clumps of bush and trees washed from the riverbanks drift far out to sea, to fetch up with their vegetation—and sometimes insects and even birds and animals—upon any reef that chances in their way. In the waters of the East Indies and round New Guinea I have many times sighted such drifting plots, some of which were almost floating islands. Debris from them, spread by the currents and blown before the winds, helps form new land.

Slowly, slowly, through the aeons, a new island grows, despite the onslaught of the sea: what is washed from one will help to build another, in an area where reefs abound. Sand becomes soil; soil sustains life; the coconut and the pandanus grow, and the wiry pine. The fragment of cay becomes an islet and then an island, while to windward still the polyp grows and its tiny tentacles wave in the sea, searching for prey. The turtle comes and lays her eggs; migrating birds find a new port of call to rest them on their flights; crabs come from nowhere, and after them that other useless denizen of too many tropic islands, the ubiquitous rat. Wandering natives, perhaps blown out to sea, while fishing from another

island, or forced from their home atoll by near starvation, in
due course come upon the new land and add a minute shell to
the grid of their stick chart to indicate its position. It might
offer only a few coconuts and a base for fishing; no sand cay or
islet can sustain much life, and even an age-old atoll is a poor
domicile.

A coral island, properly called, is formed usually by the
development of a sandspit on a coral reef, and in its early stages
it may be far from stationary, for the spit moves with the
change of seasons. An *atoll* is formed by a strip of coral on
which are isolated cays and islands, surrounding a central
lagoon. Most of these rings of coral have breaks which permit
the entry of canoes and sometimes even seagoing ships: but
there are atolls with no break. Few, if any, support continuous
areas of anything that could be called land. They have an
average height, in the Coral Sea, of about twelve feet; mangroves and coconuts may bring this to seventy. An *atollon* is a
small atoll on the margin of a larger one. A *barrier reef* is an
offshore reef, with a deep and navigable passage between it and
the land. It may front a coast or encircle an island or group of
islands, but there is always a deep channel somewhere between
it and the shore. The great reefs off Queensland and the reef
encircling New Caledonia are good examples.

A *fringing reef* is a shelf of coral attached to the land, with
no navigable area between it and the beach. The seaward face
of such reefs is usually the highest part, and the outer edge
may be a rampart to impound the water with the falling tide.
Some islands have both fringing and barrier reefs: why some
polyps colonize the neighborhood of a beach and others gather
far offshore, no man can say. The only thing certain is that it
is not the polyp's plan. The polyp has no plan.

The Great Barrier Reef is one of the natural wonders of the
world. Not only are the various forms of coral seen here
flourishing and beautiful, but all the ocean and beach life is

exaggerated. Marine animals, elsewhere small, grow here to an immense size; those which are elsewhere drab here sport gorgeous colors. Giant starfish, often a foot across, enormous anemones, crabs of every kind, tremendous sea urchins, the succulent sea slug known as *bêche-de-mer*—all these are prolific throughout the length and breadth of the reef.

The *bêche-de-mer* is much sought as an article of diet, especially for sale in the East. It is known also as *trepang*, sea cucumber, and sea sausage, though it tastes like none of these things, and real appreciation of its gastronomic excellence is confined, in general, to those who can also appreciate birds'-nest soup. The French name is from the Portuguese *bicho-do-mar*, a sea worm, and trepang is the Malayan word for the same thing. On the Barrier Reef the *bêche-de-mer* varies in length from a few inches to a couple of feet, in color from mottled creamy white to a sort of yellowy orange, brown, and black. Some are jet black above and bright crimson below. All share the unusual ability of being able, when aroused, to eject their internal organs either *in toto* or in considerable sections. They then grow new sets, though this must surely be an irritating ability, not without hardship to the big slugs.

Turtle riding is a sport on the reef islands, though the first European who reported this was derided publicly. His name was Louis de Rougemont, and for years he was held up as a modern Sir John Mandeville, for this and other statements of plain fact. Today the spectacle of huge turtles, weighing probably several hundredweight, carrying shouting tourists of both sexes on the beaches of the better known Barrier Reef islands, is commonplace, though not inspiring. The turtles there are of three types—green, hawksbill, and loggerhead; each is abundant. You can have soup, turtle steaks, or lovely shell, just as you will. But first you must catch your turtle, and take good care he flings no corraline sand into your eyes. The old turtle may look comatose, but he is no fool. A flipperful of

sand, well directed, has kept off many an amateur jockey and
saved a turtle from many pots.

Crabs of many kinds abound—giants, pygmies, armored,
soft, soldiers, hermits, death feigners, gardeners. They grow
into splendid specimens, though all are ill tempered, as is the
habit of crabs everywhere. In the northern part of the Barrier
Reef giant clams may reach nearly five feet across and weigh
a quarter of a ton or more. Waders and divers must beware
lest they catch a foot between the shells of these giants, for the
closing of such a clam's enormous mouth could crush the
bone. Squids grow to a large size; the octopus reaches six feet
across. There are fish which breathe air and are pure amphibians
and can even climb trees. Sharks, sea snakes (all venomous),
huge eels, humpback and killer whales are to be seen, though
the larger whales give the windward side of the great reefs a
wide berth, for they are well aware of the danger of stranding
there. A whale which frequents the Coral Sea must carry in
its enormous head a great store of navigational information.
It is as dangerous for a whale to strike a reef as for a ship—
more dangerous, in fact, for ships might come off again but
the poor whale, never. The humpback is a happy whale, left
to his own devices. This is the whale with long flippers, the
female of which, when attacked, takes the young ones literally
into her arms. The spectacle of a harpooned humpback cow,
swimming along with her side streaming blood and her little
one clasped in her flippers, is a pitiful one. But neither the old-
fashioned whale hunter, from his open boats, nor his modern
counterpart, gunning from the bows of an ocean-going
steamer, spares any compassion upon whales, humpback or
otherwise.

Other mammals which frequent that area include the
dugong, another peaceful though not quite silent seagoing
beast. The dugong of the Barrier Reef grows to nine feet in
length and may weigh half a ton. He is greatly hunted for his

oil, flesh, and hide. Tradition has it that the dugong is the origin of the mermaid story; all womankind should rebel at the idea, for not even among mammals is there anything more homely. He has a face and snout like a pig. Mermaids are depicted as bewitching wenches whose lower limbs unfortunately take the form of a fish's trunk; the dugong is neither fish nor woman, but a placid and affectionate wanderer, interested only in being left alone and having his fill of sea grass. Were he not so huge he would make a good pet, for his wants are few and he is capable of real affection. This he shows toward his young and to his fellows. He makes a noise like a baby crying when he is wounded, but this does not save him.

Not all the denizens of the Coral Sea are as harmless as the tasty dugong. Who walks on coral strands had best not go barefoot, for the poisonous stonefish lurks invisible, waiting to inject venom through its sharp spike. He takes the color of the rock around him and is impossible to see: a touch of his venom may mean a lost foot, and he can cut through the rubber soles of light footwear.

Sea birds abound, and on many islands the muttonbirds arrive with Christmas, by the thousand, and honeycomb the ground with their peculiar furrow nests. The muttonbird is sometimes salted down and put in casks, though in truth his flesh is not even vaguely reminiscent of any sheep. The great albatross from the Southern Ocean does not enter the coral belt; his home is on the far south islands, such as Campbell, 500 miles beyond New Zealand, and he follows only ships which keep to southern routes. But gulls and terns of many kinds, often in clouds thick enough to darken the air, frequent the reefs.

Much of the coral forming the Great Barrier Reef is indescribably beautiful. In the translucent waters round the Capricorn Islands, not far from Gladstone, fascinating grottoes of multicolored tints and brilliant hues form wonderful

coral gardens, in which swim fish as bright in color as the coral
itself, some small, some huge. Here groper, kingfish, mackerel,
morwong, red emperor, rainbow trout, coral cod and sweet-
lip—to mention only a few—are found in abundance and provide an angler's paradise. On the reefs every loose piece—every
staghorn, every fragment of coral rock—is the hiding place
of some strange flotsam of marine life. Corals exquisite in
color and in form; miniature fish as dazzling as any Chinese
goldfish, some looking as if their eyes were garnets and their
scales turquoise, flash through the clear water of the reef pools;
deeper down, the dark shape of some lurking murderer shows
for a moment as he seizes his prey, or the soft, death-dealing
tentacles of the giant squid writhe and wave. It is all color and
profusion of diverse interest for naturalist and fisherman,
bird lover and holiday maker alike. Some of these islands on the
Barrier Reef have been made into resorts, and people come
from far and wide to visit them.

Farther north, in Torres Straits, among the islands which
are the half-submerged ridges and peaks of the ancient land
bridge that once connected New Guinea with Australia, there
are pearls. Here also the coral gardens are of great loveliness,
and turtles and dugong are found in profusion. The pearls
from the Torres Straits banks are noted for their luster, though
they are not generally considered quite so beautiful as those
from the Persian Gulf.

One of the strangest inhabitants of the Barrier Reef is a fish
called the mudskipper, which basks in the sun, breathes
through its tail, has a staring eye like a periscope on a stalk
above its head, and will drown if forced too long under water.

As the waters of the Barrier Reef and all the Coral Sea
abound with strange marine life, so also the islands, from New
Guinea to New Caledonia, offer much of interest. They are
especially rich in bird life. The bird of paradise of New Guinea
has been famous since the days of Solomon, and its glorious

plumage was an article of trade in eastern markets long before the Portuguese doubled the Cape of Good Hope. Now its usage as an ornament is restricted to those natives who have worked its feathers into their elaborate masks; no Parisian lady of fashion nor Park Avenue debutante need apply. Malays and Chinese visited New Guinea for many centuries before the European ever saw that island, in quest of the plumage of the bird of paradise and other articles of trade, and slaves. So beautiful are some of the king birds of paradise that the Aru Islanders, in the Arafura Sea off New Guinea, spoke of them as God's birds.

The New Guinea forests are alive with lories, parakeets, and cockatoos, whose shrill cries resound through the dark woods, while numerous small birds of lovely form and color chirrup and sing the day long. In New Guinea more than five hundred kinds of resident land birds have already been tabulated, and doubtless more remain unlisted: there are some hundred and twenty on the Solomons. The New Guinea birds include the flightless cassowary—a big strider of a bird belonging to the emu family—the bowerbird and the mound builder (which forms groups to build large mounds of rubbish wherein to incubate its eggs), the glossy ibis, white pelicans, hawks, falcons, eagles, owls, crowned pigeons, and more than fifty kinds of parrot.

The farther south and east one travels through the Melanesian islands, the fewer species of birds one sees, but in New Caledonia lives the strange kagu, found nowhere else.

As with birds, so also with reptiles, insects, butterflies, and moths. All these exist in profusion in New Guinea, and there are many throughout Melanesia; but the farther from the mainlands of Australia and Asia, the fewer the species. The crocodile haunts the wide rivers of New Guinea and is found in the Solomons and New Hebrides; lizards range from the big monitors (often called iguanas) to the little skink and the

clicking gecko, whose ability to walk flylike across ceilings
and roofs is of great assistance in his war on insects and mos-
quitoes. The clicking call of the gecko is familiar in island
homes as the soft-footed, thick-tailed little lizard darts for
his prey. The skink is no relation to the skunk. He lives by the
seashore, and how he got his name I do not know.

Snakes are common, more of them harmless than poisonous,
though there are death adders, whip snakes, and sea snakes
enough. In Papua, pythons are found up to twenty feet long,
but they are nonvenomous.

In the insect world the profusion of types is so great that
it is most unlikely that even the greatest expert could make an
accurate guess at their number. Any inhabitant of the islands
will tell you that there are far more than enough of the
pestiferous things, most of them with bites like gnats and some
like small, bad-tempered dogs. There are flies which should
exist only in nightmares, dreadful things with their eyes on
stalks so they can see round corners, flies with things on their
faces that look like stag's antlers: all have ravenous appetites
and are useless to man. Beetles of wondrous shades, many of
them glistening bright; butterflies larger than small birds and
of brilliant coloring; spiders as large as small bats; fireflies
several inches long—all these are as commonplace as scorpions
and centipedes, and almost as nasty. Many different kinds of
moths and butterflies await the enthusiast who is fever-free
and of iron physique and indomitable will; he will find them
in New Guinea and elsewhere in the islands. There are insects
which look exactly like pieces of twigs, and in New Guinea
and the Solomons are many of the most spectacular butterflies
to be found on earth. Some approach nearly a foot in wing-
spread.

New Guinea has already disclosed more than two thousand
different kinds of orchids, despite the fact that much of that
great island has as yet to be combed thoroughly by botanists.

But there are no orchids on the atolls, which support little save the coconut and the pandanus palms, with perhaps some casuarina trees and mangroves. It would be difficult to find a sharper contrast than that existing between the volcanic islands of the Coral Sea, and its many coral atolls, those sand cays grown upon the reefs formed of the hard calcareous substance secreted by the coral polyp for its support, defense, and habitation. The volcanic island may carry a luxuriant vegetation, lush and exuberant: in its dark woods many birds sing, and the cuscus and the flying fox live in its trees. Bandicoots, bats, wallabies, and phalangers are to be found. The atoll dweller is fortunate if he can find a pig.

Yet the atoll also has its beauty. It knows the freedom of the untamed sea. Its people may lead full lives in the sunshine, wresting a sufficiency from the abundant life of the waters around them. The dank bush of the New Hebrides, the Solomons, and much of New Guinea are depressing by comparison, though all these islands are beautiful, seen from the sea, and the life in them is varied and interesting.

CHAPTER THREE

THE PEOPLES OF THE
CORAL SEA

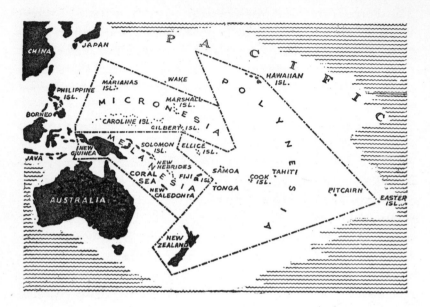

It is customary to regard natives of the Pacific islands as coming under one of three heads—Polynesians (people of the many islands), Micronesians (people of the small islands), and Melanesians (people of the dark islands). Geographers and some anthropologists have for years been labeling various areas of the Pacific with these names and placing arrows on the map to show the ways these various peoples are alleged to have come. At first they were all called Polynesians, whether they dwelt in Tahiti, Tanna, or New Caledonia: but not many years of contact with Europeans sufficed to show that there were great differences among the peoples of the Pacific.

They were derived, obviously, from the three main divisions

of all mankind: the dark, woolly-haired Negroid race whose
home was Africa, the lighter Caucasians of Europe and west
and south Asia, and the yellow-brown Mongoloid race of
eastern Asia. Just how the ancestors of any of them reached
the Pacific islands is not known, and probably never will be.
The Polynesians and Micronesians have traditions of great
voyages, and research into the legends of these peoples indicates that the Polynesians, at any rate, probably made great
migratory voyages during the last five hundred years. Both
these peoples were, and still are when given the chance, good
seamen.

It is generally accepted that they must have originated in
Asia, and that they came in their small sailing-ships against the
trade wind. In 1947 six young Norwegians drifted in a raft of
balsa logs from the coast of Peru to the more easterly islands
of Polynesia. Beyond the raft's being an interesting contribution to the postwar shipping shortage, it is difficult to see what
such a drift was expected to accomplish, for the fact that
winds and currents set that way has long been known. The
voyage was announced, at any rate on the American lecture
platform, as helping to prove that pre-Inca Indians traveled
also by rafts from South America to the South Seas.

Perhaps they did. Certainly, had they wished, they might
well have done so. Most of the available evidence, apart from a
few strange mysteries, indicates that movements of peoples into
the Pacific were all from the other side of that great ocean: but
our knowledge is limited and recent. One of the principal
"arguments" advanced by those who favor the idea of Pacific
migrations originating in the east of that ocean is the un-
doubted fact that winds and currents both favor passages
made from that side. But sailing against the wind is an ancient
art in Asia. The Arabs, the Persians, the Indians, the Malays,
and the Chinese were all experts at it. So are the Pacific
islanders today.

There seems to be general agreement that the Melanesians—really the Papuo-Melanesians—came into the Pacific by way of New Guinea, and that from New Guinea and the adjoining archipelagoes they then spread southward in an arc through the Solomon Islands, the New Hebrides, and New Caledonia. The Fiji Islands represent their furthest wandering toward the east; it is strange that they should so carefully have confined themselves to the malarial belt of the Pacific, for there is no malaria east of the 180th meridian. The people themselves have no tradition of any migratory voyages. As far as they know, the gigantic island arc they now inhabit has always been their home, and the home of their ancestors.

According to some scientists, many of them belong to a great race of seafaring people who wandered not only most of the Pacific but much of the Indian Ocean as well, and interesting similarities have been found between languages used on the coasts of New Guinea, the Fijis, the Solomons, New Britain, and New Ireland, and some of the languages spoken as far away as Madagascar, the Malay States, and southern India. It has been pointed out that this similarity of language closely follows the distribution of the outrigger canoe, and the theory has been put forward more than once that at some stage in Pacific history a race of seamen in outrigger canoes must have journeyed far and wide.

That a race of seamen wandered there is fairly obvious: but as a sailor, one hopes they knew something of other ships besides the outrigger canoe, which is an unsafe and unwieldy contraption for deep-sea voyages. If they did, there is no record of the fact. Though the coastal and river peoples of all Asia were familiar with real ships, centuries before the European, there is no evidence that the Melanesian or the Polynesian, the Papuan or the dweller of the small islands, ever built or sailed a ship. A canoe is not a ship and cannot take the place of one except with an assurance of continued good weather. For atoll hopping, it may serve; in a lagoon it is ideal. As for the alleged evidence of similarities of language, I don't know. I remember the mate of the *Joseph Conrad*, a Finn, coming to me excitedly in the lagoon at Nissan, between New Ireland and the Solomons, and pointing out some Finnish words which, he said, were used by the local Melanesians. I have heard of no expert who claims that they had the slightest connection with Finland.

The Pacific islanders, if we are frank about it, have a history that can only be guessed at: it is not my plan to add to the guessing, but I may look at what we know of their seafaring with, perhaps, a more critical eye.

The basic Melanesian (when you find him) is described as being Negroid in feature, with fuzzy hair which he often brushes outward and wears in a thick, huge mop; his color ranges from chocolate brown to deepest blue-black. His darkest hues are seen perhaps in Buka, in the northern Solomons, but in the New Hebrides he is often black enough. Papuans are not type-Melanesians, except that they are certainly very dark and inhabit a western Pacific island. Even the most casual acquaintance with New Guinea shows that it will not do to group its inhabitants under one generic term. For instance, the only thing the pygmies of parts of the interior share with the sailor-farmers of the Moresby area is that they are both natives of a place called Papua, part of New Guinea. In Papua alone there are at least three distinct types of people, who may be classified as a short Negrito type, a tall Negroid type, and a lighter colored coastal dweller, who generally has wavy instead of curly hair. In the Trobriand Islands, on Wari in the Louisiades, and on others of the New Guinea islands, there are natives who could well pass as Semitic persons: the theory has been advanced that one of the dispersed tribes of Israel may have wandered there or perhaps influenced those who did.

The short Negritos are often real pygmies. These live in the higher mountain ranges and were probably the earliest inhabitants of New Guinea of whom there is now knowledge. There is little evidence that New Guinea ever supported anything that could be called a civilization, though on the island of Ponape, in the Micronesian Carolines, there are strange ruins which may indicate that some sort of civilization flourished there before our recorded time. Queer things are sometimes dug up in New Guinea, but against any theory of comparatively recent civilization is the fact that, when first discovered by the modern European, the natives of Papua were still in the Neolithic Stone Age. They fought with stone clubs and spears and used well-polished stone tomahawks. The bow and arrow was used in some districts but elsewhere was unknown, and a coconut palm was regarded as a refuge. It provided food and drink, and missiles to be thrown down upon any assailant who tried to cut the trunk with his stone ax. To this day, many of the pygmies still shape and use the stone tomahawk, and are prepared to trade in smoked human heads.

The Papuans knew how to cultivate the soil, which is more than the aborigines of nearby Australia ever did. They grew sweet potatoes, yams, taro, sugar cane, and bananas, and they used dogs for hunting the wild pigs. On the coast they often lived in villages built over the sea, as many Moros in the Sulu Islands also do. The idea originally was for defense; the administration has encouraged the habit, for it solves most drainage problems. The pygmies often sought refuge in trees.

Many migrants bound toward the islands now included in Polynesia may have passed along the island arc of Melanesia: there are plenty of lighter strains in the blood of the dark inhabitants of the smaller islands. The light-skinned Polynesians, with straight or wavy but never fuzzy hair, splendid physique, and a highly developed culture, must surely have been able to overwhelm the Melanesians and the Papuans in their path—if they ever were in their path. It seems strange that the most highly developed and most intelligent islanders passed on to the atolls, leaving the fertility and diverse interest of the volcanic islands to a more primitive race, though they could colonize New Zealand. But that, at any rate, we are asked to believe they did: there were splendid islands in their own area of the Pacific, to be sure—the Samoas, the Friendly Islands, the Society group, and, far to the north, the Hawaiian Islands. But could they have been aware of this at the time of the great migrations, whenever that might have been? Some theorists say they doubled back, to form the truly Polynesian outposts scattered round the Melanesian islands, places such as the Banks Islands, Ontong Java, and the Carteret atolls. The Polynesians and some of the Melanesians used double canoes, lashed together, and the first-named were such daring navigators as almost to be foolhardy. An ocean passage of several hundred miles in the trade-wind zone probably meant little to them. But a fight for life at the end of such a passage, surely, must have meant a great deal.

The Micronesians are of predominantly Mongoloid origin, though they are more hybrid than most Polynesians or Melanesians. Their islands come close, in the Carolines, the Gilberts, and the Marshalls, to the fringes of Melanesia. Yet they are of a distinct type which is readily recognizable—copper-colored, comparatively thin-lipped, slight of build, often with hair as lank as the Chinese. Their culture, such as it has been discovered to be, embodies traits from both the Polynesian and the Melanesian.

The Melanesians are great gardeners and superb fishermen. Many of them can catch fish by hand. The main occupations of the men were hunting and fishing; the drudgery of gardening was normally left to the women, though the men took a great interest. Fighting was also a leading profession, and in parts of New Guinea, in Malaita in the Solomons, and Malekula

in the New Hebrides it still is. Secret societies, always confined
to males, are still an important feature of everyday life in many
parts of Melanesia, though their influence is waning. Societies
such as the Duk-duks of New Guinea and New Britain, the
bull-roarers of New Guinea, and the Qat of the New Hebrides
still practice their ancient rites as assiduously as the Elks in
Brooklyn or the Masons in Sydney, New South Wales. The
Duk-duk is a notorious "racket," based on the best Chicago
principles. One of its chief activities is to sell "protection," and
its thugs know how to deal with the unprotected. It does at
least maintain some law and order in a primitive society. Its
membership fees are high, so high that most of its members are
in debt and have to work hard to clear themselves. The fees are
raised when the membership lists become too long, possibly in
the hope that some will refuse to pay them; they provide legal
fare for a cannibal feast. Cannibalism was rife in many parts
of Melanesia until recent years, and here and there the practice
may still survive. Head-hunting—usually a low form of
miserable sneak butchery—was also fairly general.

Many of the secret societies claim to associate with spirits
in secret rites, and they do not scruple to use this "power" to
bring death and destruction to their enemies and others who
refuse to contribute to their support. Some of them really do
preserve some knowledge of the stars and the seasons, and
garden lore. But the great majority are unscrupulous and in-
genious racketeers. There were, for instance, the flourishing
members of the priesthood in the island of Tanna, in the New
Hebrides, whose specialty was spreading disease. (Curiously
enough, the natives of Tanna—which, incidentally, is a Malayan word meaning land—were accustomed to do their hair
in the manner of the priests of ancient Egypt, wearing a veri-
table head of whipcords made by growing their locks to eighteen inches in length and carefully curling them in small sections round the thin rind of a creeping plant, with the ends

trimmed and oiled. A missionary who counted such a head of hair, which was dyed red, found no fewer than *seven hundred* locks!) Tanna also had rain makers and thunder makers, fly makers and mosquito makers. The disease makers held the real power. To wreak vengeance on any islander, all they had to do was to burn some rubbish which had passed through his hands: the society had at least the effect of making the Tannese scrupulously careful about refuse, for they were most careful to collect every possible piece for burning, burying, or throwing into the sea, lest the "sacred men" get hold of it. Naturally enough, the "sacred men" took an extremely poor view of all missionaries, who interfered with their trade. They must have led an excellent life, for once it was known that they had got hold of any rubbish belonging to a family, the members were only too anxious to buy them off with as costly gifts as they could afford. These rubbish burners had so great a hold on the people that whenever a person was taken ill, it was believed that something he had discarded was being burned. If he died, it was thought that the priests were dissatisfied with the gifts offered to them. The blowing of conch shells also was part of the art, though this seems to have been merely a form of publicity.

Another custom in Tanna, at any rate until the missionaries were able to put a stop to it—and that took time—was the strangling of a chief's wives when he died. This custom seems to have spread from the nearby island of Aneityum, and the idea was that the wives would accompany their chief to the land of the departed. Most of the wives rejoiced in it, for they had a firm belief in the realities of eternity. A chief on his deathbed would address his favorite wives, "Now, who will go with me?" and it was a great slight for any wife not to receive the invitation. None refused it.

From time to time a considerable amount of nonsense is talked, and sometimes written, about the "noble savage." The cult received a great fillip from the account of Bougainville's brief visit to Tahiti, which lasted eight days. No one has professed to find much nobility about the lives of the savages in Melanesia. Until the organization of the islands by Europeans and the coming of orderly government—in most of them a recent acquisition—the natives lived narrow and frequently dangerous lives, their lot darkened by a hundred *tabus* and fears, their society ridden by a cunning and avaricious priesthood with powers of life and death, no man's authority extending beyond a gunshot of his house, no common language, cannibalism and head-hunting rife.

In the Polynesian islands there was some unity of purpose and real joy in living; there was at least a common language. But the dark peoples of Melanesia were split up in hostile isolation. Islands within sight of one another dared exchange no trade or visits, save warlike ones. The islands of Tanna, Erromanga, Futuna, and Aneityum in the New Hebrides all lie within sight of each other; yet there were different languages spoken not only on each island but in different parts of every island. There were many orators and politicians, but each harangued only his own tribesmen and was understood by no others. The common relationship with other districts was one of war, and not manly or clearly defined warfare either. Treachery walked the dank bush, and death lurked in the undergrowth. Where head-hunting was in vogue, any head would serve. To be killed meant to be eaten, in many islands. When the body of an enemy—most men were enemies—was taken, it was dressed for the oven and served up with yams for the next meal. All men went armed, and even the little boys had their tiny clubs and spears and bows and arrows. Another favorite weapon was a stone shaped like an ebony rule but twice as thick. This they threw with fatal precision up to a range of twenty yards.

But life had its lighter side, even in these islands. Night

dancing, generally lascivious to an almost incredible degree, was a frequent diversion. The men and children played with tops, kites, model canoes. They sometimes played a sort of football in parts of the New Hebrides, and hide-and-seek was a popular diversion among the Banks Islanders. The gong and drum were to be found everywhere, though rarely used for anything the European would recognize as music. Jew's-harps were used in the Solomons and New Britain, Panpipes in the New Hebrides, a sort of flute in New Caledonia. Their wants were few, and nature was prolific. The kindly coconut was the great provider, and the fruits of the earth flourished all about.

But on the whole, though isolated groups on small islands managed to live well enough, the state of savage society existing throughout Melanesia had little to commend it. A bountiful nature is poor recompense for barbarous man. As a general rule, even the white beachcombers sought the Polynesian and the Micronesian islands, when they could reach them.

CHAPTER FOUR

THE NATIVE NAVIGATORS

Beating between the lagoon of Nissan, near New Ireland, and New Guinea in a full-rigged ship in 1935, I was surprised to meet several native canoes sailing handsomely in the open sea. The southeast trade wind at the time was fresh, and there was a short, steep sea which made things uncomfortable even in my ship, a Cape Horner. There was a considerable set toward the northwest which, together with the adverse trade, threatened to embay me in a bad corner by the Lusançay reefs; the weather was trying, with rain squalls, and with so much weight in the wind at times that I was down to the forecourse and the three full tops'ls, and wondered whether I should be carrying them. Sprays drove aboard; good helmsmanship was called for, and though my vessel had proved herself an able sailer in harsh conditions through the previous fifty years, it was as much as she could do to hold her head up and go to windward.

Under such conditions I was astonished to see a skimming dish of a canoe, manned by a handful of near naked savages, come racing by. She set only one sail, and that a comparatively small one, made of matting of the pandanus leaf and shaped roughly like a small lateen. She had an outrigger out to windward, and a light platform stretched from the hull of the canoe proper to the light framework from which the outrigger hung. On this platform men and cargo were lying. The whole canoe could not have been more than thirty feet long, and even with the outrigger its beam was less than eight feet. It glided across the seas, skimming the surface, now hidden by breaking crests, now on top of them. At times the weather platform slanted steeply, and spray and spume were flying there, wetting the crew. A chance ray of sunshine turned the pandanus sail to gold, and gay white streamers flying from its foot added a yachtlike touch to the scene. In a flash, the canoe was past, the Melanesians grinning up at what, to them, must have seemed a very large ship. I wondered where she could be bound, while I admired the skill and daring of the men who manned her.

I should not have been so greatly surprised. I had sailed already, that voyage, through the Carolines almost as far as the Marshall Islands, and I knew that the Micronesians there were gallant and efficient sailors, though their canoes were then degenerate. Intercommunication over a wide area was carried on by relays of seagoing canoes until recent times, and the lateen-rigged interisland sailing canoe carried the dark mariners as far as the Gilbert and Ellice groups, and perhaps beyond. The asymmetrical double-enders of the Marianas, so shaped that the lee side is flat and the weather rounded, have been famous since the globe-circling Anson wrote of them.

Speeds of twenty miles an hour were claimed for them by
European navigators: Anson said they would lie "much nearer
the wind than any other vessel hitherto known," which was
high praise.

Yet, like many another seafaring man of European origin,
I had forgotten just how accomplished many native seamen
are.

It is a commonly accepted piece of effrontery to imagine
that all discovery was the prerogative of the white man and
that sailing skill is restricted to him. Historians speak of "finding" islands which were never lost. It is customary to ignore
completely the fact that, in the Pacific and all the East, the
white man is a newcomer. The Polynesians were making great
oceanic voyages when the European was still confined to coastal
sailing. When Captain Cook first reached the Society Islands,
a native named Tupaea had such extensive knowledge of the
islands of the central Pacific that Cook shipped him as a sort
of assistant navigating officer. Tupaea had accurate knowledge of the Society, Austral, Tuamotu, Marquesas, Cook,
Samoan, and Fiji groups, which is about as much navigational
knowledge as any man can carry in his head. When Queiros,
sailing from Peru toward the Solomon Islands in 1606, reached
the islands of Taumaco in the Duff group, not far from the
Solomons, a local chief named Tumai caused him great surprise
by the extent and accuracy of his knowledge of the islands of
the western Pacific. Tumai named over thirty islands and drew
a rough chart on the beach showing how they bore from
Taumaco.

Tumai could have gained his knowledge as the fruit not only
of his personal experience but of a strong tradition of islands
voyaging which had been handed down to him. At Taumaco,
Queiros saw ocean-going canoes hauled out under palm shades
on the beach. They could carry thirty or forty persons with
ease, and the natives said they were accustomed to voyage in

them to distant islands, including one named Manicolo (Malekula) and a "great island" somewhere to the south. They indicated the distance to Malekula by counting the number of
nights it was necessary to spend in making the passage there.

Torres, in his account of the same incident, speaks of the natives of Taumaco as "great navigators." He adds: "The vessels in which they sail are large and can go a great way. They
informed us of more than forty islands, great and small, all
peopled, naming them by their names, and telling us they were
at war with many of them."

Unfortunately, Queiros showed his appreciation of the information offered him by seizing four of the natives, to show
him where the islands lay. At this, says Torres, "they were not
much pleased."

Many other European navigators have left records of their
astonishment at the navigational knowledge and skill of the
Pacific islanders. Carteret, in 1767, was approached off New
Britain by canoes one of which he estimated to be ninety feet
long, though it was hollowed out of a single log. Matthew
Flinders was much taken with the canoes of the Torres Strait
islanders. He expressed the belief that no European sailors
could have handled their sailing canoes better than the naked
savages of Warrior Island, in Torres Strait. The fact appears
to have surprised him. The warriors of Warrior Island were
neither completely naked nor savages, in the true sense of that
term, and they had a tradition of canoe sailing that went back
at least a thousand years. Sailing, to a large degree, was their
occupation. It was also their principal means of gaining food,
their recreation (as the means of taking them to wars), and
their one link with the world they knew.

After all, an atoll is like a ship. It offers little disturbance to
the ocean winds. It is the ideal platform from which to acquire
sea lore, to study the winds and the stars. Some atolls were, in
effect, the bases of sea rovers, where they kept their canoes and

their families until they might find a better island. It was this
eternal quest of the better island that led to so many voyages
by canoe, some of the voyages great and all of them perilous,
the sagas of which live on in many an island's legend or song.

The islander was never dependent for his skill in navigation
upon such artifices as the compass or instruments or charts,
though some made use of "stick charts," made of shells and
palm fronds, the shells being islands and the palm fronds,
routes. Living so close to the sea, with a keen mind uncluttered
by other learning, he was a seaman in the true sense of that
term. Just as the aboriginal "black trader" of Australia and
the red Indians of North America are able to follow trails in
woods and over deserts which offer no evidence to white men's
eyes, so the Pacific seamen in their canoes had an encyclopedic
knowledge of the ways of the waters and the signs of the
heavens and the land. The evidence the black tracker sees is
there to see, for all who have the skill. The native has two
advantages. His power of observation has been developed
naturally, and his eyes are unspoiled.

So also with the seaman from the coral islands. He carried
his knowledge in his head, and his eyes were attuned to the
sea and the skies. His knowledge may have been limited (generally he knew only his own waters); but what he did know
was in his head always. He had no written language to bother
him. He did not overreach himself trying to know too much.
He knew a few simple things, naturally; those things sufficed
for his needs. The realities of sea life were his knowledge and
his strength. The modern European mariner, by comparison,
has managed to draw himself so far from the sea, in his big
powered ships, that the water is now merely a means to sustain
his ship afloat and to resist the thrust of the propellers by
which his vessel goes where he wills. He is almost completely
removed from the realities of the sea. Without his well-
equipped bridge and better equipped chartroom, without all

the expensive paraphernalia of instruments, radio aids, tables, nautical almanacs, and the like, many modern navigators would be as much use at sea as a child.

In the recent war, use was made of the Pacific islanders' methods of sailing and of navigation, for the assistance of those who had to undertake long voyages in lifeboats, and of airmen forced down in the sea and left to rescue themselves in rubber dinghies. For such as these, there was provided, in America, *The Raft Book,** bound in oiled silk. This was prepared by Harold Gatty, both a distinguished navigator (not only for his early round-the-world flight with the late Wiley Post) and a former sailor of the coral seas. Harold Gatty began his active sea career in an Australian three-masted schooner which sailed from Sydney to the islands. *The Raft Book* was an excellent piece of work. Birdlore, the lessons to be learned from the ocean swells and other sea movements, the use of the stars for those without instruments, the manner in which Polynesians and Micronesians went about their long canoe voyages—all these are set out in the little book. I carried a well-thumbed copy through some anxious years of the war, when my work consisted largely of making long ocean voyages in peculiar landing craft, and I found *The Raft Book* both interesting and valuable. I was never, by the grace of God, reduced to dependence on its contents. Many who found themselves adrift were much helped by the information it contained.

In a region where the wind is as steady and reasonably reliable as it is in the trade-wind zones of the Pacific during much of the year, the behavior of the ocean swells was one of the means by which the native navigator gauged his proximity to land. A break in the swell might indicate the presence, somewhere not far away, of an island or a large reef. The natives' closeness to the sea gave them a great feeling of affinity with it. It also gave them poor horizons. A coral atoll does not show

* Gatty, Harold, *The Raft Book*, George Grady Press, New York, 1943.

far, especially if there be some haze. But to the skilled eye it
shows its signs both in the sea and the sky—on the sea by the
behavior of the swells; in the sky by the reflections from the
green light thrown up by the seas breaking on the reefs.

The native seamen made considerable use of the stars and
knew the stars which passed over the islands to which they
sailed. There was no magic about the ability to navigate. Voyage making from island to island was too commonplace for
there to be much magic about it. The conduct of long journeys
to distant groups may have been entrusted to special men, or
priests, because, as specialists, they had the greater learning:
but sailing skill among the atoll dwellers was general.

"It has been recorded," says Gatty, "that accomplished
Polynesian navigators had names for 150 stars, knew their
positions, knew the position where they rose, and the times
they rose at different seasons of the year; knew which islands
they passed over, and could direct their course at sea by them
from island to island." No wonder that they had no need of
the compass: and no wonder that they had a contribution to
make, in the middle of the twentieth century, to seamen who
had become too long accustomed to reliance on manufactured
aids.

It is nonetheless a peculiar thing that the Pacific islanders,
to many of whom plenty of timber was available, never seem
to have built a ship. There is no evidence that they ever had
anything comparable with the Arab dhow or Chinese junk,
though both junks and *proas* sailed at least to western New
Guinea. Their voyages were made in canoes, sometimes double
canoes, often large single canoes with outriggers. The canoes
were frequently built up a little with washboards to keep out
the sea. Both the double canoe and the canoe with outrigger
are unsatisfactory seagoing vessels, when the material for lash-
ing is limited to creepers and coconut-fiber rope. Nor is it pos-

sible to achieve the necessary perfection in a double hull to enable the vessel so constructed to withstand all the stresses set up by the motion of the sea. In a heavy seaway the vessel built of two canoes, or of one canoe with an outrigger—no matter how large or how well secured the outrigger may be—stands an alarming chance of disintegrating. Even if it remained afloat, its least fate would be to become waterlogged, if it did not capsize. Loss of outrigger meant loss of stability. The outrigger must be to windward when the canoe is under sail, which means that the sail must be shifted end-for-end whenever it is necessary to go about. A sailing canoe is a fragile thing, no matter how well designed or admirably handled.

Consequently, the maritime achievements and the maritime history of the islanders become even more astonishing. They must have been the greatest handlers of fast vessels under sail the world has seen. It seems unfortunate that such seamen had lost all tradition of the ship, for with anything more seaworthy than canoes the sailors of the coral seas might well have made voyages back to Asia or to Europe long before the European came to them. When the European first sailed to the Pacific, his knowledge of navigation was poor. He had no means of finding longitude. He had no particular knowledge of the stars. Many of the crews were even more afraid of "magic" than the natives were, and they had just as many fears of the unknown.

Something of native sailing, on a considerable scale, survived well into the twentieth century, and it is fortunate that there is a comprehensive account of it. This is the so-called *kulu* sailing of the Trobriand Islanders and others from the islands off the eastern end of New Guinea. Because they were so remote as to be considered unworthy of the conscienceless exploitation which swept native cultures aside in the more accessible islands, the seamen of the Trobriands retained a good deal of their skill and habits. A further factor which assisted

them was the good fortune which brought their islands, and
most of the *kula* chain, under the control of a particularly enlightened and able administration for a considerable period
during their more important formative years, in first contact
with the European on a permanent basis.

The Trobriand Islands lie about a hundred miles north of
the eastern tip of New Guinea. With the reefs and cays of the
Lusançays, they form the northwestern corner of a great
system of atolls, raised coral islands, reefs, and volcanic islands
which extends eastward nearly three hundred miles and covers
some thirty thousand square miles. Within this area, in addition to the Trobriands, are the D'Entrecasteaux, Woodlark,
Louisiade, Marshall Bennett, Conflict, and Samarai groups of
islands. Until the war against the Japanese brought troops
there in large numbers, this was one of the most remote corners of the world. Away from the port of Samarai itself and
the gold workings on Misima, a few missionaries, magistrates,
and traders were the whole of the white population.

Into these waters, making his headquarters at the Trobriands, the distinguished anthropologist Bronislaw Malinowski made a field expedition in the course of the 1914–1918 war.
He found so much to interest him that he made a second expedition later, lasting some years. He spent one period of two
years constantly with the Trobrianders, learning their language and mixing with them on a free and accepted basis. He
sailed with the *lakatois* of the people called Motus in the Port
Moresby area, and he sailed with the Trobrianders in their *kula*
canoes. What he discovered about sailing even in those late
days, when the natives had had some contact with the white
man for over a century, was astonishing. He found organized
voyaging on a considerable scale, and a well-preserved canoe-
building and sailing industry.

The *kula* is a sailing–trading system that covers most of the
islands in the eastern New Guinea groups. In his *Argonauts of*

the Western Pacific * the professor describes the trade as being built round the exchange of two sorts of shell ornament, the one a necklace and the other a pair of arm shells. The necklaces move round the island groups in a clockwise, and the arm shells in a counterclockwise, direction. The ornaments are exchanged between partners in the trade, always a necklace for a pair of arm shells, never a necklace for another necklace. While the *kula* tokens are exchanged, ordinary barter continues. All exchanges are scrupulously fair and are conducted with an absence of haggling. To the sailing native, the lowest form of vice is meanness. (This probably helps to explain why many European navigators, who looked upon the islands merely as sources of refreshment for their crews, were received inhospitably. At first the natives gave generously, but it was not long before they perceived that they received no generous return.)

All this *kula* sailing is done in outrigger canoes, unlike the *lakatois* of other sections of New Guinea. *Lakatois* are large double canoes or series of canoes joined together, propelled by a distinctive clawlike sail. Each canoe forming the base of the *lakatoi* is a built-up dugout. In most of the *kula* voyaging, single dugouts with large outriggers are used. In the early 1920's there were over sixty such canoes sailing from the Trobriands alone. When I was there in 1935, there were perhaps six. In the war which ended with the Japanese capitulation of 1945, the Trobriands became an airdrome, and the canoe builders, sailors, and gardeners of the islands gained little from this first contact with the white man in his glory. Strangely enough, the natives had a tradition of canoes which fly, believing that they could produce such things had not some remote ancestors allowed the necessary magic to become forgotten. This tradition is in no way fantastic, for the designers who

---

* G. Routledge and Sons Ltd., London, 1932. I am indebted to them for permission to use this material.

could produce the almost perfect airfoil which is the sailing canoe's sail would have little difficulty producing a glider wing. Perhaps there is not much in this modern world which has not been done before, in some form.

The Trobrianders do not like to sail at night if they can help it. There are too many reefs among the islands of the *kula* ring. It is customary to camp for the night on a cay, or in a secluded spot on the beach of a friendly island. They used to be careful which islands they visited, for it is not long since to land in an area where they were not known might mean extermination. Pilotage in those waters is not simple, even to craft which draw as little water as canoes. The dangers of the sea, as the native knows them, are many—some real, some imaginary. Real dangers include reefs, sandbanks, strong races, sets, eddies, rocks, the danger of the canoe being caught aback and upset, or waterlogged in a heavy shower of rain, or overturned, or broken up in a confused sea. Imaginary dangers (which are very real to the natives) include the risk of being carried off by flying witches; having the canoe struck and sunk by leaping rocks which hurl themselves up from the sea bed with force to strike at unsuspecting vessels; meeting an octopus named *kwita*, which is big enough to entwine large canoes and suck them to the bottom, and the grave danger of being compelled to land on the island of Kaytalugi, somewhere to the north. Kaytalugi is the land of the lecherous women, whose ribald orgies spell death within weeks to any male unfortunate to fall among them. One of the most popular means of passing the time in canoes at sea is for the mariners to regale each other with stories of the viragoes of Kaytalugi and what they have done to shipwrecked men.

The significant thing about the *kula* voyaging is that it remained in existence until so recently. Elsewhere in the Pacific, in the more accessible islands, the art of passage-making by canoe died quickly after the European came. The natives of

Fiji and other groups gave up building large canoes when they saw how much better were the white man's ships, though the gondolalike canoe of the coastal Solomons is still in general use. It is purely a coastal vessel, not venturing in these days out of sight of land.

If an anthropologist (himself no seaman) discovered so interesting a field of organized and skillful native sailing as late as the 1920's, what might competent predecessors have found a century earlier? Or a century before that? But the early explorers either hurried by, like Wallis and Byron, or stayed a brief while to "refresh" their ships. They noted only that the people of the islands were dexterous in handling their canoes. The traders, when they came, were not interested in sociology, nor did they care about canoes, except to make use of them.

The missionaries who stayed among the islands and might have had a real contribution to make, too often were so fiercely determined to spread light among the "savages" that they failed to notice that some they sought to save were, in many ways, not savages at all. Far too often the early missionaries broke down cultures they never bothered to understand. Investigators since Professor Malinowski's day have found evidence, among the so-called savages of the South Seas, of highly organized social life and customs, whereof their canoe voyages and their remarkable maritime abilities were only a part.

CHAPTER FIVE

THE PORTUGUESE

THERE IS no evidence now discoverable that the ancient navigators of the East—the Arabs, Indians, and Chinese—ever sailed to the eastward of New Guinea, though anthropologists have noted traces of the Malay and the Chinese among islanders of some of the New Guinea groups. When the Portuguese first visited the spice islands of the East Indies in the first decade of the sixteenth century and took possession of the Moluccas there for the sake of their riches, they found various sultans in those islands who claimed to rule western New Guinea.

The first recorded European navigators in the northern waters of Australia speak of meeting Malay *proas* there—those swift-sailing, shallow-draft craft, so much more seaworthy than any canoe. They found the Chinese raiding parts of New Guinea for slaves, and trading there for the plumage of the

bird of paradise. But the southeast trade wind would blow in
the face of any junk or *proa* which ventured too far east, and
the dark islands of Melanesia, in their primitive state, offered
little trade. Legends of "islands of gold" persisted through
several centuries: but they were only legends. There *was* gold
enough in many of the islands, particularly in New Guinea,
but it could be worked successfully only by large-scale exploitation, a development which had to await the coming of the
European.

A chain of useful islands stretches south almost from within
sight of Tokyo Bay through Niijima, Aogashima, Sofugan, the
Bonins, the Marianas, and the Carolines practically to the
equator. The navigator could sail from Tokyo to Australia
with a favoring breeze on his port beam for most of the way
and never be more than two hundred miles from land. Yet the
Japanese, a hardy, able race of skillful and courageous mariners, seem not to have sailed there before the twentieth century. Their ocean voyaging was stopped, at any rate for a
considerable time, by a royal decree in 1636 which ordered that
no Japanese could leave the land of his birth and that seagoing
ships should no longer be constructed. Pains were taken after
this to ensure the unseaworthiness of Japanese vessels, which
were built so weakly that they were barely capable of making
coastwise passages in good weather.

Though only the Japanese adopted this queer notion of en-
couraging unseaworthiness, no Asiatic ship was strong enough
to stand up to the hard westerlies of either far northern or far
southern waters. Eastern ships were fair-weather ships, developed with a tradition of assured good sailing. From Madagascar right round to Formosa, over the east coast of Africa,
the southern coasts of Arabia and all India, the Bay of Bengal,
and the whole East Indies, monsoons could be depended upon.
They blew—and still blow—from the southeast or southwest
for half the year, and from northeast or northwest for the

other half. This is an ideal arrangement for sailing vessels,
which can stand a lot of wind, provided it is behind them.

But when real ocean voyages had to be made, it was European mariners who made them, for the harsh conditions of
European waters trained them in a hard school and forced
them to develop ships with real ocean-going, and ocean-keep-
ing, qualities. Travelers such as Ibn Batuta and Marco Polo
have left records of large Chinese ships which would astonish
the sailor of today—vessels manned by a thousand men, with
gardens aboard to grow "garden herbs and ginger," and pent-
houses built up on them in which the senior officers had their
quarters, with their wives. They kept hogs and poultry aboard,
brewed their own liquors, and were commanded by great
emirs. Such vessels may have traveled as far afield from China
as the port of Mogadishu, on the east coast of Africa: they
could make such a voyage, long as it seems, by an intelligent
use of the favoring seasons, laying up in safe ports when the
seasons were adverse.

In the same way, the Arab pilot Ibn Majid could pilot Vasco
da Gama from Malindi to Calicut, for this was a monsoon passage of no great difficulty, and he knew the way. The Arab
movement over the Indian Ocean is ancient. Malay and Swa-
hili both have been accepted languages in the Hadhramaut
district of Arabia for many centuries. Arabs certainly knew
the Aru Islands, off the south coast of what is now Dutch New
Guinea.

What else either they or the Chinese may have known about
those parts can now be mere conjecture. Navigators of their
skill who knew the Aru Islands *could* have sailed to the Coral
Sea. In the northwest season the wind is fair; later comes the
southeast season to blow the trader back again. The Arus are
almost within sight of the high mountains of New Guinea,
and Torres Straits is not five hundred miles away—which is a
stone's throw in the Pacific. Coasting eastward by New Guinea

to the north, or the mainland of Australia to the south, it would be difficult to avoid the area. But, understandably, its maze of reefs turned back any but the hardiest.

All that we now know for certain is that several maps show strange evidence of some knowledge of Coral Sea waters and of northern Australia *before* the generally accepted discoverers of those areas ever sailed there. The so-called Dieppe maps, which were prepared in the first half of the sixteenth century in the great sea pilots' school of Dieppe, sometimes show a vast continent to the south of Java. One such map, prepared in 1536, shows more than an indication of Australia. These Dieppe maps were probably—almost certainly—prepared from data smuggled out of Portugal; indeed, some of them show Portuguese flags on this strange continent, though there is no chronicle of any actual voyage there. The so-called Rotz map, of the time of Henry VIII, is surprisingly accurate, in parts, in its delineation of the northerly coasts of Australia. Ortelius's map of the Pacific, dated 1589, shows the Solomons more or less where they should be, and it shows New Guinea with a strait dividing it from a large southern continent, though Ortelius has this wandering away to the eastward and covering much that is now known to be open sea. This large continent is entitled *Terra Australis Incognita*: some of the Dieppe maps indicate a great island called *Java de Grande,* which is not to be confused with the mythical southern continent. *Java le Grande* was a real place, known to exist, though its extent was not known. *Terra Australis* was apparently very much *incognita*.

The origin of the belief in some sort of *Terra Australis* goes back to classical times, and geographers in Greece and elsewhere argued that there must be a vast land in the southern hemisphere to counterbalance the great continents known to exist in the northern. Ptolemy actually showed such a land mass on his map. In the early Middle Ages classical theories were forgotten, but the Renaissance brought a revival of interest, and many reputable geographers subscribed to the theory—so many, indeed, that one is forced to conclude that someone, by the mid-sixteenth century at any rate, must have had some knowledge of parts of it. These maps could scarcely all be products of "brilliant geographical romances," as one or two modern research workers have declared them to be. More than a good imagination, surely, was required to show Torres Straits on the map, as Ortelius does, and the Strait of Magellan or Drake Straits, as the map of Martin Behaim does.

It was no quest of *Terra Australis—cognita* or *incognita*—which set the Portuguese first sailing in the direction of the Coral Sea. They were surveying the approaches to the great spice islands of Ternate and Tidore, as intelligent mariners should. Being competent seamen and courageous navigators, steeped in the tradition of Henry the Navigator, they were not afraid of strange voyages. They took local pilots, and they learned—they *must* have learned—what the local pilots knew. Sailors from the Celebes and the Moluccas had been sailing at least as far as the Gulf of Carpentaria for many centuries. If they knew the Gulf of Carpentaria, they knew Torres Straits. It is strange that Torres, when he sailed that way in 1605, does not seem to have regarded himself as making an important discovery. The reasonable assumption—I write as a sailor, about sailors—is that he *knew* the straits were there. A sailor does not become embayed willingly in that grim corner of the Coral Sea: there were plenty of routes to the north which Torres could have used, after his vessel was to the south'ard of the Louisiade islands. He had a favorable wind to use the Jomard Passage, or China Straits.

If he knew the way, someone must have found it. That is plain sense. The only navigators who could have done so were the Portuguese. Torres was himself a Portuguese. He had access to their charts. Prior to 1600 there are references in published works to New Guinea being an island, for example in Cornelius Wytfliet's *Descriptiones Ptolemaicae Augmentum*, which appeared in Louvain in 1598. It is highly probable that some Portuguese seafaring men had sighted the Pacific from Halmahera, Morotai, and western New Guinea some years before Balboa became excited with his view of the same ocean from a hill in Darien, 9,000 miles away. Portuguese intelligence was not available to Balboa; indeed, so closely guarded was it that important sections of it must still be lost. For we know little, and nothing conclusive, about any Portuguese voyage into the Coral Sea.

Vasco da Gama rounded the Cape of Good Hope and sailed to India in 1498. At Calicut in India and later at Malacca in the Malay Peninsula, the Portuguese were interlopers in a vast field of shipping and trade carried on by the seafaring peoples of the East. It took a little while to establish themselves, to secure a share in the trade. Several years were required before they could dominate it. By 1511 the great viceroy Affonso de Albuquerque could organize a small expedition in quest of the spice islands, and to investigate the area east of the Strait of Malacca. In these days, when spices of all kinds are within the reach of most consumers and packets of them are to be had at every grocer's shop throughout the civilized world, it is difficult to realize how important an article of trade even pepper was in the sixteenth century. Pepper, cloves, mace, nutmeg, cinnamon—these things were rarities, accessible only to the rich, and there were fortunes to be made in trading in them. The point of origin of much of these spices was in the islands of Ternate and Tidore, off the coast of Halmahera: the discovery of this source of richness was the main quest of the 1511 expedition.

Command of the expedition was entrusted, apparently jointly, to Antonio de Abreu and Francisco Serrao. Serrao was a friend of Ferdinand Magellan. Magellan had taken part in

the capture of Malacca and was in the vicinity when the de
Abreu–Serrao expedition set out. There is some evidence that
he may have taken part in it, though this is doubtful. With
the Portuguese went an Arab (called, as usual, a Moor in the
contemporary accounts) named Ismael. The expedition was
gone approximately two years. Ismael the "Moor" was the man
who knew the way, who knew from which islands spices came,
and how to influence the local emirs, sultans, and kings.

According to Antonio Galvao, the Portuguese chronicler of
the *Discoveries of the World from Their First Original unto
the Year of Our Lord 1555*, at least one of the de Abreu expedition touched at New Guinea in 1511 or 1512, if not also at
northwest Australia. Galvao should have been in a position to
know, as he was one of the early governors of Ternate. This is
what he says:

> *In the end of this yeere 1511, Afonso de Albuquerque
> sent three ships to the islands of Banda and Maluco. And
> there went as generall of them one Antonio de Breu, and
> with him also went one Francisco Serrano; and in these
> ships were 120 persons. . . . They ran their course east,
> and sailed between Java and Madura. Beyond the island of
> Java they sailed along by another called Bali; and then
> also came unto others called Aujaue, Solor, Guliam, Mal-
> lua, Vitara, and the Arus, from whence are brought deli-
> cate birds, which are of great estimation because of their
> feathers: they came also to other islands lying in the same
> parallel on the south side, in seven or eight degrees of lati-
> tude. The course by these islands is about 500 leagues. . . .
> Beyond these [it is said] there are other islands, which are
> inhabited with whiter people going arraied in shirts,
> doublets and slops, like unto the Portugals, having also
> money of silver. The Governours among them doe carry in
> their hands red staves, whereby they seem to have some*

*affinitie with the people of China: there are other islands
and people about this place, which are redde: and it is reported that they are of the people of China.*

In 1512 the expedition departed from Banda, bound on the
return passage to Malacca with a cargo of "cloves, nutmegs,
and mace." Serrano (or Serrao) was wrecked, but de Abreu
returned safely with his report to the viceroy and died on the
way home to Portugal.

If not much is known about de Abreu, still less has come to
light regarding whatever voyage his countryman Christovao
de Mendoca, or Mendonca, may have made toward the same
parts and perhaps beyond. A recent Portuguese authority *
has stated that he visited the coast of Australia as early as 1522.
It is reasonably certain that some Portuguese, besides de Abreu,
was on the Australian coast—not only in the north and west—
well before the middle of the sixteenth century. The Portuguese were not the mariners to allow a great land so close to
their territories as Australia to remain completely unknown,
at any rate to themselves. That they did not publicize whatever
discoveries they made is understandable, because they could
not be sure in whose hemisphere—their own, or Spain's—they
were sailing, once east of the spice islands. They did not try
to colonize New Guinea, for there was already a satisfactory
flow of trade from there in the hands of the Arabs and Chinese.
Dom Jorge de Menezes, an early governor in the spice islands,
spent a few weeks on the north coast of New Guinea in 1526,
when blown there while on passage from Malacca to the Moluccas via the Sulu Sea. It is possible that de Menezes was having
a quiet look for gold on his own account, for stories of gold in
the vast land of New Guinea were very prevalent in the nearer
islands of the East Indies.

The next Portuguese to sail from the East Indies toward the

* Armando Cortesao.

area of the Coral Sea, of whom today there is any real knowledge outside Portuguese archives, was Manoel Godinho de
Eredia, or Heredia. Eredia was a distinguished cosmographer
and mathematician who lived and worked for some time at
Goa, when the Portuguese had their central administration for
the East at that port. No full account of his voyage to Australia, which was made in 1601, has yet been published, but
there is a map in the British Museum which experts regard as
evidence of his work. This shows the outlines of the New
Guinea and north Australian coasts as far as Torres Straits. It
does not show the strait. The Solomon Islands are shown much
closer to the eastern end of New Guinea than they actually lie,
but the delineation of the coasts of both New Guinea and
northern Australia is fairly accurate.

There is a record, in a reprint of a rare pamphlet issued by
the Royal Press at Lisbon in 1807, that Eredia was sent by the
Portuguese viceroy Ayres de Saldanha on a voyage to seek an
alleged island of gold somewhere south of Timor in 1601. If he
sailed south of Timor a few days—very few days—then he
came upon the coast of Australia. Of that there can scarcely
be any doubt. If he found Australia, it was merely a matter
of his own endurance—and his ship's—how far he followed
that continental coast line. There was nothing elusive about
it. It is prominent enough. Followed to the east, it leads to the
Coral Sea.

Like so many other voyages of those days, Eredia's was not
publicized. When the two great maritime nations of the world
spent money sending out ships in quest of knowledge, neither
was interested in making discoveries in the other's hemisphere.
There was no reason for Portugal to spend money to develop
what might ultimately prove to be Spain's. Eredia found
neither the island of gold nor any other gold, but—if the
British Museum map is any guide to the fruits of his work—

he must have added a great deal to the knowledge of the waters adjacent to the Coral Sea.

There is no doubt that the Portuguese would have opened the Pacific, too, had they thought this ocean was within the hemisphere allocated to them by Pope Alexander VI. The precise position in eastern waters of the line of demarcation laid down by the pope, later revised—in the light of fresh discovery —by the Treaty of Tordesillas in 1494, was known neither to the Spaniards nor to the Portuguese, since neither was able to establish longitude. Both knew that by all the rights then recognized by the Christian world, they controlled the trade of the world between them—half to each. To the Spaniards was given the western hemisphere, and to the Portuguese the eastern. But where did west become east, or east west? The great area of the Pacific Sea, to both immeasurable, had not been bargained for when the hemispheres were allocated. The pope's original line of demarcation had simply been a meridian of longitude cutting the Atlantic 100 leagues west of the Azores. All lands discovered by Europeans in the hemisphere which extended to 180 degrees west of that line were in the domain of Spain; all within 180 degrees to the eastward, Portugal.

This was all very well, before the rich spice islands were brought directly under the control of Europeans. Since nobody could measure even one degree at sea with accuracy, calculations as to the position of the dividing line in the Pacific between the two zones were merely academic. At that time, errors of 500 and 600 miles in longitude were commonplace on such ocean passages as were made. Moreover, the convention of 1494 had moved the line in the Atlantic another 270 leagues west of the Azores, to give the Portuguese the right to colonize Brazil, which was their discovery, though not then publicized as such. This had moved the line another 270

leagues to the westward in the Pacific also, and there was no
doubt, then, that the greater part of the Pacific, all the Coral
Sea, and the east coast of Australia lay within the Spanish
hemisphere. So the Portuguese withheld their information of
that area.

There were many geographers and politicians who claimed
that the spice islands were rightly in the Spanish zone. Among
these was Ferdinand Magellan. As a Portuguese, Magellan had
no business worrying whether his own country's discoveries
were outside or inside its pope-given rights. But Magellan
was an ambitious man, said to have been disappointed by
what he regarded as the inadequate rewards offered him after
his service in the East and his exertions at the siege of Malacca.
Knowing from Serrao that the Moluccas lay a good 500 leagues
to the east of Malacca, and not having the least idea that the
Pacific was 3,000 leagues across; knowing further from the
maps of Martin Behaim that there was a way from the east into
the South Sea, Magellan shook the dust of Portugal from his
boots and in 1517 went off for secret conferences with Charles
V of Spain, at Valladolid. His subsequent voyage, in 1520–
1521, is history; but it did him no good, and Spain very little.
The route he found was of small practical value in the days of
sail. He would have done better to find Cape Horn, for the
Strait of Magellan was never of much use to the sailing-ship.

Magellan sailed the way he did in order to avoid *Terra Australis.* The maps available to him showed this land as an enormous sprawl across the nether portions of the earth, larger than
Asia and blocking the way across the South Sea completely,
except to the north of New Guinea. Therefore, Magellan, a
determined and knowledgeable navigator who knew quite
well what he was after, stood toward the trade-wind zone of
the Pacific, as soon as he had sailed through his strait, and made
his way before the favoring easterly winds to the westward and
west-northwest. What Magellan did was precisely what he set

out to do. He made a successful voyage across the Pacific to the Portuguese spice islands in the East Indies. That this was also a great voyage of discovery was incidental. It was the spice trade he was after, and he knew where to find it.

Magellan's voyage, thanks to Pigafetta, is well chronicled, but it is difficult to check up on other early voyages—for one reason, because the names given to places visited were altered by their later "discoverers." But as a seaman with considerable respect for the seafaring Portuguese, I think there can be no real doubt that at least northern Australian waters were known to them. A certain Rebello, who lived in the Moluccas in 1569, wrote, "According to the information existing about these islands [the Papuan Archipelago] they run along a great land. . . ." What sailors who had been there knew of that land, we can only guess; but it would be worth while investigating Portuguese records on the subject, if these could be made available. It is well enough established that de Abreu, Mendoca, and Eredia probably knew North Australia. But what about the east coast? Who was there? A Dieppe map in the possession of Sir Joseph Banks, dating from the sixteenth century, showed a tolerable indication of the coast of New South Wales. It even marked a section as the *Coste des Herbaiges* in the area where Botany Bay now lies.

If this was the product of a "brilliant geographic imagination," as at least one expert has declared such evidence to be, then all I can say is that it was brilliant indeed. The early navigators were concerned with promoting trade. They kept their own counsel and reported only to those who sent them: such reports were filed with the utmost secrecy, and some remain to be discovered. The "brilliant and imaginative" cartographers of the navigation school of Dieppe, I think, had somehow had access to Portuguese records which have since been lost or forgotten.

CHAPTER SIX

THE SPANIARDS

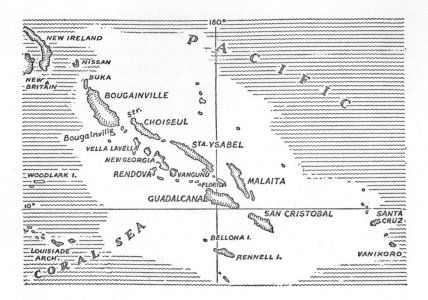

To SEE for myself how the sixteenth-century navigators fared, I took the *Joseph Conrad* over the route of one Alvaro de Saavedra, a cousin of Cortes, who sailed from Mexico to the Moluccas in 1526 and made the passage without too much difficulty. But when he tried to return, he wore his ship and crew to pieces trying to beat against the trade wind, and he died after making a few hundred miles along the north coast of New Guinea. Perhaps he thought the trade winds were monsoons and would change at the proper season.

The passage de Saavedra attempted is a difficult one, as I learned on passage from Singapore toward the Solomon Islands and Australia. I sailed by way of the South China Sea, the Sulu Sea in the southern Philippines, and over the North Pacific on

66

about the 6th parallel of latitude. By making careful use of an east-setting counterequatorial current, I was able to make some tedious easting, generally against doldrum conditions.

I had the aid of the latest navigational publications, both British and American; the limits of the favoring current were well defined; there was no excuse for my navigation not being precise; I had excellent charts, and I knew where I was going. Two other great advantages I had which were denied the seamen of the sixteenth century. I had ample food, fresh water, and galley fuel; and since I did not have to fight my ship (the area being clear of pirates), I had what would have appeared to them an extremely small crew. Nonetheless, my passage was trying. It took more than five months, and I arrived at last in Australia with a serious fever, brought on board in the Solomon Islands.

If the passage was difficult for the *Joseph Conrad*, it was infinitely more difficult for the early navigators, who had no knowledge of the counterequatorial current. In due course they learned to pass to the north, outside the tropics, and to make their easting there. This led to tolerable voyages but no discoveries, and it kept them away from all Melanesia—and Polynesia as well.

If there is still some mystery about early Portuguese voyages toward or in the southwest Pacific, the work of the few Spanish navigators who ventured there is documented reasonably well. As the Portuguese developed their trade with the spice islands of the East Indies, the Spanish exploited the resources of the west coasts of South and North America. Early in the sixteenth century there was already a considerable passage of ships between Spain and the Isthmus of Panama, whence goods and passengers traveled on mules or afoot to the Pacific side to take passage in country-built craft sailing in those waters. By 1521 Magellan had shown the back way into the Pacific, but this was too stormy and too dangerous for normal trade. The

Isthmus of Panama continued to be used, and the trade of the
Pacific was restricted almost entirely to vessels which were
built to Spanish design, of local woods and material. After
Magellan's voyage Spain kept the Philippines, though these
were largely within the Portuguese hemisphere, and soon there
was some passage of vessels between the Philippines and Mexico.
Spain also retained the Ladrones, or Marianas, as a possible half-
way stopping place for her Pacific galleons.

The trade between the Philippines and the west coast of
America, such as it was, was carried on by ships which made
their passages entirely in the North Pacific, and it was some
years before the Spaniards discovered that the only way to
make easting there was to get out of the trade-wind belt entirely. The trade winds blew them nicely to the westward,
but they had to face sterner, more variable conditions for the
return run.

Before they had been long in Peru, the Spaniards were hearing of strange Inca traditions of a civilization somewhere far
out in the Pacific, to the west of Callao. One would have
thought that there was gold enough already to hand in Mexico
and Peru, but there are always ambitious persons for whom
there is not a sufficient share, and the persistent legends that this
lost civilization included an "island of gold" caused more than
one adventurer to become deeply interested. One such adventurer was a navigator named Pedro Sarmiento de Gamboa. Sarmiento was a pilot with an international reputation, and he
had made himself something of an expert on Inca legends of
the Pacific. Exactly what he knew or thought he knew about
South American Indian—or earlier—voyages to the west, it
would be interesting to know; but he knew enough, at any
rate, to be keen on getting hold of a ship to sail in their tracks.
Unfortunately, Sarmiento had fallen foul of the Inquisition. A
ruthless and resourceful adventurer who in the course of a
varied life had tried many things, it was his misfortune, and

Spain's, that his pleas to be allowed to take an expedition to test the Inca legends so impressed the viceroy of Peru that the viceroy decided to keep the command in his own family. The expedition was organized more or less in accordance with Sarmiento's plans, but the leadership was given to Alvaro de Mendaña de Neyra, the viceroy's twenty-five-year-old nephew, untried, inexperienced, fresh from Spain. Mendaña was no seaman and had no knowledge of navigation.

Whatever may have been Sarmiento's faults (he is said not to have been above torturing the Incas for information, and to have caused the deaths of many of them), he was at least an excellent seaman. Sir William Monson, that hardheaded officer of Queen Elizabeth's navy who left, in the form of his *Naval Tracts,* an interesting maritime document of his times, knew Sarmiento personally. He refers to him as a "choice and perfect navigator": Monson knew a seaman when he met one. Sarmiento showed his nautical excellence by being the first to sail down from the Peruvian ports and enter the Strait of Magellan from the westward—no easy feat in a weakly built ship along that unmarked and dangerous coast.

Records of Mendaña's voyage have been unearthed in the Spanish archives and have been published by the Hakluyt Society. He sailed with 2 ships, of 250 and 107 tons, from Callao on November 19, 1567. Just how good those ships were, is a matter of conjecture; but the conditions were not such as to lead to the building of strong, fast vessels. Good weather, quiet winds, gentle seas such as predominate off the coast of Peru and Central America, would permit the survival of indifferent sailing vessels: it is probable that Mendaña's ships would horrify any seaman asked to cross the Pacific in them now.

The avowed purpose of the expedition was to convert infidels to Christianity, and for this a number of friars was embarked. Mendaña's was therefore the first missionary voyage in the South Seas. The land where the infidels were supposed to

live was said to be in 15 degrees of south latitude, some 600
leagues west of Peru. In addition to the friars, the ships carried
seventy soldiers, as well as a number of mariners and black
slaves. The slaves were entitled to a meal of meat on six days a
year, but for the mariners and soldiers a sufficiency of good
food seems to have been provided, at least for the first six
months.

From the records available, it is obvious that the two ships
had not gone far before Sarmiento found himself at odds
both with his leader and with Hernan Gallego, the chief pilot.
After sailing westward about 600 leagues and being within
striking distance of Tahiti, Mendaña, on Gallego's advice, altered course in a more northerly direction. Sarmiento pro-
tested strongly, but Mendaña was adamant. Perhaps Gallego
was concerned about the flukiness of the trade wind, which
begins to grow feeble in the area of the Tuamotus and the
Society Islands at certain times of the year, and counseled an
alteration to the north thinking to hold a better wind. But to
leave the latitude to which they were committed was foolish.
The expedition thereafter performed the astonishing feat of
sailing right through the maze of Polynesia and seeing next to
nothing. Mendaña's sail across the Pacific almost appears to
have been a passage *to* the Solomons, with prior knowledge of
their approximate position, but this does not seem to have
been Sarmiento's intention. If Mendaña had followed his advice, the expedition could scarcely have failed to find the high
islands of Tahiti and the rest of the Society group, which lie
between 15 and 18 south. In clear weather Tahiti can be seen
for 60 miles, even from the poop of a small sailing-ship. Tahiti
would have been a much more worth-while discovery to the
Spaniards from Peru than any Isles of Solomon, with or without gold.

For eighty days Mendaña led his small fleet westward toward
the setting sun, and Sarmiento followed him. Night after night

Mendaña caused a large stern lantern to be lit, to aid his second-in-command in his station-keeping. Day after day, night after night, the pair of small Peruvian sailing-ships creaked and rolled on gently toward the west, while the wondering soldiery began to fear that the great ocean had no end. By night, sail was shortened, lest they come upon dangers in the dark hours. Morning after morning the ships closed and hailed one another, and sometimes the chief pilot consulted with his juniors in the smaller ship about the state of their reckoning and other such things. With cumbersome astrolabes, the pilots did what navigating they could, but it was mostly guesswork. Hourly they scanned the sea for signs of seaweed and drifting things, and the sky for signs of birds, that they might observe the course of their flight. But they saw few birds until they came along what must have been the Ellice Islands. There was a chance to land and perhaps replenish their fresh water, but Gallego let the ships drift past. Once down to leeward, they could not get back. They were seeking a high, great land, not a group of atolls.

On the eighty-first morning they sighted the high land of the central Solomons, having first seen the atolls of Ontong Java. They shortened sail. The friars chanted the *Te Deum.* Even the protesting voice of Sarmiento, who for so long had decried the decision to alter course to the north, was temporarily stilled. Before nightfall of that day both ships were at anchor in a bay on the northern side of an island which Mendaña called Santa Ysabel. It was February 7, 1568: and this is the first unquestionable record of any European landing on a Coral Sea island. The prospect of the land about them was lovely, seen in its full beauty on the morning after arrival, and Mendaña was delighted. True, the land was much farther to the west than had been thought (at any rate by Sarmiento): but here it was. True, too, the natives seemed suspicious and were far from being the civilized and clothed humans the

Spaniards had hoped to find. The wild, dark Solomon Islanders watched from the woods and wondered what kind of invasion had come out of the sea upon them.

The first thing to do was to find whether the land was an island or a mainland; if an island, how large, and how close to others; and what sort of economic possibilities it presented. Disgusted with the poor sailing qualities of the ships from Callao (which had averaged something under seventy-five miles a day for the passage, with a favorable wind and generally good conditions), Mendaña, on the advice of his professional seamen, laid them up as accommodation ships. The shipwright's gang began immediately to construct a small vessel for exploration. This vessel is referred to as a "brigantine," but it can hardly have borne much resemblance to the modern craft of that rig. It was undecked, registered about five tons, and could carry thirty men under crowded conditions. It can have been little more than an open boat, about forty-five feet long, with a foremast carrying one square sail and the main some sort of fore-and-after. Some of the material for it had been brought from Callao, but it took nearly two months to put the boat together.

Meantime, Sarmiento and others had made some ventures inland. They discovered they were on an island by climbing to a mountaintop and seeing the Pacific on the far side. The natives were hostile and tried to ambush them as they returned. On the whole, the natives of Santa Ysabel were a great disappointment. Though a few of them could be induced to chant odd psalms without the least idea of what they were doing, and sometimes went through the motions of divine service for the novelty of the thing, there were no converts either to Christianity or to the cause of Spanish colonization. At first, when the visitors' needs had been pointed out, a market was established to which natives brought in fruits and vegetables. Before long the demands of the white men were making heavy inroads on the native gardens, for the Solomon Islander was not accustomed to produce much more than his immediate needs. One morning a canoe approached the Mendaña flagship and threw the forequarter of a freshly killed boy aboard: whether as gift or warning, the islanders did not stay to tell. Perhaps it was meant to indicate that this was all the food remaining. The horrified Spaniards (who might have killed the boy) hastily buried what was intended as the makings of a meal and hardened their never soft hearts toward the people of the Solomons.

When at last it was ready, the brigantine made several useful cruises round Ysabel and the adjacent islands. Mendaña did not make these voyages, which were the really interesting contributions of his expedition: it is a measure of the man that he did not. To sail the lengths of Ysabel, Malaita, Guadalcanal, and San Cristoval, as the brigantine did, must have been enchanting, despite the risks and the hardships. Just what Mendaña did with his time during the six months of his stay in the Solomon Islands, it is difficult to say. Attempts were made to compile a vocabulary—apparently with a measure of success, for such a document turned up in Holland many years afterward and was used on Tasman's voyage. Traces of gold were found in the mountain streams. Odd natives were kidnaped (Mendaña was the first blackbirder, as well as leader of the first missionary ship) with the idea of teaching them Spanish and so acquiring whatever information they might have had. This could scarcely have been much. The Melanesian of inland Ysabel and Malaita was a primitive with a mainlander's outlook: he had not the sea knowledge of the Polynesian or Micronesian.

Yet Mendaña must have learned something to convince him that the islands he had found were the outposts of a continent, as in fact they are. But why did he not send the brigantine on longer passages? Sarmiento continued to implore him to extend his researches to the southwest. A week's sail would have brought the vessel to Australia, and the wind was favorable. But the voyage was not made. The brigantine stayed in the Solomon Islands and sighted only some of them. Mendaña shifted his ships to Malaita and to Guadalcanal and later sailed along the coast of San Cristoval and to the small islands of Santa Anna and Santa Catalina. He seems to have hated the idea of losing sight of land, once he had found it. With the real hardships of a trans-Pacific voyage behind him, with a continent a few days' sail away and a sea of islands about him, with his ships and his people still largely intact, he chose to sail away. He burned the brigantine and departed, and the Solomons dropped out of sight for 200 years.

It seems odd that this young Spanish nobleman became for the next quarter of a century an enthusiastic promoter of colonizing the hot, fever-ridden, and hostile islands he had found, when he took no steps to form a settlement or even thoroughly to investigate the vast field of new discovery open to him when he was there. In later years many a beachcomber ruled an island with fewer resources.

On the way back to Callao, Sarmiento found it convenient to disappear. That was the last that is heard of his connection with the Isles of Solomon, nor is there any record that he was ever heard exhorting anyone to go there. Strange figure of the South Seas, Sarmiento later failed to distinguish himself when he was sent to look for Drake; later still, his attempt to found a Spanish settlement to block the English from the Strait of Magellan was a tragic failure, for he seems to have sailed off and left the settlers to their fate. When Thomas Cavendish came through, the stench of the dead at the settlement was overpowering; and there was no one to contest his passage. Yet it was unfortunate for Spain that Sarmiento did not lead the Mendaña expedition.

Returned to Callao, Mendaño found a hostile world, which

was not interested in organizing a further expedition for him, nor indeed much impressed with the report of his first. His uncle was superseded within a few months of his return, and the pair went back to Spain. Mendaña had brought neither gold nor spices, and his last surviving converts—a Solomons mother and child—died at Lima shortly after their arrival there. They are reported to have died "devout Christians, invoking the name of Jesus many times." But they were none-theless dead, and no information about gold or anything else could be obtained from them.

What Mendaña did manage to find and to present in a favorable light in his secret report, it would be hard to say. But his report to Spain was preceded by another, by no means favorable. This was the letter of Don Juan de Orosco, into whose administrative area the ships first returned from the voyage which Orosco describes as "to the Western Islands in the Southern Ocean, commonly called the Isles of Solomon." Orosco expressed the opinion that the "advantage which might be derived from exploring these islands would be to make slaves of the people, or to found a settlement in some port in one of them," whence the continent said to be not far away (and inhabited by people who wore clothes) might be discov-ered.

There is much that remains mysterious about Mendaña's voyage. Who "commonly called" his islands the Solomons? Nowhere in his own accounts does he use the name, which appears to have been taken for granted. Perhaps that name would have been given to any large group of islands, or large island, which was first found in the Pacific to the westward of Callao, in accordance with the tradition that somewhere from such islands King Solomon had shipped gold. There *was* gold in Mendaña's Solomons, as in many other Coral Sea is-lands. But there were nowhere reefs with large nuggets to be picked up from the earth. The gold they offered was to be obtained only by those who were prepared first to expend a great deal of capital setting up the machinery and plant necessary for its recovery—and that, no Spaniard of Mendaña's day proposed to do.

CHAPTER SEVEN

THE COLONY AT SANTA CRUZ

DESPITE DIFFICULTIES, Alvaro de Mendaña did succeed in making another voyage toward the Coral Sea. This second voyage is remarkable for several things. It was the first attempt to found a settlement on any island in the South Pacific; a considerable proportion of women took part in it, and the second-in-command and chief pilot was that strange Portuguese mystic and navigator, Pedro Fernandez de Queiros.

The bald facts of the voyage are plain enough. In April, 1574, after long campaigning, Mendaña received authority from the king of Spain to colonize the islands he had found. His commission was to take 500 men, of whom 50 were to be married; wives and children, as well as horses, cattle, goats, sheep, pigs, and vegetable seeds, were to be taken; he was

to found three fortified cities within six years of the first settling: he was to have the governorship of all the islands for life,
and this position was to remain in his family as its privilege for
two generations. He was to be styled marquis and would enjoy
the customs monopolies and so forth. He was to establish and
maintain communications with Callao and with the Philippines.

For twenty years after receiving the king's consent, Mendaña tried to organize his expedition. It was April, 1595,
twenty-seven years after he first returned there from the
Solomons, before he was able to sail from Callao. With him
went Doña Ysabel de Barreto, his wife, and too large a proportion of her relatives. These included her sister and her three
brothers, all of whom occupied privileged positions in the
afterguard.

There was little enthusiasm in Peru for the second Mendaña
expedition. It was looked upon as a repository for undesirables,
and some of the women came off the streets. The four small
ships were ill chosen, poor sailers, and in bad condition. One
of them was so bad that, before it had crawled 100 miles along
the coast of Peru, the people in the ship bored a few gimlet
holes below the water line to expedite its sinking, in order that
the leader would be compelled either to get another vessel or
to leave them behind. They obtained another vessel by turning out the rightful owners. When there was some remon-
strance, answer was made that God would provide the purchase
money, in due course, for the voyage was being made and the
ship requisitioned by His will. They completed their stores in
the same spirit and, apparently, in much the same manner,
for the viceroy sent the fleet from Callao short of many necessities.

There were quarrels, bickerings, and sometimes near riots
the whole way along the South American coast. It must have
been obvious to anyone who was capable of judgment that the

whole expedition was ill conceived and, to say the least, un-likely to succeed. Doña Ysabel soon showed herself as the power behind her husband. The master of the camp—a military man of sorts, aged sixty; overbearing, tactless, stupid, but ap-parently honest; by name Don Pedro de Merino—began at once to disrupt the discipline of the ship by interfering with the deck duties, though his function was to conduct affairs ashore when a landing was made. Some of the riffraff sent aboard proved so thoroughly disorderly and disreputable that the others refused to sail with them, and the worst were turned out of the ships. Queiros himself became so disturbed by the constant bickering, the ominous manner in which a power-ful clique of the Mendaña relations began to form round Doña Ysabel, and Mendaña's own obvious lack of grip that he asked to be allowed to resign. Mendaña implored him to stay. Why anyone remained with such an expedition passes modern com-prehension, unless they had been misled with hopes of gold. But Queiros was not there for gold.

On June 7, 1595, sixty days after sailing from Callao, the ships were at last able to leave Peru and head off toward the setting sun. In accordance with the custom of those days the best two ships were known as the *Capitana* and the *Almirante*, since the fleet captain and the admiral sailed in them. In the *Capitana* were Mendaña himself, Doña Ysabel and relations, Queiros the chief pilot, the master of the camp, two priests, as well as a large ship's company and a proportion of the prospective settlers, who included children. In the *Almirante* sailed Lope de Vega, about whom not much appears to be known, and since he was lost on the voyage, there is not much to be found out. The other craft were the *San Felipe*, described as a galeot, and the *Santa Catalina*, which is called a fregat. In the four ships were 378 souls, "whereof 280 were capable of bearing arms." There must have been nearly 100 women and children, and there were not many children.

Exactly how the women and the married couples were ac-
commodated on board these small ships, and what kind of life
must have resulted from cooping up so wild a party on so
curious a project, is not recorded. The lives and the fate of the
females seem to trouble the chroniclers of the expedition not at
all. It is mentioned that there were some fifteen marriages in the
first month at sea, "scarcely a day passing without someone
wanting to be married the next day," and the vicar was kept
busy. Women were expected to take life as they found it in
those days, afloat and ashore. Apparently all went well enough
for the first six or seven weeks, while the four little ships with
their queer assortment of humanity and kine wandered westward before the steady easterly breeze. All was jollity at the
various weddings. Mendaña left the navigation to Queiros and
gave himself up, perhaps, to dreams of grandeur when he
should become ruler of the Solomon Islands and all the southern
lands as far as the South Pole. If he was to organize a government on which a great colony was to arise, he should have been
busy enough.

Each evening before the night came quickly down, the
other three ships closed the *Capitana* and hailed her for their
night's orders. Through the balmy, starlit nights four great
stern lanterns bobbed curiously upon the lonely sea as the ships,
their tops'ls furled, spritsails clewed up, and lateens lying
brailed in their gear, creaked along, rolling gently, slowly on
their way. Each morning their canvas was set again, and they
sailed up to hail the *Capitana* once more, to report all's well.
Sometimes on these occasions there were shouted conferences
between the pilots about their approximate position, which
became more approximate as they proceeded toward the west.
The days were pleasant, the weather good. There was food
enough, and for the time being, sufficient fresh water. Flying
fish flew over the bulwarks in the low waists of the ships, and
these were a welcome change in the diet. There was a double

lookout at the masthead in each ship through the daylight hours: by night, lookout was kept from the heel of the bow-sprit in the smaller ships, and from the forecastles in the larger ships.

Two months passed. Land was sighted on the sixtieth morning. This was high land, and as the ships sailed slowly closer, the friars leading the chanting of the *Te Deum*, its pleasant aspect was noticeable. These were the islands now known as Hiva Oa, Tahuata, Moho-tane, and Fatuhiva, of the Marquesas. Mendaña named the group Las Islas Marquesas de Mendoza.

After the Marquesas were sighted, the voyage continued toward the west. Day after day was much the same—same good weather, same poor progress of the small, crowded ships. There began to be murmurs from the fainthearted and the soldiery, who had never imagined that there could be so much sea. Having little to do, the soldiers had plenty of time for grumbling. The state of affairs aft did not improve. The master of the camp found himself in a minority of one against Doña Ysabel and her relations: Queiros, then only thirty years of age, kept to himself; Mendaña showed no evidence of the strength of character and capacity for inspired leadership which alone could have held the crazy fleet together.

After three months the Isles of Solomon still lay somewhere far off, below the setting sun. Day after day, week after week, the wind blew from the east, and the soldiers began to say that never again would a breath of air come from any other direction and the ships would sail on forever, until they disintegrated, or came to China, or slipped from the sea's edge. They began to question the existence of the Isles of Solomon. There were frantic examinings of the compass, lest they sail daylong in circles: yet the direction of the sun's path remained constant over them, and there was no real doubt of their course. West, west, west, and never a westerly breeze: day after day, week after week, month after month, the blue sea

opened gently to permit the four small ships to sail along, and
the four slight wakes were soon lost in the infinite maze of
waters.

On September 7, 1595, they sighted the volcano of Tinakula, a volcanic island near Santa Cruz. It burst suddenly upon
them out of a fog which had hung about the ships all day and
dispersed only in the last hours of light. Into that fog, four
ships had sailed: out of it, three ships emerged. It was a local
fog of small extent and no real danger, but the *Almirante* was
never seen again. It seems probable that she deliberately deserted, taking the opportunity of the bad visibility to turn tail
and make for Peru. There was not a pilot of real repute in the
ship: if they tried to beat back against the trade wind, they
would soon have been short of food. There were many reefs
across the meandering track of a beating ship which the
straight-sailing vessel, with a favoring wind, might have the
luck to avoid. Yet it is an extraordinary thing that this vessel,
crowded with men, women, and children, should vanish within
a few hours. The other three vessels remained for two months
in that area, yet nothing was heard again of the *Almirante*. Her
fate is one of the mysteries of the Pacific.

The sighting of Tinakula, which he had not seen before,
seems to have been sufficient for Mendaña. He ordered the
friars to chant, the soldiers to be confessed, and Queiros to
take the ships into anchorage at the nearest land. This was the
large island of Santa Cruz, which can be seen, on a clear day,
from a ship which is also in sight of Tinakula. Queiros took
the fleet into a bay on the northern side of Santa Cruz, and
this was called Graciosa Bay.

The ships were met by a party of islanders in seagoing canoes
who approached the fleet in strength and with so much caution
that it seemed they must have heard of the dangers of white
men's guns. There were at least fifty canoes, manned by
woolly-haired natives with their teeth stained and their dark

bodies darkened the more by smears of war paint. They let loose a volley of arrows at the ships as they approached the anchorage. Then the Spaniards opened fire, killing some and wounding many more. The fleet ran into the anchorage, while the soldiery, their morale up, now they had someone to shoot, stood ready with their arquebuses.

The natives of Graciosa Bay, on the whole, were not unco-operative, and an arrangement for a real settlement might easily have been made. The pleasant shores of the bay were well peopled with cheerful, stalwart natives who built good canoes, fished well, and seemed to delight in the growing and wearing of sweet-smelling red flowers. They had good gardens and fair houses. The chief of these natives, an upstanding Melanesian named Malope who wore brightly colored plumes in his hair, called on Mendaña and offered a welcome which, if a little dubious, was at any rate peaceable. Malope arranged a market at which food was bartered.

But it did not suit the soldiers to be at peace. They began to kill some of the natives deliberately, in order to foment trouble and to make settlement impossible. The natives "showed them-selves to be valorous, so that it was understood we had met with a people who knew well how to defend their homes," as the Spanish chronicler has it. But the Spaniards guffawed as they returned the flight of arrows with musket fire and held up the arrows jeeringly and thrust their points against the stout leather protective clothing they wore and broke them against their breastplates.

Having come upon Graciosa Bay fortuitously, Mendaña decided that it would do for the first of his three cities. Under direction of the master of the camp, the soldiers began half-heartedly to clear some land for gardens and houses. This was not the kind of work they had bargained for, and there was serious discontent. There was land enough to till in Peru with-out crossing the South Sea to find more, said the soldiers:

where were the gold and pearls their leader had talked about?
Were these the Isles of Solomon?

Mendaña made the stupid error of remaining aboard his
ship while the master of the camp led the parties ashore. The
official reason for his continued residence afloat was that no
house had been built for him ashore, but the natural conse-
quence was to foster the division between the military and the
seamen and to promote discord. Before long the soldiers, "to
whom a limit to what they are permitted to do seldom or ever
seems good" (as the chronicler shrewdly remarks), began to
make serious trouble. In that fertile spot, as soon as they had
cleared land the jungle began to creep in again: gardens needed
constant care, and they were not gardeners. No persons skilled
in tilling the tropic soil had been brought, nor does it seem that
any proper organization for a settlement had been thought out.
That sort of thing was the domain of the master of the camp.

Rightly or wrongly, that embittered old soldier took the
brunt of the blame for the state of things ashore. The soldiers
were afraid that the ships would go off and leave them, even
after Mendaña had all the sails unbent from the yards and
stowed in a locked place under armed guard. Not even the
makings of a brigantine had been brought, this voyage, so the
seamen lacked the interest and the occupation of putting a
small ship together and making prospecting voyages. The small
vessels of the fleet spent much of their time looking for the
Almirante.

On Santa Cruz were pigs and fowls "like those of Castile,
many of them white," which ran wild and seemed to exist in
abundance. Edible roots and coconuts were plentiful. Fish
teemed in the bay. An excellent small colony could have been
founded there. But some wanted to go to Manila and be done
both with this place and all the Isles of Solomon: many grumbled that they wanted to be taken to the islands in search of

which they had sailed, where gold and pearls existed in abundance. Others sought to return to Peru.

What form the trouble finally assumed, it is difficult to understand from the chronicles, for a writer in those times had to be careful of any criticisms, real or implied, of members of the aristocracy. But it is obvious that Doña Ysabel took an active part. She wanted the master of the camp executed. Mendaña temporized, sending Queiros to address a meeting of the soldiers and settlers. The stock of Queiros did not stand high at the time, for the soldiers were aware that Santa Cruz was a new discovery, and they blamed the chief pilot for missing the Solomons. There were disorderly shouts asking him where the great lands were, and the wealth whereof they had come in quest. Where were all the great things of which they had heard back in Lima and Callao? Queiros answered these doubters by pointing out that when Columbus discovered the new world, at first it seemed that little had been achieved, "there being only a few small islands of little or no value. Yet, through the constancy of the discoverers, there were afterwards found the great and rich provinces of New Spain and Peru."

The soldiers, having perhaps heard of the fate of Columbus and most pioneers, were far from convinced. They shouted at Queiros to play at being Columbus himself if he liked; for their part, they wanted to go to Manila, or Peru, if he were able to take them there. From that time there was a conspiracy to murder the chief pilot.

The natives tired of providing their garden produce for the unfair exchange offered by the colonizers, and the shore party was jealous of the comparative freedom from want of those who stayed in the ships. The spirit of the whole camp was mutinous. Mendaña sickened, while his wife continued to urge him to have the master of the camp dispatched. At last

Mendaña landed from his sick bed and did her bidding. The
master of the camp was butchered in cold blood when he came
out, unarmed, to greet his leader, and a drummer stole the
clothes from the bloody body. His head was cut off and put on
a picket by the entrance to the camp stockade.

But his death achieved nothing. Some of the soldiers had
already gone off to kill Malope, the friendly chief, on the
grounds that if he were murdered, the settlement would have
to be abandoned and they could return to Peru. Malope's
murder aroused the whole island. The junior officer who led the
murderers was summarily executed, and his head joined that
of the master of the camp on the picket fence. Doña Ysabel
landed, saw the heads, and went to Mass. There were further
executions, until even the vicar began to tremble for his life.

Mendaña at last moved ashore into the house of the master
of the camp. It was too late. He was sick unto death; and so
was his settlement. All hope of controlling the soldiers and the
settlers was gone. Within a few days Mendaña was dead, having
left control in the hands of Doña Ysabel and her elder brother
Don Lorenzo. Sickness became general. The natives began to
attack the survivors with boldness, choosing moments after
showers when they knew the Spanish guns were useless. Now
it was the islanders' turn to laugh, as they aimed their stout
arrows carefully from the treetops at the soldiers' exposed
knees, legs, necks, and arms. They aimed well, and sometimes
their arrowheads bore poison. No member of the camp knew
from which tree or bush a wretched poisoned death might
come winging at him. None dared to leave the camp. No natives now brought food.

Don Lorenzo died not long after Mendaña, of the same
fever. Several of the friars died. The surviving priest drew up
a petition to Doña Ysabel, on behalf of all, imploring her to
leave Santa Cruz. Her family, however, had guaranteed 10,000
ducats for the successful accomplishment of the voyage, and

that was only the beginning of their expense. Let the priest petition and the soldiers complain: she would remain. Queiros then added his influence to the request to leave, and did no better. Did he pay for the ships? she snapped. But that night three of the four cables holding the *Capitana* chafed away: and in the morning it dawned upon the lady that perhaps, after all, she might not have the final word.

Reluctantly she decided to permit what she hoped was the temporary abandonment of the settlement. On November 7, 1595, they withdrew from Graciosa Bay, leaving the dead behind them.

Even then, Doña Ysabel was in no mood to give up the whole of the undertaking. She planned to continue toward San Cristoval in the Solomons, to see if the *Almirante* was there. If the *Almirante* was not found, then she would agree to go to Manila to engage more priests and people "to return to complete the discovery."

In this ambition, she stood alone. It should be added that she and her immediate entourage also stood alone in having had, at all times, plenty of provisions, for the lady had seen that, whoever else went short, she did not. Her store of food and other essentials was a private one in which the ship's people had no share, and even when they were dying of scurvy, she would not willingly part with as much as a drop of olive oil. It was her misfortune, and the expedition's, that Doña Ysabel had less feeling for the ship's needs than for her own.

They hove home the one good cable, hoisted in the boats, set the ripe sails, and departed. The gear was in such a state that the boatfalls carried away three times before the boat was in. At Santa Cruz they had been close to the Solomons. San Cristoval then lay about two hundred miles almost due west of them: but they sailed west-southwest and saw nothing. They continued on a west-southwesterly course until reaching the 11th parallel of south latitude. Then, seeing no land and no sign of their lost consort, they altered course to the northwest in order to pass round the north of New Guinea.

Within a month of leaving Santa Cruz, forty-seven persons had died. Long before then the few sailors who were still fit to stand, exhorted Queiros to let the ship drive up on the next reef, atoll, or island they came across, for they no longer cared whether they lived or died, and wanted only an end to their sufferings, which continued intense while the rotten ship skirted the blue-green waters of the Coral Sea and made painful easting to the north of New Ireland. There was a lot of calm. One night the galeot disappeared. The *Capitana*'s mainmast was sprung. The daily food of all hands except Doña Ysabel and a favored few of the afterguard consisted of half a pound of flour made into a paste with salt water and baked in ashes.

"There was not much good fellowship," states the chronicler, with masterly understatement. Two or three people died every day; but the women, on the whole, seemed to stand up better than some of the men. A letter from one of those women on that voyage would make interesting reading, but they could not write.

The ship had to be pumped four times a day, for the tropic worm had eaten away her timbers while she lay at Santa Cruz, and they had no wood for replacements. Her hull was filled with filth, for her people were too worn out by sufferings to care about cleanliness. The rigging and sails, never good, were practically useless: and there was more than a thousand miles to go before they could hope to reach the Philippines. Sewing the burst seams of the rotten sails went on continuously. All the cordage in the ship was worn out, and the standing rigging began to carry away. The bowsprit was sprung. One night the spritsail yard carried away, taking with it the spritsail and all its gear. The mainstay parted. They unrove some backstays from the mast, spliced these the same length as the mainstay, and rigged them; these stood a few days and then they too parted. Sometimes for three days at a stretch the topsail hung in untidy, chafing folds in and across the maintop, because it had collapsed there through the parting of the halliards, and no man had strength enough to furl the sail or the heart to splice the halliards yet again, when they had already been spliced thirty times.

At length the ship could set only the two courses, fore and main. The spritsail had gone and they could not replace it; nor could they set the lateen, lest the ship, with insufficient sail set for'ard, fly up into the wind. Long grass clung to the rotten planks, and gay-colored fish fed upon the sea growth that stank upon the ship's undersides. The foul stench in the hold sickened even those long grown accustomed to it, so that few went below, and those who died down there sometimes were suffered to lie for days awaiting burial. The ship was literally floating upon her beams, for the sea ran in and out of the many gaps in the warped planking of her sides. The sprung mainmast threatened to fall upon them whenever there was a breeze: a shower of rain was enough to burst the seams of the two remaining sails.

"The sailors, from the hard work, their weakness, and from seeing the ship in such a state, set no store by their lives," one reads. "One of them said to the chief pilot that he was tired of being always tired, that he would rather die once than many times, and that they might as well shut their eyes and let the ship go to the bottom."

Queiros answered that if they cast themselves away, they gave themselves to the devil. It was God's will that they go on: and therefore as God-fearing Christians they must bear all things and accept their fate. To this, the men said that there was honor for a chief pilot to bring in a ship from such a voy-age, but for them there was no honor but only suffering and work. They were better dead. But Queiros said God gave them

life, and God would take life back from them when it was
ordained.

Through all this, Doña Ysabel, keeping herself to the
spacious quarters of the great cabin aft, where the stern windows stood open to the cleansing wind and the filth from the
rest of the ship rarely penetrated, lived a life apart. She still
had abundance to meet her needs. At her orders, her servants
took much of the remaining supply of fresh water to wash her
clothes. Queiros remonstrated, but she answered that surely
she could do what she liked with what was hers. It was of no
interest to her that others went short of drinking water. Perhaps it would rain and they might have the sense to catch the
water: when they grumbled too much, she suggested that if a
couple were hanged, the rest would be quiet enough.

Queiros pointed out that either the sailors must have their
share of water, and live, or she would not live either, for there
would be no one left to work the ship. At this, the lady grudgingly parted with two jars of oil. She took the key of the stores
and kept that; she even refused to allow the slaughter of the
beasts which had been brought to provide stock for the settlement.

Before the ship sailed from Santa Cruz, Mendaña's body had
been disinterred from its temporary grave and was being carried toward Manila in the small fregat. Time and time again
Queiros implored Doña Ysabel to allow him to relieve those
in the smaller ships by taking them into the *Capitana;* but she
would not have it. The pilot of the fregat had no chart and
would not have known how to use one, for the poor man could
not read. One night the fregat disappeared, not far from the
Marianas. It was never seen again.

At the Marianas they could find no succor. They went on in
wretchedness toward Manila, the ship making scarcely two
knots, a loathesome, waterlogged hulk, spewing swollen bodies
over the side. At last, on February 11, 1596, ninety-six days

out from Santa Cruz, the battered, miserable little ship arrived off Manila Bay; and as it does so often there, the wind blew fresh directly out of the bay, in their faces, and they could not work the ship in nor keep her up for the entrance.

"For the love of God, cast now this dreadful ship upon the rocks," the survivors implored Queiros: but the chief pilot refused. He knew that at the first embrace of any rocks, that rotten hull would collapse in a ruin of worm-eaten planks and drown all on board. He stood on.

At last a boat came within hail, and Doña Ysabel was able to send in a message to relatives who held positions of importance in the port. These sent out a crew arrayed in silks to work the death ship in; and the silken mariners of Manila held their noses as they climbed aboard, and stared with astonishment at the poor, fever-ridden skeletons who remained to man what once had been a ship of great adventure. All the crew were sick, in tattered rags, covered with boils, their teeth dropping out of bloody mouths in which the swollen, ulcerated gums smelled horribly, their hands raw from the work of pumping, and their forearms blackened. The stench of death and sickness was appalling. High on the sloping poop, right aft, stood Doña Ysabel, in silks as gay as any in Manila, her proud, hard face as fleshed as the day she sailed from Peru. Before her, on the main deck, scampered two pigs, and the Manila men looked at them in that ship of starvation with great astonishment. Asking why they were not eaten when there was so much want, they learned they were Doña Ysabel's.

"What, is this a time for courtesy to pigs?" shouted one, and the beasts were slaughtered at last to make a feast for the well-fed town dwellers who worked the ship in.

Within a brief while, Mendaña's widow was married again, and the waterfront winehouses ran with rumors that her ship had sailed from Peru to the Isles of Solomon to fetch the Queen of Sheba, but had missed the way. The surviving widows, who had left Peru only some nine months earlier, were "received into the houses of the principal residents, and afterwards they were all married to their satisfaction."

As for Queiros, he remained in the service of Doña Ysabel and her new husband, Don Fernando de Castro. With them, he sailed from Manila back to Mexico. They reached Acapulco on December 11, 1597, whence he returned as a passenger to Peru.

There he called immediately upon the viceroy and set before him a plan for a further expedition in a ship of seventy tons manned by forty sailors, to return to the Coral Sea and discover the other lands which he suspected to exist in that part of the Pacific.

Where Mendaña's remains may rest in all the wide Pacific is unknown. The great ocean is a fit grave for him, strange wanderer, who, if he had only strength of character enough to control the situations he created, might have taken rank with the great explorers.

When, centuries later, the British came to Santa Cruz, there seemed a brooding curse over Graciosa Bay, and twentieth-century colonists fared little better than Mendaña's misled mariners of 1595. Blackbirders used Graciosa Bay, and more than one was murdered there. Before that, the French discoverer La Pérouse touched there on his way to death at nearby Vanikoro. A great copra combine made a station there but gave it up after sixteen years. Trader after trader left the place. Almost three hundred years after Mendaña's men had foully murdered Malope, natives of Santa Cruz killed a British naval officer with poisoned arrows at Graciosa Bay. This was Commodore Goodenough, Royal Navy, then in H.M.S. *Pearl* and commodore of the Australian station.

There has long been a story that either on Vanikoro or on Santa Cruz there is buried treasure saved from the lost ships of

La Pérouse. Men have died from fevers, in quest of this, but beyond a few French coins found near a timber camp, the search has yielded no more treasure than the islands gave to Alvaro de Mendaña de Neyra, three and a half centuries ago.

CHAPTER EIGHT

THE QUEST OF QUEIROS

Q̲ueiros returned from his voyage with Mendaña more
saint than sailor, a combination as impractical then as it is
now. But the third Spanish South Pacific expedition was
largely due to the saintliness of Queiros.

Who was this Pedro Fernandez de Queiros, last of the Portuguese and Spanish discoverers? Not much is known of his
career, beyond the bald facts. He was born at Evora, Portugal,
in 1565. There was no taint of treachery in his subsequent
voyages for Spain, as there was with Magellan, because in his
time a voyage for Spain was equally one for Portugal.

He went to sea as a young man, sailing in ships from Lisbon.
According to his enemies, he was bred in the slums of Lisbon,
but if this had been so, it is hardly probable that he would
ever have become enough of a mathematician to study the arts

of pilotage and navigation, crude as they were at that time. In any case, it was not long before he established a reputation as a first-class pilot.

Pilots in those days were experienced and skillful seamen, well versed in the art of sailing by landmarks, local knowledge, and dead reckoning. They were also navigators, in so far as any seamen could navigate: they could read charts and often made them; they were students of marine life and all the natural phenomena of the sea and the sea-sky; they could lay off a compass course and use the astrolabe to give them a fairly accurate idea of the sun's meridian altitude, and they possessed a wealth of knowledge of landmarks, ocean winds and currents (though they were somewhat vague about these), and the general behavior of sailing-ships at sea. In their hands rested the success of voyages. They were important officers, whose ranks did not open easily to welcome the newcomer.

In 1589 Queiros married. Shortly afterward he moved with his family to Peru, intending to earn his livelihood by serving as pilot in vessels engaged in the extensive coastwise trade between Lower California, Mexican and Central American ports, and Peru. Here his abilities and excellent character brought him to official notice so that he was recommended to Mendaña. His voyage with Mendaña was the turning point of his life.

Of all persons, Queiros should have had his fill of the southwest Pacific. But he returned from the second Mendaña expedition almost a fanatic for the idea of further discovery in the Coral Sea. He made no secret of his objective. He had come to the conclusion that Santa Cruz, the Solomons, and New Guinea must all be fairly close together, and that these islands were probably the Porto Rico, Haiti, and Cuba of the great *Terra Australis Incognita*. This would have been sound enough had there been any *Terra Australis* of the dimensions then ascribed to it, but Queiros was a little wide of the mark. However, his fundamental idea—to make again for Santa Cruz and

establish a base there from which to find the southern continent—was sound.

His intention was to claim the new continent for Spain and
to begin the conversion of the heathen who presumably inhabited it, to the true faith. He found little support for either
of these ideas in a Peru which had already sent two costly and
abortive expeditions, and he had to return to Spain before he
could make any progress.

There was not much welcome for him or his ideas in Spain,
until he thought of making a pilgrimage to Rome and enlist-
ing the support of the pope for the great project of bringing
the Christian faith to the Australians. Unfortunately for the
chances of success of his expedition, he thought Australia was
a much greater land than it is, for like most of the geographers
of his time, he had no idea that there were really two undis-
covered continents in the southern hemisphere, the real Australia and the frozen Antarctica. He supposed there was one
enormous land embracing both of these, and half the southern
Pacific Ocean as well, with its east coast stretching somewhere
from Tierra del Fuego toward New Guinea.

Apparently, the further Queiros traveled from Santa Cruz,
the more convinced he became of the existence of his continent, not far from that island. The council of cosmographers
and geographers called by the pope to consider Queiros's sub-
missions was much impressed by the fervor of his arguments,
and they were in no position to judge their substance. The
papal council listened to exciting stories of the extent of the
heathen domains to the far south, while to the pope, as to
Queiros, the idea of many millions of lost souls awaiting the
salvation that could come to them only through the hands of
Rome was enough.

Queiros left Rome, still in the poor garments of a pilgrim,
as he had traveled there. But in his satchel there was a papal
letter to the king of Spain and a piece of the true cross. Armed

with these, he returned to Madrid, where he had little trouble
in getting a royal warrant calling upon the viceroy of Peru to
fit him out with ships and men for his expedition and to give
him all possible aid. After all, it cost the king nothing to send
a royal warrant to Peru; while the pope's letter made ample
amends for the Church's old antipathy to what was once regarded as the heretical idea of the existence of the antipodes.

In the summer of 1603 Queiros sailed from Spain in a
ship bound for the Isthmus of Panama. The ship was wrecked
on the South American coast not far from its destination,
and Queiros was destitute in La Guaira for months. It took
him a long time to reach Lima, and not one of the colonial
officials whose duty it was to give him help paid the slightest
attention to the king's letters. The king was far away, and
gold was scarce. When he arrived at last in Lima, with two
orphan nephews he had found somewhere on the way, Queiros
had only the clothes he stood in. What manner of man was this
to lead great expeditions? The courtiers and the sycophants
of Lima laughed. His only shelter was with a potter in a poor
quarter of the town, but the friars gained him admittance to
the great viceroy, and at length he was able to put the king's
letters before the count of Monterey.

The count of Monterey was not pleased. If there was further
profitable adventuring to be done in the South Seas, he felt that
he was the man to put the idea before the king. It was galling
that this scraggy Portuguese should come, in his poor clothes,
penniless, and bringing peremptory orders. However, he must
pretend to do the king's bidding for the Church was powerful. So the viceroy gave reluctant instructions, much delayed,
that two indifferent vessels be prepared and something done
about manning and provisioning them.

The obstructive tactics everywhere employed in a decadent
Spanish Peru must have been exasperating even to a saint, and
when Doña Ysabel Barreto, claiming the Mendaña rights to

the Isles of Solomon and the lands beyond, added her intrigues
to the serious weight of opposition against him, a lesser man
than Queiros might have felt inclined to abandon his idea.
Mendaña's widow was now a member of the powerful de
Castro family, and she was mindful of the thousands of ducats
her departed husband had sunk in the Coral Sea. Before he
could go ahead with his plans, Queiros had to win her support.
A compromise was reached by which the Mendaña "rights"
were protected, for Queiros sought no material gains. But he
had plenty of enemies. It was said that he was a Portuguese, an
ex-supercargo, a waif from the Lisbon slums: he had lost
Mendaña at an unknown island, when he should have found
the wonderful Isles of Solomon. If he could lose what Mendaña had found, what manner of man was he to seek what
no man had seen? If he was a capable man with the driving
force necessary to conduct long expeditions, why was he so
poor?

Slowly and laboriously, with a few friends, Queiros pushed
on with his preparations. At times he was exasperating even to
his friends, for the strength of his religious fervor overcame
the need to solve worldly problems, and he often blinded himself to men's evil. The problems he had to solve were, unfortunately, extremely worldly ones. The viceroy, seizing the opportunity of the unwanted expedition to rid himself of some
questionable characters, filled the ships with evil men. Through
all this, Queiros was sustained by the devotion and untiring
aid of his secretary and companion, the Spanish poet Luis de
Belmonte Bermudez, who had joined him in Spain and remained his constant friend and assistant until his death.

The viceroy provided two small ships, one about 150 tons
and the other less than 100. They were poorly fitted out. With
them was a launch called a *zabra,* a small staunch fore-and-
after which had lately arrived from the Galapagos. In accordance with custom the two larger ships were known as the

Capitana and *Almirante,* the *Capitana* being senior. In the ships were nearly 300 men, with whom were six friars and four brothers of the order of Juan de Dios, to cure the sick. Though her timbers were unsound and her rigging far from good, the *Capitana* was a brave show, with a large painting of the Virgin above the stern windows of the great cabin, and banners of the blue and gold of the Knights of the Holy Ghost fluttering from the tops and the mastheads. Like most of the country-built sailing-ships in the Peru of that day, she was a poor sailer and required a great deal of maintenance. Her sails and cordage were indifferent and far from durable.

Subordinates who were ordered by the viceroy to accompany the expedition included several of the worst characters in the public life of Peru. Prominent among these was Juan Ochoa de Bilboa, whose appointment was as chief pilot, though he had no knowledge of any waters other than those on the tropic coast line of South America, and he was well known as a disaffected and trouble-making person. With him, as purser of the fleet, went Juan de Iturbe, a scurrilous self-seeker who was dumbfounded at the idea that any man should so value his religious convictions as to be unable to profit by whatever opportunities came his way. There was also Don Diego de Prado, about whom not much is known, except that he was a sworn enemy of Queiros and can scarcely have been much use on the expedition.

The second-in-command, or at any rate the commanding officer of the second ship, was a Portuguese pilot named Luis Vaz de Torres, an able navigator who may have been selected by Queiros himself. Torres was a forthright man, unable to suffer fools gladly, and a source of strength to an expedition which sadly needed it. As the difficulties that assailed the flesh grew, Queiros was inclined to leave their solution to the Almighty. A deep feeling of piety and overwhelming religious convictions, though sources of great strength to himself, were of little value to ships he commanded and of no influence whatever with such persons as Bilboa and Iturbe. Torres found himself looking upon his commander with grave doubts even before they sailed from Callao.

He probably felt even graver doubts when at last the sailing day arrived—December 12, 1605. The little fleet sailed through Callao Roads with a great show of ceremony, and Queiros had all hands attired in the garb of friars to impress the better upon them, and on those who beheld them, the essential pilgrimage of the voyage. He was bound on no idle search for islands whence King Solomon might, or might not, have obtained some gold, but on a great voyage to discover lands hitherto hidden from the European, to disperse forever the fog which still lay upon the vast continent of the South Sea, and to bring to the dwellers thereof the revelation of Christ's teachings. This was an atonement for Europe's long neglect of these millions of poor heathen. Banners streamed on the afternoon breeze, and the friars led in chanting and in prayer. Here came Queiros, master of his fate at last, with two ships and a launch, bound for the Unknown: and so great was his devotion, and so abundant his strength and his sincerity that, for the moment at least, even the bickering Bilboa and the scurrilous Iturbe held their peace and, in their pilgrims' garb, chanted with the rest.

But beyond Callao Roads lay the cold sea, thousands upon thousands of miles of it: and the sea listened to no chanting, paid heed to no strivings after grace, eased the paths of no pilgrims. The sea hid no *Terra Australis—cognita* or *incognita—* save the useless frozen land of the great Antarctic wastes— much of it beyond 70 south, where sailing-ships could not go —and the continent of Australia, nearly 8,000 miles away, where such aborigines as survive their contact with the ennobling White remain bewildered heathen, in great part, until this day. Poor Queiros! Yet his idea was a great one.

As the sea winds weathered the soft face of the Virgin on the counter and the banners faded, troubles came. Queiros's standing orders to his brother pilot Torres were voluminous and comprehensive, but it was he who ought to have studied some of them. Torres was to throw overboard all playing cards and dice, to maintain "Christian, political, and military discipline," to see that there was no cursing or blasphemy and that daily prayers were properly conducted and attended. He was to be strict about the issue of proper rations and the conserving of food and water. Rations to be served daily to each person on board were listed as follows:

> 1½ lb. of biscuit
> 1 lb. of meat
> 2 oz. of bacon
> 1 oz. of pulses
> ½ gal. of fresh water for drinking, with sufficient for cooking

On fish days, when meat was not issued, the ration was to be "one fish or, if it is large, part of one; 6 ounces of pulses; a measure of oil, another of vinegar, and biscuit and water as on meat days. If there is no fish, 4 ounces of cheese is to be substituted." These are generous rations and would be much appreciated even by the postwar Europe of 1948. The food was ample and good, for Queiros had had enough of short rations. He was determined to preserve the health of his people, and his was the first expedition to carry a distilling apparatus to make fresh water from the sea. This was a "copper instrument," which was used in a "brick oven built over one of the hearths." Beyond the fact that it was capable of producing two or three jars of drinking water daily and must have consumed a lot of fuel, we know nothing further of this device.

His preventives against scurvy were cleanliness and good food, with as many fresh fruits and vegetables as the islands could afford. The Brothers of Juan de Dios had charge of the antiscurvy campaign, which was highly effective. During the nine months the *Capitana* was at sea only one man died, and he was over eighty.

The plan of the voyage was to sail toward the west-south-west from Callao until they reached the latitude of 30 degrees south, where Queiros hoped to sight the coast of *Terra Australis*. Torres advised going to 40 south. Perhaps he had picked up some special knowledge, or thought he had; in those days a pilot kept much of his knowledge to himself.

Before they reached 30 south, Bilboa was stirring up discord about the cold. There was a blow from the westward with a big sea, as there so often is in that area. The father commissary spent the night "conjuring the sea and winds," and the sailors saluted St. Elmo "with great devotion three times." It was all very well to salute St. Elmo, but Bilboa started the rumor that the saint had sent his fires to warn them against the folly of standing on. Next morning the other vessels closed the *Capitana* as usual for the daily orders and to pass news of the night. These sunset and dawn hailings were an excellent means for a man with a loud voice to spread subversive propaganda. Bilboa shouted across to the other ships that winter was near and it was time they altered course toward the north in order that they might not freeze. There were ominous murmurings when the people in the *Capitana* heard this. For several days there had been a sharpness in the air which mariners from the Peruvian coast did not like. It blew fresh that afternoon, with squalls of rain that lashed the little ships and caused them to strike their topmasts and remove the bonnets from the courses. There were savage looks at Queiros as the cold sprays began to drive on board with greater weight, and the loose gear on the decks clattered about as the vessels jumped and leaped in the rising sea.

After a few days of this, and an open rupture with Bilboa, Queiros altered course to west-northwest. This was on January 26, 1606. It was a wise decision. Though no one in the little fleet could know it, there was no point in standing on toward the south. There, the ships would be battered to pieces. To stand to the westward in the zone of the wild west winds, in weakly built ships manned by disaffected sailors used to the milder sailing of tropic seas, would be to seek shipwreck.

Queiros turned away from the land that was not there, and soon the fleet was in good weather again. This made the discontented the more morose, since they had more time for grumbling. Queiros began to regret that he had sailed without irons or any other of the corrective and disciplinary aids of the day. He had deluded himself with the belief that the mood of religious exaltation which inspired him was also the ruling force of the greater number of the others on board. It was not; with reluctance he had the boatswain lash a block to the main yardarm. But that was as far as he went. No rope was ever rove through the block to string Bilboa's neck, not even when the same Bilboa, arrogant after the change of course, drew his sword upon the quarter-deck and menaced those who were still loyal. Bilboa's sword was taken from him and he was confined to his cabin for a day or two. Queiros, disheartened by the daily evidence of man's disgusting infirmities, became sick.

They sighted Anaa Island, in the group of atolls now called the Tuamotus. Queiros was not far from Tahiti then; if he had sailed west instead of west-northwest, he would have come upon that island and the others near it.

Bilboa now insinuated that Queiros had sailed too far to the west and had overrun his objectives. Again by means of loud remarks at the dawn and dusk assemblies, Bilboa spread his calumnies, and the crews listened, as they were meant to do. In the great cabin of the *Capitana,* Queiros sought communion with his God and, with his poet-secretary, continued his plans for the founding of a New Jerusalem in the Coral Sea and pressed on with the preparation of blue crosses for his Knights of the Holy Ghost.

Men accustomed to shorter, simpler passages on the American coast began to grow fearful of the immensity of the ocean they continued to cross. Day after day it stretched interminably before them: day after day they sailed toward the rim of the unbroken horizon: sunset after sunset and dawn after dawn, the same horizon, unbroken as ever, beckoned them on. Toward what? Bilboa said to their destruction, for he was genuinely fearful of the outcome of a voyage the like of which he had never known.

"Worse things were said of Queiros than if he had been a Turk," wrote the poet-chronicler. "The Captain replied to all this that it was not a new thing to him, for on other voyages he had sailed with men who were easily wearied. What such men wanted was good health, plenty to eat and drink, little work, many complaints, much grumbling together, and as little love as possible for the voyage. . . ."

By the end of March, when they had been little more than three months at sea, Bilboa was out of hand. He called a council of pilots, the ostensible purpose of which was to discuss dead reckoning and longitude. Queiros estimated that Santa Cruz was some 1,850 leagues to the westward of Callao: Bilboa had shouted only that morning that they had already sailed 2,000. He added that they had been sailing for 94 days continuously, and on the previous passage the island had been sighted in less than 70. He made no allowance for the long leg toward the south, which added weeks to the passage. Torres thought they had sailed not much short of 2,000 leagues, all told, and were then about 1,800 leagues west of Callao. Queiros gave his reckoning as 1,700. It was found that Bilboa's workings included an error of 600 leagues. He was turned out of the ship for that and for gross insubordination, and the unfortunate Torres was commanded to take him to the *Almirante* forthwith. He took a meaning look at the block at the main yardarm and objected strongly to being made Bilboa's keeper, saying with some heat that it was more punishment for himself than for the mutinous chief pilot.

The fortuitous discovery of the island of Taumaco in the Duff group, a few days later, distracted attention from boredom, intrigue, and incipient mutiny. They landed at Taumaco and a priest celebrated Mass, while the natives followed them attentively and aped all they did. It was here that Queiros was astonished by the geographical and general maritime knowledge of Tumai, the chief, and his seafaring people. Tumai had heard of the death of Malope at Santa Cruz, and he had a great respect for Spanish arms. He told the Spaniards about many islands to the south, and one which Queiros took to be a continent. At this, Queiros abandoned his intention of going to Santa Cruz, seized four of the local geographers to show him where the great island was, and got under way again, banners flying.

A brief northwest breeze sprang up fresh; for a few hours the ships were driven from their course. When the wind drew back again to its customary quarter of east-southeast and the weather cleared, the pilots asked Queiros what the course was to be. Their leader's reply, "Put the ships' heads where they like, for God will guide them as may be right," is surely the strangest recorded course ever given to a helmsman.

It was not so crazy as it sounds, for the clearing wind had shown the islands of the New Hebrides to be close aboard, and from the position where the ships then were, the overlapping coast lines of the several islands gave the appearance of a continuous mainland, high, wooded, welcoming, pleasant. *Terra*

Australis at last! No wonder Queiros did not quibble about the precise point of the compass to be steered. God had brought him that far: God would bring him to anchorage now. God did. But there was little that was godly about it, save beauty. They came into the great bay which Queiros called the Bay of St. Philip and St. James, in the island which he named Austrialia * del Espiritu Santo, thinking it a mainland. His stay was so brief and his mood so exalted that he did not even discover that this was an island.

An occasion such as this must be marked by proper ceremony. He had not been permitted to hold a religious festival before departing from Peru. Now things would be done properly. First, the Order of the Knights of the Holy Ghost was established and the insigne of the order issued to almost every man in the three ships. The insigne was a simple blue cross, meant to be worn on the breast over a taffeta robe. All were confessed. They fired artillery, rang bells, beat drums. An advance party landed to rig an altar on the beach. By night the ships were illuminated with lanterns, and they fired rockets and fire wheels. There was music and dancing.

Next morning they landed, Queiros leading. He fell upon the warm sand of the beach above high-water mark and kissed it, while the friars chanted and the mariners stood by solemnly, the blue cross of the new order at their breasts, their hearts full of hope that at last, on this third attempt, Spain had solved the problem of the South Sea. Queiros, when all was ready, recited in a strong and deeply moved voice the formula for taking possession of new lands. For the king and for the pope, he claimed the great bay in which the ships were anchored and "all the lands which I sighted and am going to sight, and of all this region of the south as far as the Pole, which from this time shall be called AUSTRIALIA DEL ESPIRITU

---

* *AUSTRIALIA*, not Australia. The intention was to mark the king of Spain's connection with Austria, of which he was archduke.

SANTO, with all its dependencies and belongings; and this for ever, and as long as right exists. . . ."

The ships again fired all their artillery, the father commissary and his five barefoot monks said three Masses; and the services, the processions, and later the jollifications went on all day and far into the night. Queiros had the block rigged down from the main yardarm, and a friar brought Bilboa before him, asking pardon, the wily Bilboa well aware that there would scarcely be a better opportunity. He was restored to some measure of grace, which was unfortunate.

In the meantime Queiros's grandiose schemes for the founding of his New Jerusalem made haste slowly, except in such manners as required only the effort of the mind. A river debouching into the bay was called the Jordan; the officers of the city of New Jerusalem were elected, twenty-three strong. They set about building a church of wood on a spot carefully chosen to provide a fitting site for the great cathedral Queiros said would soon arise there. They sowed a little land with maize, cotton, onions, melons, pumpkins, beans, and pulse. Torres was now master of the camp, and an able one. But there was not much for him to do.

There were troubles soon after landing. The natives were not impressed by the chanting and the processions, though doubtless they enjoyed the extraordinary show. The Spaniards cut down their trees and seized their land without recompense. The natives showed reluctance to bring food, for they had no desire to encourage the strangers to remain. In return, the Spaniards seized some children in order that their parents might bring food to ransom them, which they did. But the children were not returned.

Torres had difficulty in obtaining precise orders from his leader, who seemed like a man in a trance. Bilboa and his kind, after a few days, began to ask where the gold was. And where were the clothed people? Some soldiers asked for permission to prospect for precious metals, saying this was their trade. Queiros answered that the expedition was to save souls, not gold.

This was received with loud murmurs, and some of the men threw their crosses in the Jordan. Native restlessness grew when the children were not returned. New Jerusalem had to be fortified.

For a bare five weeks Queiros remained in the bay of his continent. Exactly how he came to leave is still a mystery. The few accounts are contradictory and may be biased. The main account is from the pen of the poet-secretary, who says that they sailed, after five weeks at the anchorage, to complete the discovery of the southern continent. He implies that both Queiros and Torres sailed, according to some mutually agreed-upon plan. But, he says, when they were outside the bay, it blew hard from the southeast with considerable sea. It was decided to return to the anchorage. Torres managed to beat his ship in again, but Queiros was badly set down to leeward. The *Capitana* would not go to windward, and after beating for six days, the attempt had to be abandoned. Santa Cruz was the agreed rendezvous in case of accident, and Queiros now wished to make for that island. Even the loyal poet can no longer gloss over the fact that the management of the ship was taken out of Queiros's hands. They did not try to make for Santa Cruz or to look for any further part of the coast line of their "continent," but instead sailed back to America.

From other accounts it seems probable that there was mutiny; at any rate, Queiros was quietly deposed while the ship sailed away. Torres states quite clearly that the *Capitana* sailed out of the innermost part of the bay in the middle of the night, after they both had returned from a brief exploratory passage spoiled by bad weather. Torres adds that the *Capitana* made no signal or any other indication of her intention to leave, and showed no lights. In his opinion there was certainly mutiny.

Queiros never lost hope of returning to his "continent."
He gave himself to the effort without stint but also without
profit. He was back in Madrid by early October, 1607, again
destitute. He arrived with two small coins, which he gave to a
deserving beggar. His poet-secretary was still with him. What
an extraordinary pair they were! The story of their long and
unselfish association, their devotion to a common and great
ideal, must stir even those who find it hard to overlook the
incapacity for leadership which spoiled Queiros's otherwise
great voyage and greater vision.

Queiros busied himself writing memorials about his discoveries and about *Terra Australis,* with which to impress the
Court and the influential Council of State. He produced fifty
memorials in as many months. Of these, some eight are known
to exist. They became more flamboyant and extravagant in
language as time went on. There was soon nothing that his
Terra Australis could not produce. Its climate was temperate,
its produce tropical, its wooded glades and gardens like Eden.
Before long, Queiros began to be regarded as a nuisance. More
than that, he was a danger. It was feared that so industrious
a producer of memorials might not always be careful into
whose hands they fell, and foreigners, already casting jealous
eyes on the colonies of Spain, might learn more than was good
for them. Queiros might even give his services to the upstart
English, or the Dutch.

In truth, nothing could have been further from the great
pilot's mind, for both the English and the Dutch were heretics,
and the idea of their faith, or the lack of it, spreading to the
peoples of the great lands of the South Sea was anathema to
him and to all good Catholics. But a scheme was hatched to
delude the dreamer. He was sent off at last, after seven years
of memorials and general agitation. In his satchel was a royal
letter instructing the viceroy of Peru to provide him with
ships and men for another expedition. Not in his satchel, not

even in the same ship, but in a faster one which sailed earlier, was a *contra-despacho* ordering the same viceroy to "entertain Queiros, but not to despatch his business." With him on this last voyage were the faithful poet and the navigator's wife and children.

At Panama, in 1615, Queiros died. He was fifty years old. He did not know about the *contra-despacho;* in keeping that knowledge from him, the God he had served well was merciful.

CHAPTER NINE

LUIS VAZ DE TORRES

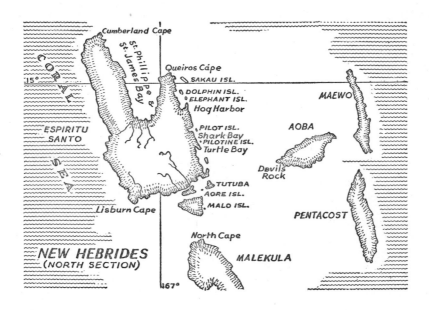

LUIS VAZ DE TORRES, Portuguese pilot and discoverer, was under no delusions as his little ship sweltered in the anchorage at Espiritu Santo. He would have hung Bilboa long since had he been allowed. When the ship with Queiros aboard disappeared from the bay, he knew that he would see neither her nor his leader again. But he dutifully waited fifteen days, during which his own crew became steadily more mutinous. The only good thing about Queiros's disappearance was that he had taken Bilboa with him. Torres quelled the spirit of insubordination in his own ship, and though his people wished to return to Peru, he carried them with him down into the Coral Sea and onward to Manila.

We would have no idea of his subsequent movements if the

only source of information were the archives of Spain. Torres's
"Letter to the King of Spain, Giving an Account of His Voyage to Manila After Parting Company with Queiros" was
written at Manila in July, 1607, but was buried in the archives
there until the British took the town in 1762. The letter came
into the hands of a man named Dalrymple, who realized its
value and made known its contents. Torres says that he wound
up the brief affairs of New Jerusalem and took off the ordnance
that had been landed. His own crew had no heart for the
further prosecution of the voyage. But Torres stood no nonsense from them.

"My temper was different from that of Captain Pedro
Fernandez de Queiros," he says, adding that opportunities
for such voyages do not occur every day. Sealed orders were
opened, and he was disappointed to read that Don Diego de
Prado was to assume command in Queiros's absence. Nonetheless, it is evident that practical leadership remained with Torres, despite the orders. Instructions were that they would continue westward until reaching 21 degrees south, and then sail
northwest and so to Manila, round the north of New Guinea.

Torres first tried to examine Espiritu Santo more closely,
and he nearly succeeded in sailing round the island, but the
currents and fresh trade wind prevented him. So he stood away
and made a long tack down into the Coral Sea. Again the real
Australia narrowly missed discovery (or perhaps a visit from
another Portuguese mariner), for had Torres continued on
this course a few days longer, he must have come to the coast
of New South Wales. As it was, he came very close to New
Caledonia and then altered course more to the north. But he
found himself in the great gulf that stretches from the north
Queensland coast to the south coast of New Guinea. He then
sailed westward along the south of New Guinea. Here his account is laconic in the extreme, so much so that he might have
been describing a sail along a well-known route.

I fell in with the beginning of New Guinea the coast of which trends from east to west [he says]. *I could not go up the east side, so I went coasting to the west, and on the south side it is all the land of New Guinea. . . . Having run three hundred leagues of the coast . . . we could not go forward on account of the numerous shoals and strong currents which there are throughout, so we had to go on by the south-west course. There were some very large islands and more were seen to the south. . . . We found ourselves in twenty-five fathoms of water and five degrees latitude, and ten leagues from the coast, and we had gone four hundred and eighty leagues. Here the coast trends to the north-east. I did not reach it, because the bank is very shoal, so I went on running to the north . . . as far as four degrees, when we fell in with a coast which also stretched from east to west. . . . We understood that it joined on with the coast we had left behind. . . . Lastly we ran along to the west-north-west beside this coast. . . . Here it was in this country where I found the first iron and bells of China . . . by which we understood more certainly that we were near the Moluccas, and so we went following this coast.*

All the coastal districts of New Guinea, he found well populated by people "not very white." He kidnaped some twenty of these from various places, the idea being to compel them to learn Spanish and then impart information, preferably about gold. In western New Guinea he also found "Moors" who had artillery "such as falconets and swivel guns and arquebuses." These Mohammedans "go conquering the people who are called Papuas, and preach to them the sect of Mohamed." They sold Torres some fowls, goats, fruit, and a little pepper. He could not properly replenish his stores, because all the trade goods were with Queiros in the *Capitana*.

"From hence to the Moluccas it is all islands," says Torres. He continued to Ternate and thence to Manila, where he was scurvily received. The officials of colonial Spain were not interested in voyages except those which brought them direct profit. Torres reflects sadly that he found them more interested in their private gain than in the public business.

With that remark he fades out of history. The Spanish officials lost his letter; within a few years Torres was dead. He had sailed across the Coral Sea, and he had seen the real Australia, either without being aware of it or well knowing that it was no new discovery.

The voyage of Queiros and Torres was a notable one. With Mendaña, they had found the Solomon Islands and the New Hebrides, the Duff and Banks groups, and at least thirteen other islands, mainly in the southwest Pacific. They had blazed the way toward Australia. Had either Spain or Portugal then been in a position to follow up these voyages, Pedro Fernandez de Queiros would without doubt be reckoned now as the Christopher Columbus of the great South Sea, though his Austrialia de Espiritu Santo was 1,000 miles from Australia and was considered of so little worth that it remained unvisited by Europeans, after its discovery, for more than one hundred and fifty years. These great voyages were made too late. The glory of Spain was in decline. The defeat of her war fleets by the weather and a handful of English sailors in the English Channel in 1588, the chaotic state of her colonies in Central and South America, and the inevitable consequences of her own shortsighted policies, caused her by the beginning of the seventeenth century to draw in her reins. Her aim then was to assimilate rather than colonize.

Drake had been in the Pacific before 1580, and others of the upstart and too successful English followed him. Of what use was it to colonize the Solomons or settle the New Hebrides,

when these might well become staging points for the maraud-
ing English? Either group was well placed to provide refreshment for pirates bound from Peru toward the Philippines.
"The maine Ocean by right is the Lord's alone" was the English view; from the time of their King Henry VIII they cared
nothing for papal orders. Their espionage of Spanish—and
Portuguese—navigational and economic intelligence was becoming increasingly good. From the time that Mr. Robert
Thorne, a Bristol merchant residing in Seville, fearfully forwarded a stolen chart of the route to the spice islands to his
ambassador in 1527, the English had learned far more than
was good for them to know, from the Spanish point of view.
Using the information furnished by Thorne, the British ambassador forwarded a report on the wealth of the spice trade to
his king. Knowledge of Mendaña's Solomons reached England
through a trader in Mexico. There were other nations anxious
to share in the great wealth which had been tapped by Spain.
The Portuguese were themselves fully extended in India and
the East Indies: even had they wished, they could scarcely
have developed the new lands discovered by their nationals
sailing for Spain. At the vital period—1580 to 1640—Spain
and Portugal were under the same crown.

The Solomons then slipped from the maps, after a brief appearance upon them: before they were found again there were
geographers who declared them mere figments of Spanish
imagination. This they were not: today, many of them still
bearing their Spanish names, they stand, 700 miles long, across
the eastern end of the Coral Sea. At the pretty island of Santa
Catalina, off the southeastern end of San Cristoval, the islanders
still remember in dance and legend the landing of Mendaña's
men there nearly four centuries ago. Austrialia del Espiritu
Santo, known merely as Santo for many years, still has no New
Jerusalem, though in the 1941–1945 Japanese war 300,000
Americans were on the island, which was then an advanced base

for the Pacific campaign. Santo is a rich island with good harbors, broad fertile valleys, and heavy forests. Queiros's dream
that a great city could arise there may yet come true one day: in
the meantime a wooded headland at the eastern end of his great
Bay of St. Philip and St. James still bears his name and is his
only Coral Sea memorial.

CHAPTER TEN

THE HOLLANDERS

CORAL SEA, *Mar del Coral, Koral Zee?* It might have been any of these. The mantle which was thrown down by the Spaniards was taken by the Dutch, who before the close of the sixteenth century were already cutting into the trade of the rich East Indies. They sought spices and the wealth that spices brought: like the Portuguese, they were too good seamen to leave their flanks exposed. Shortly after they had established themselves in Java and the Moluccas, they were sending picked men in the tracks of Antonio de Abreu and Manoel de Eredia. The Hollanders, like the English, were insistent in their attempts to find out what the Portuguese knew. There is evidence that they had heard of Australia before their own sailors, coming a new way, began to be wrecked on the west coast of that continent, and they knew New Guinea was an island, though no sailor of theirs ever found the way through Torres Straits.

A Hollander named Jan Huighen van Linschoten was one of the more successful early agents. He had served for some time as secretary to the Portuguese archbishop of Goa. In this capacity he learned a great deal about the fabulous spice trade, and what he learned he passed on. Before 1590 he was exhorting Dutch merchants to send their ships around the Cape, "especially to Java, an island not yet frequented by the Portuguese, but abounding in diamonds, frankincense, and spices." This trade, he added, was in the hands of "Moors" who used Malacca as their principal market: there should be little difficulty in wresting it from them.

Dutch merchants knew already of the fortunes to be made in the spice trade, for they were the chief distributing agents for goods from the East to northern Europe. In this capacity they did very well, and they might have continued satisfied and successful handlers of products which were brought to them in others' ships had not a foolish edict banned them from the trade in 1594. The intention was to punish the Dutch for declaring their independence. The Dutch answer was to seize the trade at its source. The first Dutch ship was in Java by 1596, and although the first voyage was not successful commercially, the Dutch East India Company was founded in 1602, and Dutch ships thereafter quickly ousted the Portuguese from the trade. The Portuguese had had to fight their way over the whole Indian Ocean, and they were spent. The Dutch merchants had little difficulty in establishing themselves. Between 1602 and 1614 the Dutch East India Company paid annual dividends which averaged 37 per cent. One year the profit was 160 per cent. They had found—or rather seized—a gold mine.

This, they proceeded to exploit with such thoroughness and efficiency that they soon took over the whole East Indies, building the area into a compact and immensely successful colonial enterprise which endured, to their great profit, for more than three centuries. They might easily have extended their dominion over the whole southwest Pacific.

It was necessary for the Dutch to have knowledge of the eastern approaches to Java and the spice islands, that they might at least be aware of the quarter whence interlopers might come. They had to be assured that there was no easy way to Batavia via the Coral Sea (as in fact there was), and that Australia offered no real possibilities for colonizing by another power (as in fact it did). They did their best to ensure both things; it was the fault of their navigators that they failed. They were unable, in spite of repeated attempts, even to find Torres Straits. They made several voyages from the further East Indies ports to examine the possibilities of New Guinea and northwestern Australia, and to push a way through into the Coral Sea.

This way the little *Duyfhen* sailed, under Willem Janszoon, who was sent in 1606 to see what offered. In the very year that Torres, commanding a considerably larger, much more unhandy, and somewhat decrepit ship, passed successfully through the strait to the westward, the small and handily rigged *Duyfhen* could do no better than become embayed in the Gulf of Carpentaria. She sailed from Bantam on November 18, 1605, which ought to have brought her to the Torres Straits waters with northwesterly winds. Her instructions were to explore the *island* of New Guinea, but she bore away to the south'ard somewhere about Cape York and ran down the western side of Cape York Peninsula, apparently thinking this to be New Guinea. The letter of proceeding, which survives, states that they "sailed along what was thought to be the west side of New Guinea to 13 ¾ degrees of South Latitude" and found nothing but desert inhabited by "wild cruel black savages" who murdered some of the crew.

As for the "wild cruel black savages," one of Janszoon's
chief activities was the kidnaping of natives in order that they
could be taught Dutch or Malay and so disclose what knowledge they might possess. The aborigines on that coast were accustomed to attempts to kidnap them, for the Malays in quest
of *bêche-de-mer* were never against seizing an aborigine or
two and turning them to work. Jan Carstenz, commanding
the *Pera*, also tried his hand at kidnaping when he followed
in the *Duyfhen's* tracks in 1623, with more success in the seizing of blacks though no more at discovery. He managed to
secure one poor aborigine by lassoing him round the neck.

> *By showing them bits of iron and strings of beads we
> kept them on the beach till we had come near them* [reads
> Carstenz' log], *on which one of them who had lost his
> weapon was seized round the waist by the skipper, while
> at the same time the quartermaster put a noose round his
> neck, by which he was dragged to the pinnace. The other
> blacks, seeing this, tried to rescue their brother by fu-
> riously assailing us with their assegais. In defending our-
> selves we shot one of them.*

A little later the same log records, apparently with astonishment, that "in spite of our special kindness and fair semblance
the blacks received us as enemies everywhere." Probably the
bush telegraph had been working.

Mariners who hoped to probe the secrets of *Terra Australis*,
or any other secrets, from the minds of a few Australian
aborigines must have been optimists. Though many natives
were taken in this manner both from northern Australia and
from New Guinea, and some were required to learn Spanish
and some Dutch, there is no record anywhere that any of them
ever disclosed anything useful. These were no Polynesians: the
Australian black never built anything water-borne save the

frailest of bark canoes, and his knowledge was that of the Stone Age Bushman.

"They are in general utter barbarians and coal black [ran Carstenz' summary]. They are utterly unacquainted with gold, silver, lead, tin, iron or copper. Nor do they know anything about nutmegs, cloves and pepper."

In short, they offered no prospects of trade; there was no way through to the Coral Sea; and with his lassoed aborigine more or less patiently learning Dutch, Jan Carstenz returned to his East Indies base and never again approached the Coral Sea.

In 1636 a third expedition under Gerrit Tomas Pool did no better. Pool was murdered.

If Dutch seamen could not find the way to the Coral Sea round the north of Australia (which they early called New Holland), then they must go there another way. An enterprising Dutch governor of the East Indies named Antony van Diemen conceived the bold move of sailing down the west coast of Australia and then eastward to the Pacific. A voyage along these lines was planned by one Frans Visscher, a "pilot of renown," but though Visscher sailed on the expedition, its leadership was entrusted to Abel Janszoon Tasman, who was perhaps the greatest of the Dutch navigators and certainly the most fortunate.

Tasman's orders were to sail from Batavia, pass through the Straits of Sunda, and make a long tack through the southeast trades to Mauritius; thence run through the west-wind zone further east than any Dutch or other ship had been before, with leave to pass 800 miles beyond the longitude of Mendaña's Solomons: thence he was to sail to the nor'ard, look for the Solomons, Austrialia del Espiritu Santo, and Santa Cruz and examine the east coast of New Guinea. He was to return to Batavia. This was an excellently planned voyage, both for the new area it penetrated and the seamanlike use it made of the prevailing winds.

Tasman sailed from Batavia with the two ships *Heemskirk* and *Zeehan* on August 14, 1642, and from Mauritius on October 8 of the same year. Mauritius was Dutch at the time and offered a convenient port for refreshment and repair before entering the Roaring Forties. It was a convenient weatherly departure point for the voyage proper. Leaving Mauritius, he stood down at once toward the west-wind zone and reached 47 south, but it was early summer in the far south, and the southwest wind blew cold from the nearby icebergs. Tasman's crews, too long accustomed to the kinder weather of tropic seas, complained, and he altered course northward to 44 south.

Here he ran to the east, the first in a long and glorious line of square-rigged ships to run that way, and for that, perhaps the most famous of them all. The route he took was to become, two centuries later, the way of the early convict transports to Botany Bay, and after that of the immigrant clippers and the racing wool ships and the grain ships. Here in later days those lovely wooden square-rigged ships *James Baines, Lightning, Thermopylae,* and *Cutty Sark* (in their wool-clipper days), and after them the great iron and steel four-masted barques and full-rigged ships of the last of sail were to race in the squalls toward the ports of Australia. Tasman's little *Heemskirk* and *Zeehan,* under prudently shortened sail, ran onward with only the albatross and the mollyhawk for company, and dawn after stormy dawn, Tasman and Visscher anxiously searched the eastern horizon for sign of land.

They ran almost 4,000 miles before they saw any. On November 24, forty-six days out from Mauritius, they sighted the high mountains of the west coast of Tasmania. With that auspicious beginning it ought to have been a simple matter to discover eastern Australia, which was only a few hundred miles away—thousands of miles of it. But Tasman skirted the tip of Tasmania, which he called Van Diemen's Land, and did not so much as sight a single aborigine or seriously try to follow the trend of the land. He made a running survey of the southern portion of the island, very rough, though he fixed his longitude with surprising accuracy, for like all navigators forced to sail without an accurate chronometer, he was dependent on dead reckoning and lunar observations. The longitude of his landfall, he computed as 146 degrees 46 minutes east of Greenwich. (His actual figure was 163: 30 east of the peak of Teneriffe, which is 16; 46 west of Greenwich).

The precise longitude of his ship when he made this computation must have been within 20 miles of the position he gives. This excellent result was likely the work of Visscher, who had not gained his reputation for nothing. Even today, a navigator with a chronometer in a small sailing-ship would be pleased enough to come out of a 4,000-mile run in the west winds and find himself not more than 20 miles out in his longitude.

Tasman set up a pole with the Dutch flag on it, "took possession of the said land as our lawful property," weathered a blow or two, and sailed away. This seems to be extraordinary conduct on the part of a discoverer, even one with so large a commission as Tasman had. What he had come across was no barren piece of harborless desert such as other Dutchmen had discovered on the northwest of Australia. His Van Diemen's Land was a rich, lovely, and fertile island, well forested and abounding in minerals, and containing in its lovely coast line one of the best harbors in the southern hemisphere. But he scarcely looked at the place.

From Tasmania the *Heemskirk* and *Zeehan* crossed the Tasman Sea in 41 degrees south and came next upon New Zealand. This, Tasman concluded, was probably the west coast of *Terra Australis*. Had he sailed a little further to the eastward here, he would have come upon the open Pacific, which stretched before his ships from that point right to Cape Horn. It is difficult to explain why Tasman failed to find that the passage he was in was a strait and not a bay. Though Cook Strait can be a difficult place for a square-rigged ship, with eddies, strong tides, and frequent heavy squalls, it should have presented little real trouble to ships which had already sailed 5,000 miles in the west winds and were less than three months out from a good base. The *Heemskirk* and *Zeehan* must have been handy ships and smart enough. They had sailed from the east coast of Tasmania to New Zealand in little more than a week, though they shortened sail by night.

Some of the people from the *Heemskirk* were murdered by the Maoris at Golden Bay. These Maoris had taken New Zealand by assault and were not prepared to allow any newcomer to repeat the performance. But they had only hand weapons and spears; their "ships" were canoes. Some understandable opposition on their part ought not to have been enough to deter a discoverer with a pair of well-armed and well-manned ships. Tasman's conduct is the more inexplicable in that he himself was more or less convinced—at the time, at least—that he was then upon the west coast of the long-sought *Terra Australis*. If the land he saw did indeed stretch away more than 4,000 miles toward Cape Horn, then he had found a continent. But he did not even bother to land to examine it.

He says that, when some canoes approached the Dutch ships, the natives "called to us several times, but their language had nothing in it like the vocabulary of the Solomon Islands given us by the general and council at Batavia." The council at Batavia could have obtained a vocabulary of the "Solomon Islands" only from Mendaña's records, through a nice piece of espionage in Spain. One wonders what else they had hold of. It would have been extraordinary if a Polynesian Maori in New Zealand had understood anything that a Dutchman with a

Malay accent shouted at him from a book compiled by a Cas-
tilian who had spent six months in the Solomon Islands almost
a century earlier.

Tasman sailed away to the north, along the west coast of the
north island of New Zealand. If he had landed at Onehunga,
he could have walked across the island in an afternoon and
have seen the Pacific to the east. He named a place or two—
Three Kings' Islands, Cape Maria van Diemen. He called the
whole land Staten Landt, in honor of the States-General. Then
off he went to the nor'ard and came upon some of the Friendly
Islands. He was well received by the natives of Tongatabu, to
whom he gave some nails, beads, and cheap looking glasses from
the goods he had brought for trade. For this rubbish and some
cloth, he stocked his ships with coconuts, yams, bananas, plan-
tains, hogs, and fowls. The chief, says Tasman, "behaved to us
with great friendship, and inquired of us whence we came and
where we intended to go? We told him that we had been more
than one hundred days at sea, at which he and the natives were
much astonished. We explained to them that we came to their
country for water and provisions; and they answered that we
should have as much as we wished for. . . . We saw no arms
among them; so that here was altogether peace and friendship."

Tasman, however, can hardly be accepted as an observer
without reservation. Despite the friendliness of his reception
in the Tongan islands and the good behavior of the people, he
comments that "among these people, who have the form of the
human species, but no human manners, you may see traces of
reason and understanding." This of the Tongans! Perhaps
Tasman was as good an observer of the peoples of the South Sea
as he was a discoverer of straits.

He visited Tongatabu, Eua, and Nomuka, of the Tonga or
Friendly group, which is nearly 300 southeast of the Fijis. Then
he stood northwestward and soon found himself among the

off-lying reefs of the Fiji Islands, where he met an experience
which completely dispelled whatever appetite he may have
had for venturing among coral islands. The reefs round the Fijis
are notorious both for their dangerous abundance and for the
sets that drift sailing-vessels toward them. One afternoon, the
wind fresh and some sea running but visibility not good, Tasman was alarmed by the ominous shout of "Breakers ahead!"
He was running before the wind at the time, and he immediately hauled his wind on the starboard tack, to get away to
the nor'ard.

Within a few minutes of altering course, the dreadful shout
came from the masthead again.

"Breakers ahead!"

Tasman went aloft himself. There seemed to be breakers
everywhere but in the wake of the ship, and it was not possible
to go back that way. The ship was embayed in reefs; she was
inside an arrowhead of them and fast approaching the point.

In this extremity there was only one thing to do. That was
to choose the place in the reefs where there was least sea breaking, and therefore most chance of sailing over, and make boldly
for it under a press of sail. This they did: they drove the ship
right across the reef, barely managing to scrape her over (the
smaller *Zeehan* did a little better), so anxious and so thoroughly
concerned with the seamanship side of it that they did not
take soundings. But they could see the colored coral grinning
at them in the calmer patches of the shallow water; all round
and about, the sea lashed white and green as if angrily determined to grind the ships upon the reef. Beyond were more
reefs. It was two days before any of them dared draw a free
breath again: these were nightmare days. Bad enough to get
close among charted reefs, knowing full well what to expect:
no wonder that Tasman kept away from the Coral Sea.

He kept the southeast wind on his starboard beam and drove
the ships to the nor'ard for some days, keeping them under

a press of sail by day and almost lying to by night, until a succession of long sunny days showed him that he was clear of reefs. But the scar of that experience stayed with him. He was reef-shy after that. His instructions were to search the Coral Sea: he went up as far as 4 degrees south as fast as he could go, though this was against Governor van Diemen's orders. Then he turned westward, missed all the islands save the unimportant atolls of Ontong Java, which had been seen by Europeans before, and hurried on westward round the north of New Ireland and so to the East Indies again.

He reached Batavia on June 15, 1643, having been absent barely ten months. His principal achievement was to give a demonstration of how much better his voyage might have been. One would like to find some of Frans Visscher's letters describing it and giving his views of Tasman. What a round of discoveries! Tasmania, New Zealand, Tonga, the Fijis—and except for Tongatabu, he sailed past the lot. There is no excuse whatever, except his lack of nerve after the incident with the reefs at the Fijis, for not rediscovering at least the Solomons. There is no shadow of excuse for passing to the north of New Guinea instead of to the south, as he was instructed to do. The view is often put forward that Tasman's was intended essentially as a quick surveying voyage, not a voyage of detailed discovery, and that the Dutch were interested only in trade. Finding no peoples who offered possibilities for exploitation comparable to the industrious millions of the East Indies, say these apologists, Tasman hurried by.

But this is not the view of Anthony van Diemen. His disapproval is thorough and his censure outspoken. In a letter to the company at Amsterdam, van Diemen writes: "The said Commander has been somewhat remiss in investigating the situation, conformation and nature of the lands discovered, and of the natives inhabiting the same, and as regards the main point has left everything to be more closely inquired into by more industrious successors." Later, when the same Tasman had again let him down, van Diemen angrily wrote: "We intend to have everything more closely investigated by more vigilant and courageous persons than have hitherto been employed in this service, for the exploration of unknown regions can by no means be entrusted to the first comer."

Governor van Diemen did not have to charge great ships at reefs in the hope that they might sail over them: but his criticisms are warranted. Discoverers bound for the Coral Sea would do better to stay home if the proximity of dangerous reefs unduly alarmed them.

Nonetheless, van Diemen had to select Tasman as leader of his last large-scale expedition. As soon as the *Heemskirk* and *Zeehan* were back with their report, van Diemen began to plan another expedition which was to find, once and for all, what secrets the Coral Sea might hold. The broad idea was to sail eastward from Batavia along the chain of the East Indies, thence to coast along the south of New Guinea, pass through to the Coral Sea, and find and survey the eastern coasts of New Holland as far south as Tasmania, returning thence along the southern coast of the continent and so through the Indian Ocean to Java again. It was to be an eastward—clockwise—circumnavigation of New Holland, since Tasman had spoiled his passage the other way. Van Diemen's instructions under date of January 29, 1644, are that Tasman must "endeavour by all means to proceed that we may be certain whether this land [of New Guinea] is divided from the great and known South Land or not, and you shall try [if possible] to run to the south-east as far as to the new van Diemen's land, steering along the east coast of the known South Land according to its trending. . . ."

How van Diemen knew that the coast of the "South Land" trended toward the southeast from Torres Strait, he did not

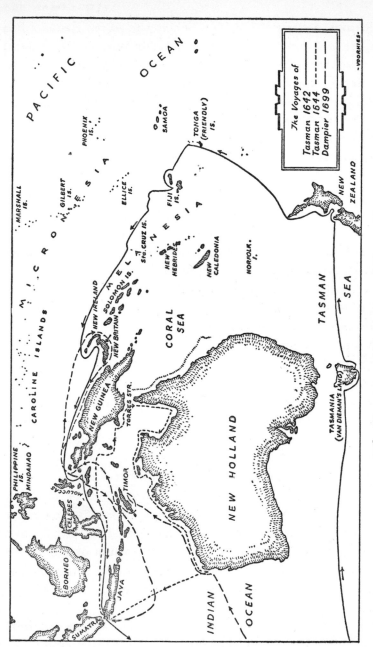

The Voyages of Tasman and Dampier

say. Tasman let the whole idea go by default, for he failed as completely as did his predecessors to find any way through, between Cape York and the south of New Guinea, though there are three channels and he was actually in the mouth of one of them. By that stage, he was putting his ship about whenever he saw a reef, and his escape in the Fijis was a constantly recurring nightmare. It is perhaps as well that he did not reach the Coral Sea in that frame of mind, for there he would have died.

When he returned to Batavia, Governor van Diemen made no secret of his chagrin, but in due course the directors of the Dutch East India Company expressed their disapproval of the governor's plans for further exploration. The company, they said, could obtain gold and silver enough from the trade it already enjoyed, and they were quite unable to "anticipate any great results from the continuation of such discoveries, which entail further expenditure from the company." This in a year when the company made 110 per cent!

Still as firmly convinced as ever that there must be some substance in Queiros's enthusiastic optimism for his great lost land, in the following year Anthony van Diemen died. The reef-haunted Tasman was not employed in command of the company's ships again, and the company made no more expeditions. It was left to others to penetrate the fastnesses of the Coral Sea and rub off the map both New Holland and *Terra Australis Incognita*. It must be a matter of regret, particularly to Holland, that their enterprising van Diemen was not better served. Three hundred years after he made his voyages, it is perhaps a little difficult to give a fair appraisal of Abel Tasman's worth. Some of his journals are missing. But the facts against him stand; and they are formidable.

Tasman's second voyage marked the end of Dutch attempts to explore the Coral Seas by ships sailing from the west. From the east their principal contribution was to open a new route into the South Sea by way of Cape Horn.

The first Dutch voyage into the Pacific through the Strait of Magellan was made in 1598, when five ships left the Texel, bound for the East Indies. Only one survived, and none returned to Holland. The same year a sailor turned innkeeper, Oliver van Noort, set off with another four ships manned by 240 men. He did not fare much better. His object was to harass Spanish trade in the South Sea, but he took fifteen months to reach the Strait of Magellan and another three months to get through. He did very little on the Peruvian coast: the only prize of value threw overboard its gold—five tons of it—before surrendering. This is said to have affected van Noort far more than any hardships of the voyage, and he never recovered from the disappointment. Van Noort crossed the North Pacific and refreshed his ships at the Marianas. Thence he sailed to the Philippines, where he failed to distinguish himself. He was almost three years on his circumnavigation, and he brought only one of his ships back to Holland.

The Dutch sent other fleets through the Strait of Magellan, none of which contributed anything to geographical knowledge of the Coral Sea, or indeed of any other part. The best voyage was that of Joris van Spielbergen [or Spilbergen], who took six well-armed ships from the Texel in August, 1614. He lost no ships, and his voyage accomplished its objectives.

The really interesting Dutch voyages, and the only ones—besides Tasman's—to touch the fringe of the Coral Sea, were made by two interlopers, who, although more than a century separated their efforts, had a number of extraordinary features in common. Both voyages were made by sons of wealthy merchants who wanted to break the monopoly of the Dutch East India Company; both sons inherited their fathers' plans and did their best to carry them out; both used the Cape Horn route (one of them discovered it) to make voyages across the

South Sea; both made interesting discoveries and came near to making great ones. The reward of both was to be flung into jail.

The first was Jacob le Maire, the son of Isaac le Maire, an opulent merchant of Amsterdam. Isaac le Maire had a passion for geography and an abhorrence of the monopoly held by the Dutch East India Company. Somehow or other, he gained access to one of the memorials of Queiros, which had been smuggled out of Spain. This fired him with the ambition to make a voyage into the South Sea and open up trade with the great South Land. The terms under which the Dutch government had granted a monopoly to the East India Company were that it should have the exclusive right to send ships to India by the Cape of Good Hope and the Strait of Magellan. The government was also keen to discover new routes to the Indies, and for this purpose it had issued a decree that, if any man discovered a new passage and made a successful voyage, he should have as his reward the profits of the first four voyages by his route. The idea was to foster the discovery of a northeast passage, where the Dutch had already done valuable pioneering.

But to Isaac le Maire, an avid student of voyages in the neighborhood of the Strait of Magellan, and fired by the memorials of Queiros, the new decree seemed to open the possibility of trying for a route round the tip of South America. He was not alone in holding that there might be a passage there. Isaac le Maire had money and he had learning, but he had no practical experience of the sea. He therefore took into his enterprise one Willem Corneliszen Schouten, "a man well experienced and very famous in navigation, as having already sailed three times to nearly all places in the East Indies as captain, pilot, and merchant, and still very eager after strange voyages and the visiting of new and unknown lands." With Schouten as the real leader, but not the practical performer, of the voyage, went Isaac le Maire's eldest son, Jacob. They fitted out at the town of Hoorn a ship named the *Concord* and a *jaght* which was called the *Hoorn*. The crews were engaged to go where the ships went, and there were many rumors as to their intended destination. The directors called the enterprise the "Australian Company"; the water front called them the gold-seekers, and it was rumored that they knew of islands of fabulous treasure. There was no dearth of volunteers.

The two ships sailed from the Texel on June 14, 1615. As soon as they reached the equator, Jacob le Maire told a muster of the hands of both ships that they were bound to *Terra Australis* by a new passage into the South Sea. The mariners had never heard of *Terra Australis,* and those who could write scrawled the name on bits of paper which they thrust into their caps.

They coasted down the eastern side of South America, but unlike all their predecessors, stood boldly past the entrance to Magellan's strait. At the eastern tip of Tierra del Fuego they found a strait and passed through, naming this place the Strait of Le Maire and the land on their port hand Staten Landt, since they did not observe it was an island. The *Concord* was therefore the first ship to pass through a difficult strait in one of the stormiest areas in the world, which in later days was to be used by many a square-rigged ship bound to the westward round Cape Horn.

Beyond the Strait of Le Maire they found a "great sea," in which "sea mews, larger than swans, with wings stretching a fathom across, flew screaming round the ship." A few of the more superstitious sailors were alarmed at these, saying they were the spirits of the South Sea, who did not want the ship to sail on. The wind came from the westward and blew hard, with savage squalls: but the *Concord* was a stout ship. In due course they came to another extremity of land, which they called Cape Hoorn, after the town of Hoorn in Holland. They made a better passage to windward here than did countless ships that followed them in later days, for they were round in little more than a week. First round the Horn! It was a famous voyage if it had done no more than that.

The *Concord* ran for Juan Fernandez to refresh: but the surf ran strongly when they reached the island, and they could not land. They stood toward the west, and the mariners plucked the bits of paper from their caps again and began to ask, where was this place *Australis?* Where was this great south land? With the people from the *Hoorn,* which had been lost, there was a crowd aboard the *Concord,* and there were too many officers. There was much time for asking questions and, as time passed, for deriding the idea that the waste of sea around them hid anything so substantial as a great land.

Schouten turned the ship's council against Jacob le Maire. Schouten was keen to reach the East Indies, which he knew, and where he was eager to indulge in trade upon his own account. The ship crossed most of the South Pacific in about 15 south, finding a few islands; just as they were approaching the eastern waters of the Coral Sea, the council led by Schouten forced Le Maire to permit the ship's head to be turned toward the west-northwest. They passed within a few miles of the range of visibility of Queiros's Espiritu Santo, and again of his Santa Cruz, and they were near enough to Mendaña's Solomons to see the low atolls of Ontong Java, which now are attached to the administrative area of that group.

And so in their turn they passed to the East Indies along the northern coast of New Guinea and in due course reached the Moluccas and thence Batavia. Here the company's governor seized the ship and sent Le Maire and Schouten back to Holland with Spilbergen, who sneered at the idea that they had found a new way into the South Sea. They had, he said, taken fifteen months to sail one ship from the Texel to Batavia: and they said they had come a "short" way. He had brought six ships through the Strait of Magellan and fought actions on the coast of South America on the way: yet he had done all this in little more than fifteen months. The log of the *Concord* was declared a forgery. On the way back to Holland for trial, Jacob le Maire died.

Jacob Roggeveen was sixty-two years old when, the second famous interloper, he sailed from the Texel with three ships on August 21, 1721, on a voyage which had been planned by his father fifty-two years before. The idea he inherited was to search for *Terra Australis* in the waste of waters that stretched from Cape Horn to the coasts of New Zealand, and his enterprise had the backing of the Dutch West India Company. Jacob Roggeveen had promised his father on his deathbed that he would carry out this plan, but he had to wait until he made a fortune before he could do it. He waited too long. His ships reached the South Pacific with no great difficulty, and the old merchant-turned-mariner began to search first for the alleged Davis-land, a smear upon the charts which a buccaneer named Davis had caused to be put there. While searching for the "continent," he stumbled on a mystery which has never yet been solved, the curious idols of Easter Island.

Disappointed that Davis's large land should shrink to a miserable and apparently useless island, and having permitted his people to commit some atrocious cruelties upon the unfortunate islanders, old Roggeveen sailed off along the tropic's edge, with the favoring east winds which dulled the desires of so many other discoverers, and seems to have given up his idea of finding any more new lands. Exactly where he did go it is now almost impossible to discover, for the old man was embittered by the experiences of his voyage and suffered little to be written about it. He got among the atolls of the Tuamotus, where he lost a ship. Later he sighted something of the Samoas.

Roggeveen must have been very much in the hands of his

professional seamen. Jacob le Maire had been too young to argue with Schouten; Jacob Roggeveen was too old and too inexperienced in the things of the sea to carry real authority with the council of his ships. In those days a ship's council upon an exploratory voyage was a powerful body, and few leaders, if they asked for its decisions, cared to stand against them. Moreover, his navigators had knowledge of several previous tracks, including Le Maire's. After the old gentleman had seen what reefs could do with one of his ships, he was impressed by the argument that, having crossed the Pacific as far as Samoa without seeing anything new, it was time to get on to a safe track and make for Java. So once again the outer belt of great islands which guarded the eastern approaches to the Coral Sea and to Australia remained unseen. The Roggeveen expedition followed what was by then almost a beaten track, well north of the Solomons and to the north of New Guinea.

At Batavia his ships were seized by the East India Company and sold at public auction. Poor Roggeveen was sent back to Holland under virtual arrest and spent his last days claiming damages for his ships. The last of the Dutch explorers, harassed by his countrymen, his fortune lost, he died soon after his return: and the Dutch left the Coral Sea and all the Pacific alone.

Tasman had made the first circumnavigation of Oceania, without being aware of it. He had stumbled upon rich lands which, centuries afterward, were to become great in their own right in the far South Sea. Jacob le Maire had rounded Cape Horn.

But these achievements were far outweighed by the great trade of the East Indies, and the Hollanders confined their efforts to exploiting and consolidating their position there.

CHAPTER ELEVEN

WILLIAM DAMPIER, BUCCANEER

THE DUTCH were not alone in their desire to share the wealth of the Pacific. When the British ambassador in Spain wrote his report on the spice trade, in 1527, it aroused great interest, though nothing was done about it for the following half century. But when intelligence began to reach the English that the Spaniards were on the threshold of discovering a great new continent in the South Sea, enterprising men considered that England might at least have some share in its trade.

The early center of English interest in discovery and exploration was in Devon, and a syndicate of West Country gentlemen gained a sort of permission from Queen Elizabeth to form a company for the exploitation of the Pacific, with particular reference to the unknown continent. Sir Richard Gren-

137

ville was their leader. He was making plans to lead a voyage
of discovery via the Strait of Magellan when the queen, for
reasons best known to herself, suddenly withdrew the half
permission she had given. This was in 1574.

But Queen Elizabeth did not forget the idea entirely.
Within three years it was under consideration again. More
than that: in that very year, the first English ships sailed for
the South Sea. It is now known that one of the objects for
which Sir Francis Drake sailed with his small fleet was to discover and examine whatever parts of the coast of *Terra Australis* might conveniently be accessible, in order to establish a
base for English trade. In fact, he made little attempt to find
Terra Australis; had he done so, a seaman so boldly competent
and fearlessly independent must surely have exploded the
myth of the vast south land and, likely, have put the east coast
of the real continent firmly on the map 200 years before it
actually got there.

But in Drake's day there was nothing for a pirate in the
Coral Sea. Elizabeth, at the time, had little money to spare for
exploration. The main thing was that the voyage should pay.
If there really was such a great south land as the geographers
loved to talk about, the Spaniards could be left to get on with
the discovery and exploitation of it. Then they could be relieved of it, in due course. When Drake reached the South Sea
at last, in 1578, he was blown away from the western end of
the Strait of Magellan and saw enough of the tip of South
America to conclude that the Pacific and Atlantic met near
there. With this surmise he contented himself, and he stood
away to the north as quickly as he could go, to begin his
piratical cruise along the coasts of Peru, Central America,
and Mexico. The wealth that he removed from Spanish colonial
towns and ships must have convinced him that, whether *Terra
Australis* existed or not, there was excellent value in the com-
merce already available.

There is evidence that he sought information about Mendaña's discoveries from the many Portuguese and Spanish pilots he kidnaped, but it is not recorded that he obtained any fresh knowledge in this way. He certainly did his best to augment his navigational information by taking charts, books, and pilots wherever he could find any who seemed likely to be of use. When the little *Golden Hind* (ex-*Pelican*) sailed round the world, the English were good seamen and they had stout ships, but they had access to little navigational information away from the North Atlantic, beyond such as could be filched from Portugal and Spain. Geographical theories were one thing, navigational data quite another. Drake relied greatly upon the data that he seized.

Since in those days navigational knowledge was usually limited to the pilots who had obtained it, he had to seize the pilots too. He had not gone far before he took the Portuguese Nuno da Silva from his ship, off the Cape Verde Islands, in February, 1578. He also took the ship, but he valued the pilot more and kept him longer. A dark and silent little man with a big black beard, this da Silva remained a figure of mystery aboard the *Golden Hind* for many months, down the lengths of both Atlantics, through the Strait of Magellan, up the west coast of South America, and on to Central America. He saw Drake wax fat and boastful as he sailed from success to success along that unguarded coast; he listened to the fiddles playing as he ate at the captain's table.

Precisely what use he was to that famous captain, only Drake and da Silva know. Drake did not publicize it. Da Silva was tried for it in Mexico, and naturally denied having been of any use. Drake had a chart several feet wide which had been prepared for him at Lisbon, and some books which included an account of Magellan's voyage. Perhaps he needed da Silva to interpret Portuguese directions and help him to use Portuguese charts.

The whole of his way up the west coast of America, Drake kidnaped local and deep-sea pilots. At Valparaiso he seized Juan Griego, who knew the South American ports (though these are easy enough to enter). At Payta he persuaded one Custodio Rodríguez, a pilot, to ship aboard the *Golden Hind* by the simple means of seizing his ship and offering him no alternative. Off the island of Cano, from the barque of Rodríguez Tello, he took an old pilot named Alonzo Sanchez Colchero, an official navigator for the China trade, who was traveling to Panama with his charts and instruments. Colchero denied he was a navigator and was clapped in irons for his pains. A noose about his neck and a couple of swings off the deck were intended to persuade him to disgorge information, but the old man could not have given much, despite this treatment, for he was soon exchanged for the pilot of another vessel.

With all this information, in due course Drake crossed the North Pacific, following the Spanish route toward the Philippines. With so much booty, he was not interested then in finding new islands.

Making a call at the Moluccas and the Celebes, Drake took the *Golden Hind* across the Indian Ocean on a long board, with the southeast trade on his little ship's port beam, and so rounded the Cape of Good Hope with the west-setting Agulhas current —the way square-rigged ships went to the end of sail—and ran through the South Atlantic with a favoring wind. On September 26, 1580, he was back in England. He had brought great treasure, and he had added something to what was known in England of Pacific navigation.

After Drake, many others tried to organize raiding voyages to the Pacific. The Devonian idea of colonizing the great southland was in abeyance, though early in the seventeenth century it was temporarily revived. Of those who tried to emulate Drake, only one succeeded. This was a dissolute young man-about-town named Thomas Cavendish, or Candish, of Suffolk. Having squandered most of the fortune he had inherited, Cavendish fitted out two ships for a piratical cruise against the Spaniards in the South Sea. He reached the Pacific by the Strait of Magellan, plundered several towns, took a treasure galleon, kidnaped a number of pilots [including one Sanchez, a "pilot well acquainted with the South Seas"], crossed the North Pacific from the coast of California to the Ladrones, continued on to the East Indies, and sailed back to England by way of the Cape of Good Hope.

Cavendish also gave a wide berth to the Coral Sea and did not pretend to any interest in *Terra Australis*. He brought back some useful observations on ocean winds and currents, and on the navigation of the East Indies. It did not take him long to spend the proceeds of the treasure he had stolen. Setting off to repeat the performance in 1591, he lost control of his companions in the passage of the Magellan straits. Compelled by his crew to put back, Cavendish died miserably at sea on the voyage home.

Interest in South Seas voyages of real discovery slipped back to the realm of the academic. Many of the more venturesome English seamen moved to Holland and began to sail for the Dutch. English interest in the whole Pacific remained dormant, until it was revived almost a century later by a book written by an unusual buccaneer named William Dampier.

William Dampier was a strange man by any standards; though it is doubtful whether, if he had not such a good style of forceful prose, and if his first travel book had not appeared at an opportune moment, he would now be much remembered as a discoverer. Sailor in the East Indies trade, able seaman in the Royal Navy and later captain (temporarily) of a king's ship; plantation clerk in the West Indies, buccaneer, pirate, privateer, as occasion suited; skillful cartographer and student of the ocean winds; writer, lion of London society (briefly), and protégé of the Royal Society; thrice a circumnavigator; twice associated with the marooning of fellow mariners on Juan Fernandez and twice assisting with their rescues—here was an adventurer! He commanded the first ship which the British Admiralty sent on an exploratory expedition. He commanded one of the least successful of the British privateering ventures to the South Seas and was pilot of one of the most successful. He was marooned once himself, probably for excellent cause, and he was perhaps the first producer of best-selling travel books. His predecessors in this field were not numerous and on the whole had been dull fellows. None had dealt with the South Seas, since none of them had been there. Dampier was the first man to write popular accounts of his own voyages; he had had many adventures, and he was an observant and talented writer.

The facts of Dampier's extraordinary career are set forth plainly enough in his own books. He was born in 1652 on a farm at a place called East Coker, near Yeovil, England. His father was a tenant farmer. He went to sea as a boy, his first voyage being to Newfoundland. This ship was poorly built, and the weather was bad. Dampier took permanent dislike to the bleak cold of the Newfoundland banks and to the hardships of westbound crossings of the North Atlantic. Next he shipped as a hand in an East Indiaman, in which conditions were very different, and made a round voyage to Bantam, in Java. From this he returned to England as a young man of twenty, just as another war broke out with the Hollanders. He either joined, or was pressed into, the navy as an able seaman. As such, he saw service in at least two actions, but the bleak North Sea pleased him as little as the wild North Atlantic had done, and before long he was invalided out of the navy at Harwich. He went back to Somerset, where he recovered his health.

His next move was to Jamaica, as assistant manager of a

plantation there; from this, he graduated to the West Indies interisland trade, which was carried on in small vessels, and had some part in the logwood business. He had a much larger part in various unrecorded piratical enterprises managed by the local buccaneers.

Here at last Dampier seems to have found a career after his heart. The free and easy life of a sailor of fortune in the warm sun of the West Indies and Central America, wandering and freebooting at will, had a great appeal to him. He had developed into an able pilot, largely through his own efforts, for he had considerable mathematical skill. It was this which made him a useful man to the buccaneers, and it was not long before he gave up all pretense of leading a lawful life and wholeheartedly threw his lot in with the pirates. He paid a brief visit to England in 1678, and it was noted that he had more money than could normally be earned in the logwood trade. He was soon back in the West Indies, this time to take part in an amazing adventure which began in a march across the Isthmus of Panama, including a piratical cruise of the South Sea, and ended with a holiday in Virginia, which he and his friends had reached by sailing round Cape Horn. There were excellent hide-outs round Chesapeake Bay. Dampier sailed from the Chesapeake in August, 1683, with a fellow pirate named Cook, in a brig which Cook had stolen.

This voyage took him to the Pacific again, where they joined forces with a Captain Swan and his ship the *Cygnet*. It had long been Dampier's idea to extend these South Seas cruises to the East Indies, of which he had some knowledge. He tried to influence Cook to conduct such an enterprise, but Cook died and was succeeded by one Davis, who thought the west coast of South America good enough and remained there. This was the Davis who sighted *Terra Australis* in a part of the South Pacific where other navigators have been able only to find Easter Island. Dampier left Davis in 1685 and sailed with Swan toward the East Indies. Piracy on the American coasts had ceased to pay, for the Spaniards were sending their treasure by land routes and had combined several times to inflict severe defeats on the pirate bands.

From the American coast the *Cygnet* sailed to the Ladrones, and to the Philippines, where Swan was marooned with some thirty-six of his brother pirates. The *Cygnet* then cruised about the East Indies. They visited New Holland, with which Dampier was far from impressed. Not long afterward he was himself turned out of the ship, at the Nicobar Islands. According to his own account, he chose to leave the *Cygnet* at the Nicobars, but this is difficult to believe. Whether it was at his own choice or not, he did not stay there long. He made a canoe voyage to the Sumatra coast, not far away, in the course of which a severe storm is supposed to have shown him the error of his ways. Perhaps it did: if so, he made little effort to correct them. He reached Achen and seems to have engaged in legitimate trade for a year or two, sailing to India, the Malay Peninsula, Siam, and Indo-China. Inside two years he was master gunner of the fort at Bencoolen, not far from the Straits of Sunda.

In 1691 he obtained a passage to England in the East Indiaman *Defence* and returned home after an absence of twelve years. He should have been a rich man then, but the only evidence of his possessions refers to a tattooed Malay whom he proposed to exhibit as a side show at fairs. The unfortunate Malay died of smallpox at Oxford. After this, Dampier disappeared from public view for half a dozen years, presumably living upon the proceeds of his piratical voyages.

He was also writing his first book. In 1697 this was published, with a dedication to the president of the Royal Society. Dedications meant something in those days, and Dampier became the first literary "lion" who owed his status to a travel book. His first book ran through four editions in two years and led to the production of two more. One of these was a *Discourse on Winds,* which showed that Dampier was a serious student of the movement of the surface air at sea. Buccaneers sailed far from the beaten tracks, and he had ample opportunity to learn about the trade winds of the North Pacific, North Atlantic, and Indian oceans, as well as the monsoons of the East Indies and the China Sea.

The success of his books, and his personal charm, together with the fact that English circumnavigators who were not also pirates were somewhat scarce at the time, gained Dampier command of the first expedition officially organized in England for exploration in the South Seas. Dampier's talents and experience should have fitted him admirably for this job; but he had not gone far before he showed some qualities which had escaped the observation of his patrons of the Royal Society. The granting of a commission to such a man as Dampier to command a king's ship seems strange in these days; but it was probably a temporary commission, and his status was likely that of the modern wartime temporary Reserves lieutenant. Dampier brought more specialized knowledge to the South Seas, probably, than any other Englishman then living. A studious man, he had had opportunities to learn something of Spanish and Portuguese knowledge at first hand. He had been to northwest Australia, and he know the behavior of the ocean winds. He had experience of the conduct of ships on long voyages far from bases. He knew of Mendaña's achievements and of Queiros's two voyages. He knew what Tasman had done and had failed to do; he had studied Schouten's account of the voyage round Cape Horn.

But he did not know how badly the British Admiralty could choose its ships, and how appallingly they were sometimes officered and manned. It is a reasonable assumption that there was no rush among ambitious young gentlemen to serve under this buccaneer, no matter how well he had been received by

the Royal Society. The experience might be interesting, but it
could scarcely be expected to further the interests of a serious
naval career. The Admiralty showed what they thought of it
by first offering Dampier a wreck named the *Jolly Prize,* in
which he refused to sail, and then by giving him a former
fire ship which was but little better. This vessel was H.M.S.
Roebuck, whose principal qualification for the job in hand
was that she was of little use for any other. As soon as he saw
the *Roebuck,* Dampier revised his plans and left Cape Horn
out of them. He had hoped, originally, to round the Horn to
the westward and then run across the South Pacific in the
trade-wind zone, standing on into the Coral Sea. But it was
obvious that, if the *Roebuck* faced Cape Horn, neither she nor
any member of the expedition would get any further. The
ship was rotten. After fruitlessly trying to get another vessel,
he decided to try to round the Cape of Good Hope and make
thereafter for the west coast of New Holland.

> *From thence I would range towards New Guinea* [he
> wrote of this changed plan]. *There are many islands in
> that sea between New Holland and New Guinea . . .
> and it is probable we may light on some that are not with-
> out spice. Should I meet with nothing in these islands, I
> would range along the main of New Guinea, to see what
> that afforded; and from thence I would cross over to
> the island of Gilolo* [the modern Halmahera], *where I
> may be informed of the state of those parts by natives who
> speak the Malayan language. From Gilolo I would range
> away to the eastward of New Guinea and so direct my
> course southerly, coasting by the land . . . and having
> made what discoveries I could, I would return home by
> way of Tierra del Fuego.*

This is a peculiar plan for a man of such experience and

such specialized knowledge of winds and weather in the parts
he proposed to visit. Dampier was proposing to try—among
other difficult and intricate pieces of sailing-ship navigation—
what the Spaniards had failed to do nearly two centuries before. It is possible to pass to the eastward along the northern
coasts of New Guinea under sail; but it is tedious, difficult,
and trying. Dampier would have done better to modify Tasman's tracks, which by that time were shown in the *Stadthaus*
at Amsterdam for all men to see. If he wanted to reach the
Coral Sea and to examine the eastern coasts of New Holland,
then the way to do it was to run eastward in the west winds
first, until he was to windward of the known van Diemen's
Land. Then he could sail through the Tasman Sea and "see
what afforded" there. To try to get into the Coral Sea and out
again by entering the reef-strewn maze round the eastern end
of New Guinea was to seek a lot of trouble.

Dampier must have known this. One is driven to wonder
what he was really after. He was a strange man, and not always a scrupulously truthful one. For the Admiralty to finance
a jaunt by author Dampier to look for pieces of eight on the
barren coasts of northwest Australia—there must have been
some special reason for the *Cygnet* to go there years before—
would be in keeping with that extraordinary career. Dampier
ought surely to have been seaman enough to know that his
revised plan was doomed to failure before he ever sailed.

However, sail he did, on January 14, 1699. He had not gone
far before there was serious trouble with his officers. He
clapped his first lieutenant into a Portuguese jail in Brazil,
with what now seems reasonable cause. Regular naval officers
are unaccustomed to such treatment from those placed temporarily above them with acting commissions, however much
they may deserve it; Dampier was to pay heavily for this.

With his first lieutenant left to fume in jail, many of his
other officers discontented on board, and his pressed crew next

to useless, Dampier sailed the rotten *Roebuck* 12,000 miles. He anchored for a time in Shark's Bay, on the coast of Western Australia and near the tropic's edge. Here he saw sharks, whales, kangaroos, and a few aborigines. Although, from the results of his previous visit, he expected little, he remained some time on the Australian coast. He next ran across to Timor, and on New Year's Day, 1700, was off the western coast of New Guinea. This was during the northwest season, which is, however, not sharply defined in that area. He made what easting he could, often out of sight of land, and swept round in a wide detour that brought him along the north coast of New Ireland. He coasted round New Ireland, missed the channel that separates New Ireland from New Britain, and, finding open water between New Britain and the coast of New Guinea proper, proceeded to return the way he had come. He had thought the north coast of New Ireland to be New Guinea itself; when he found what is now known as Dampier Strait, he called the island so discovered, New Britain.

> *The east land* [he says] *afforded a very pleasant and agreeable prospect. We saw smoke, but did not strive to anchor there, choosing rather to get under one of the islands, where I thought we should find few or no inhabitants. We looked out well to the north, and seeing no land that way, I was well assured that the east land was not joined to New Guinea: therefore I named it Nova Britannia.*

He went no further. So much for his great scheme of unraveling the secrets guarded by the Coral Sea: so much for England's first Admiralty-organized expedition. Dampier hurried back through his straits westward to Ceram and Batavia, and so home again round the Cape of Good Hope. At least, he tried to take the *Roebuck* home. She sank beneath him

when in sight of the island of Ascension, and he was stranded
on the beach there for weeks before a small squadron of British
ships chanced to call. They picked up him and his ship's company, and home he went—to face a court-martial which took
all his pay and declared him a person unfit for employment
in command of the king's ships.

It was a poor end to what might have been a great voyage.
There was excuse enough for going back from the eastern end
of New Guinea in a ship so ripe and so full of malcontents as
the wretched *Roebuck*. But it is difficult to understand why a
seaman of Dampier's knowledge and experience ever went that
way. If the *Roebuck* survived the west winds as far as the
longitude of Western Australia, then she would have done so
the week or two more that were required to get to windward
of that continent. Dampier knew the way. Tasman had blazed
it.

The end of the *Roebuck* and the finding of the court-
martial were not the end of Dampier, by any means. Within
a year he was on his way to the South Seas again, in command of
a ship. This was the privateer *St. George*. The voyage added
nothing either to geographic knowledge or to the wealth of
those optimists who had financed him. The *St. George* and her
consorts made one of the poorest privateering voyages ever
undertaken in the Pacific. It was during this voyage that
Alexander Selkirk was marooned at Juan Fernandez, to become prototype for Robinson Crusoe. In the East Indies Dampier was unable to produce his privateer's commission and was
thrown into jail. It took some time—even for him—to talk his
way out of this. When he contrived to get free, he took passage
back to England, where he found himself, naturally enough,
unpopular with the sponsors of the voyage.

He was not entrusted with another command. On his next
voyage he was specialist navigator for the Pacific and East
Indies in the privateering expedition which circumnavigated

the world under the command of Woodes Rogers, in the years 1708–1711. The expedition took a good deal of loot, and its captures included a treasure galleon.

What happened to Dampier in his remaining years is not known. He died in 1714. The share-out of the takings from the *Duke* and *Duchess* was not made until 1719. Troubles with the British East India Company, who viewed the voyage as an infringement of their monopoly; litigation in Chancery; difficulties in disposing satisfactorily of so large an assortment of rich goods, and quarrels among the owners led to long delays. The crew presented a petition to the House of Lords; Woodes Rogers was declared a bankrupt because he could not pay the debts his family had incurred while he was on the voyage; and Dampier died. His executrix, apparently, received £1,050 in 1717. It was then stated that he had agreed to go for a lump-sum payment of £1,500.

Almost two and a half centuries after his jaunts to North Australia and the islands of New Guinea, it is difficult to make a just appraisal of Dampier's worth. But his failures stand against him—above all, his failure to take the *Roebuck* to Australia's eastern coasts; his many failures with his brother officers and his men, and his incompetent command of the *St. George*.

Queiros, Torres, Tasman, Dampier—one after the other, they had been within an ace of dispelling the mysteries of the Coral Sea and of stumbling on the eastern coast of the real southern continent. Of them all, Dampier's failure is the least excusable. He was the last; knowing what was there to find and almost where to look, he turned away.

CHAPTER TWELVE

THE ENGLISH—I

BY THE time Dampier died, the world had a fair idea of the southwest, west, northwest, and north coasts of New Holland. The place must have an east coast somewhere. Tasman had confirmed the area in which this should be sought. Something of the myth of *Terra Australis* persisted, even among serious geographers. There was another and much more important land, they said, besides New Holland. Its southern borders stretched across the Antarctic wastes, but much of its area, said the academic geographers, must be in the temperate zone, if not in the tropic. As Dutch sea captains caught sight of more and more of the real continent, its further exploration was neglected almost as though there were a conspiracy to suppress the place. One after another the discoverers beat round the Horn or struggled through the Strait of Magellan, dissipated their energies, and wore out their ships and crews in the vain endeavor to make westing where the winds always blew from the west and the seas raged mountainous from the gales that roared unchecked right round the world. One after another they gave up the fruitless attempt and stood up into the trade-wind zone, which they were the more anxious to reach as stories of its idyllic islands became known.

When the English again began to send out official expeditions, more than half a century after their first had been entrusted to a buccaneer, it does not appear that they had much interest in the exploration of the unknown coasts of New Holland. Their aims were the discovery of *Terra Australis* and the northwest passage to the spice islands, the possible fortifying of Juan Fernandez and parts of New Britain, and accumulating vague additions to Pacific knowledge generally. The leaders of the early expeditions were badly chosen.

The first was Commodore John Byron, second son of the fourth Lord Byron and known throughout the service as "Foulweather Jack." He was promoted to commander at the age of twenty-three and was a captain soon afterward. For a while he served under Lord Anson in a squadron off Brest, but his big chance was command of the voyage of discovery, which was given him in 1764. It is possible that a worse choice might have been made, but there could have been many better. His appointment was as commander in chief, East Indies; his ship, the *Dolphin*, a copper-sheathed frigate, his consort the *Tamar*, commanded by Captain Mouat. The real purpose of his voyage was to take possession of the Falkland Islands, search for *Terra Australis*, and find the northwest passage.

This was a large program. What in fact he did, was to look hurriedly at the Falkland Islands [which the French had already settled], sail through the Strait of Magellan into the Pacific (having had more than enough of Cape Horn on a previous voyage with Anson), and hurry across the Pacific in the beaten track almost like a man afraid of what he might find there. He did not make a voyage of discovery in the Pacific. He made a passage across it; and because the *Dolphin* was a smart ship, it was the fastest passage that had been made up to that time. He sailed from Plymouth on July 3, 1764, and was back in London on May 9, 1766. This was the fastest circumnavigation that had been made and remained the "record" for many years. It was also the most fruitless long voyage of discovery.

It is difficult to believe that Byron could have earned any praise for the manner in which he had flouted nearly all the orders given him. But within a brief period he was appointed governor of Newfoundland. Later he became an admiral. His later service was mainly on the Atlantic station, and for a time he led an indifferent fleet which was based on Sandy Hook. He sired two sons and seven daughters. His elder son was John Byron, known as "Mad Jack," who was the poet's father.

Possibly the governorship of Newfoundland was not considered one of the plums of the service in 1766. But whether he incurred any form of official displeasure or not, there were influential bodies in England highly incensed at Byron's useless voyage. It was known that the French were also keen to extend their influence to the South Seas. Byron had met a French ship in the Strait of Magellan, under the command of Bougainville. This Bougainville, though not a seaman, was known as a painstaking and resourceful officer. If Byron saw him in the Strait of Magellan, there was no knowing what he might do in the South Seas. It was decided, for this and other reasons, to send a further expedition as soon as it could be got ready. Since the *Dolphin* had shown herself an excellent ship for the purpose, she was hastily recommissioned.

Unfortunately, the Admiralty again made a poor selection of the officer in command. This time they sent a Cornishman named Wallis. Captain Samuel Wallis, Royal Navy, may have been an excellent officer for more ordinary naval employment, but as a discoverer he proved little better than Byron. He had the good fortune to hit upon Tahiti: after that, in his turn, he hurried toward Tinian and avoided the whole area where discoveries were to be made.

Before that, he had abandoned his consort, the *Swallow,* in the Strait of Magellan, leaving his junior officer to make such voyage as he could. After Byron and Wallis, it is a pleasurable relief to consider the voyage of Philip Carteret, commanding officer of H.M.S. *Swallow.* Carteret was an excellent example of a type of officer by which, to its infinite benefit, the British Navy has always been abundantly served. He was a competent and courageous officer—resourceful, reliable, and full of plain guts. When he was appointed to command the *Swallow* and accompany Captain Wallis on a voyage of discovery to the South Seas, he had been in England barely a month after being in the *Dolphin* under Byron. As soon as he saw the *Swallow,* Carteret's heart sank. She had been in the navy thirty years; beyond a "slight sheathing," she had no protection against worm (though the *Dolphin* was coppered). She had not even a forge to repair her ironwork, nor any iron. She sat heavily in the water like the sluggard she was, and the experienced petty officers in the depot dreaded the idea of being drafted to her. She was altogether so poor a ship that Carteret, who had been full of enthusiasm for the voyage, began to think she could not be intended for the same employment as the *Dolphin* but was to remain in the Falkland Islands. When his request for a few essentials was turned down curtly, with the remark that "the vessel and her equipment were very fit for the service she was to perform," he was confirmed in this suspicion.

He had not even stores enough nor the common necessities of a sailing-ship to get so far. In those days, ships made their own cordage as they required it, from junk. Even when the writer went to sea in sail in the early 1920's, this was still done to some extent in British and Finnish deep-sea sailing-ships. But to make cordage, there must first be a good supply of junk. The *Swallow* was allowed none, Carteret's demands being handed back to him with the note that the *Dolphin* had enough for both ships. When he asked Wallis for junk, he was grudgingly given five hundredweight, and that was all the stores the *Swallow* ever received from the senior ship's supply. Five hundredweight lasted scarcely a month. Long before he was out of the trade winds in the Atlantic, Carteret was reduced to cutting up his cables to save his rigging.

The unusual quality of their captain's character was brought home to the *Swallow's* crew by an incident at Madeira, where nine of the crew, having heard that it would be a long time before they returned to any place where they could spend money, and still having a little with them, tried to swim ashore to get a "skinful of liquor." They found that they could not land, as the surf ran too high. They therefore swam back to the *Swallow* and climbed, crestfallen, on board. They were brought up before their captain in due course, charged with the serious offense of breaking out of the ship. From almost any other officer, this would have brought them a severe flogging. But these were nine of Carteret's best seamen; he was well aware that the deficiencies of his ship could be offset only by the morale and perseverance of his men, who had already shown that they were not lacking in skill or courage. So Carteret "admonished them and told them to put on some cloaths and lie down," adding that, if he ever needed good swimmers, he now knew where to look for them.

"Having thus dismissed these honest fellows from their fears," he said, "I was infinitely gratified by the murmur of satisfaction which instantly ran through the ship's company, and was afterwards amply rewarded for my lenity." Murmurs of satisfaction from ship's companies at the leniency of commanding officers were rarely heard in those days, or any others; Carteret must have possessed in abundance the qualities of true leadership.

It was after this that Carteret, for the first time, was shocked to receive from Wallis a copy of the secret instructions for the voyage. These were to search for *Terra Australis*—in the *Swallow!* Wallis was allowed to make his own choice of the Magellan or Cape Horn routes into the South Sea, but once the Pacific was reached his instructions were explicit. He was to "stretch to the Westward about One Hundred or One Hundred and Twenty Degrees of Longitude from Cape Horn, losing as little southing as possible, in search of Lands or Islands supposed to lie in that part of the Southern Hemisphere."

To one who had been there, these instructions had an ominous sound. The *Swallow* was scarcely fit to go to windward in a millpond: to ask her to beat to the west'ard in the high latitudes of the South Sea was preposterous. Whoever drew up those orders had thrashed no ship to wind'ard round Cape Horn or tried to make westing in the world's breeding place of westerly storms; nor could he have given much consideration to the fitness of the *Swallow* for such a voyage. Anson's fleet of great ships had been smashed up off the Horn not thirty years earlier; the design of ships had changed little in the interval. It made no difference whether the Pacific was reached via the Horn or the Strait: the storms were the same.

However, there it was. The Admiralty wanted *Terra Australis* discovered. "I was now convinced that I was sent upon a service to which my vessel and her equipment were by no means equal," writes Carteret, "but I determined at all events to perform it in the best manner I was able."

Once in the Strait of Magellan, Wallis ordered the *Swallow* to keep ahead to pilot him through the shoals, despite the fact that the *Swallow*, under all sail, could not keep up with the *Dolphin* under reefed topsails; the sloop handled so badly

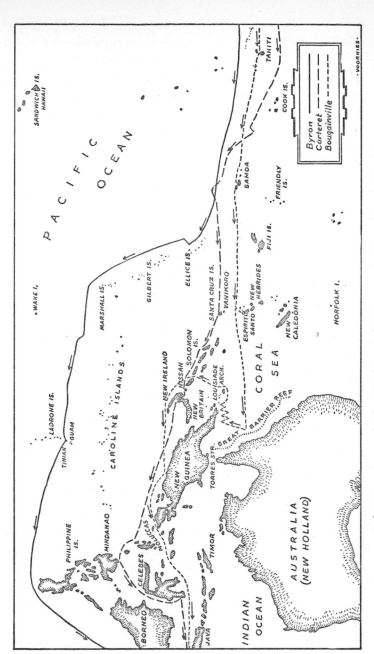

The Voyages of the Eighteenth Century Circumnavigators

Byron
Carteret
Bougainville

PACIFIC OCEAN

INDIAN OCEAN

CORAL SEA

AUSTRALIA (NEW HOLLAND)

SANDWICH IS. HAWAII

WAKE I.

LADRONE IS.
TINIAN
GUAM

MARSHALL IS.

CAROLINE ISLANDS

GILBERT IS.

ELLICE IS.

SANTA CRUZ IS.
VANIKORO
ESPIRITO SANTO
NEW HEBRIDES

NEW CALEDONIA

NORFOLK I.

SAMOA

FIJI IS.

FRIENDLY IS.

COOK IS.

TAHITI

VOORHIES

NEW IRELAND
NISSAN
SOLOMON IS.
NEW BRITAIN
LOUISIADE ARCH.

NEW GUINEA
TORRES STR.
GREAT BARRIER REEF

PHILIPPINE IS.
MINDANAO
CELEBES
MOLUCCAS
BORNEO
JAVA
TIMOR

that every time she got under way, they wondered how they would ever bring her to anchorage again. This sort of thing must have been intolerable to Carteret and Wallis alike, but the senior officer turned down every proposal his junior put before him. Since the *Swallow* was obviously retarding the *Dolphin,* Carteret submitted that she be laid up in a safe anchorage while her crew helped work the *Dolphin* through and he did the piloting. His idea was that the boats should take sufficient people back to the *Swallow* to sail her to England, while the *Dolphin* continued the voyage in accordance with orders. Carteret offered to give up command of the *Swallow* to the first lieutenant of the *Dolphin* and to take that officer's place, so that his knowledge of the South Seas would be available. To all these proposals, Wallis made a stern refusal.

And so the *Swallow,* having led the *Dolphin* through the straits, was left behind. No plan of operation had been settled, nor any place of rendezvous appointed. "I thought myself the more unfortunate in this separation," writes Carteret, "as no part of the woollen cloth, linen, beads, scissors, knives and other cutlery-ware, and toys, which were intended for the use of both ships and were so necessary to obtain refreshments from Indians, had, during the nine months we had sailed together, been put aboard the *Swallow,* and as we were not provided with a forge or iron, which many circumstances might render absolutely necessary to the preservation of the ship."

But he had a good crew. He mustered them and put their situation before them frankly. They were far down to leeward in the ugliest corner of the ugliest and most dangerous ocean in the world; charged with the discovery of *Terra Australis;* having not even any spare cordage or trade goods or sufficient tools and spares; deserted by their leader, and in a ship which must have been the worst sailer in the navy. "I had the satisfaction, however," writes Carteret, "to see no marks of despondency among my people, whom I encouraged by tell-

ing them that although the *Dolphin* was the best ship, I did
not doubt but that I should find more than equivalent advantages in their courage, ability, and good conduct."

It never occurred to Carteret to give up, though he had
every excuse for abandoning the voyage. Instead, he fought
his dreadful ship somehow to windward in the South Pacific.
A succession of heavy gales almost overwhelmed his vessel,
which had grown so lubberly that she would no longer work.
That is to say, she was little better than a wind-blown hulk
and could not be relied upon to answer her helm or respond to
the handling of her sails in the manner of a normal sailing-ship.

Nevertheless she had some good qualities, for she showed
that she could stand a lot of punishment. She pitched her bow-
sprit end into the great gray seas, which broke over her as if she
were a rock. Sails blew to ribbons. Important ironwork carried away, and they had no tools to repair the damage. There
was other damage. Carteret ran for Juan Fernandez to carry
out repairs and get wood and water, but the Spaniards had
fortified the island, and he tried Mas-a-Fuera instead. Here,
bad weather made refreshment impossible. Then he did what
none of his predecessors of any nationality had had the guts to
do: he set out to cross the Pacific south of the trade-wind belt.
Carteret alone, prior to Cook, forbore to run his ship up into
the trades, to romp across the blue South Seas the lazy man's
way. He set out to make a real search for *Terra Australis,* and
he made westing on 28 degrees south for close on 3,000 miles.
This, despite the fact that it was then the depths of winter, and
he was forced to drive his sluggard ship day and night under
all the sail she could carry, unlike the feeble Wallis, who, 500
miles and more to the north, was lying-to every night to get a
good sleep. Carteret dared not accept the delay caused by
lying-to at night, for his people would starve.

He discovered Pitcairn Island on July 2, when Wallis had
already been some time at Tahiti. Then scurvy soon began to

make itself felt; ever afterward, until they arrived months later in the East Indies, all hands suffered dreadfully. Not until July 22, when his ship had been over two months in the South Sea, and he had sailed more than 4,500 miles since leaving the Strait of Magellan, did Carteret seek the trade wind. By that time, his ship was in an alarming state and his people far gone with scurvy. Even then, it was his intention to find a suitable island at which they could be refreshed and thence return to the southward once more to prosecute discoveries.

But this was not to be. He never came across an island which offered both anchorage and refreshment to Europeans without trade goods. He looked for the Solomon Islands, where the charts of the day alleged they were, and found nothing; but he came upon Queiros's Santa Cruz and was able to recognize it from the Portuguese description. There, the *Swallow* sprang a serious leak. Though the natives were hostile, Santa Cruz ought to have supplied fresh fruit and food enough to combat the scurvy, had Carteret possessed the means to gain the natives' good will. But he did not, and the master of the *Swallow*, by stupid disobedience of Carteret's instructions, threw away the slim chance they had. Sent off in a boat to find an anchorage, the master returned with three arrows in him. From all accounts, he himself was the direct cause of hostilities. The natives received the boat's crew quite well, but the master ordered a coconut palm to be cut down and persisted in having this done despite the natives' protests.

By this time the carpenter was the only man aboard who was in tolerable health. Carteret himself was so ill that he could scarcely stand. There was only one lieutenant, and he also was sick. The master was dying of his wounds, and the gunner and thirty men were completely incapacitated. The crew began to be worried, for the only persons capable of navigation were Carteret, the master, and the lieutenant. It began to look as though all three might die.

Having gained nothing but fresh water and a few coconuts from Santa Cruz [which he named Egmont Island],
Carteret weighed and stood on. To his own intense chagrin and
almost the despair of the crew, the ship passed close by clear-
ings of vegetables and fruit which they desperately needed.
They saw fowls and hogs but could get nothing. There were so
few people fit for any sort of duty that the *Swallow* was fast
approaching the state of Queiros's ship when he sailed from
Santa Cruz toward Manila, after the death of Mendaña.

Carteret was forced to haul to the nor'ard, though he wished
to stand on westward into the Coral Sea. For the first time in
two hundred years a European had at last arrived again at the
Spanish discoveries; and because of the wretched manner in
which he had been equipped, and the base desertion he had
been subjected to, he was too ill to pursue his discoveries and
too weak to risk becoming embayed. Carteret sailed by the
Solomons, not even aware that he had rediscovered Mendaña's
islands. He recognized his Egmont Island as the Spanish Santa
Cruz, but he did not recognize the northwestern end of
Malaita, which he also sighted. Most of this time he was unable
to walk. He stood on toward the northwest, hoping to come
upon Dampier's New Britain, which might offer wood and
water. He hoped, also, that he would be able to carry the east
wind as far as a civilized port in the East Indies, where the ship
could be repaired and the crew restored to health.

He named Gower Island, in the Solomons, after his first
lieutenant, and sailed past the island now known as Bougainville. At Gower Island the natives showed that, though it was
nearly two centuries since Europeans were in the area, they
remembered the use of muskets. There was no anchorage at
Gower, and no refreshment. "There is certainly much land
in this part of the ocean not yet known," wrote Carteret in
his log. It was his misfortune, and England's, that he was in no
state to search for it.

Just northwest of Bougainville he came upon the lagoon now known as Nissan, which he called Sir Charles Hardy's Island. There was a good channel into that lagoon, and sheltered anchorage inside, had he been able to work the ship in, or even if he had had enough fit men left to man his boats. By that time his whole crew could not manage to weigh the anchor, and his ship was almost completely unmanageable. From Nissan, Dampier's New Britain was practically in sight. Carteret stood on and sailed through the middle of Dampier's island. The buccaneer had not noticed that the "bay" he called St. George's was in reality a strait, splitting his island into two. Carteret sailed through it and named the strait St. George's Channel. The northern island, he renamed New Ireland. He found an anchorage here, with coconuts and fresh water, but he dared not stay long enough to give himself a real chance to recuperate, for fear the easterly winds would give out. He was then in the area of the northwest monsoon. It was August, 1767. The season of variables and westerly winds might be expected to set in about October. If this happened while the *Swallow* was still to the eastward of a proper place of refreshment, Carteret knew it would be the end of her. He said, ruefully, that the time was enough for any other ship to sail three times the distance between New Ireland and Batavia, but he doubted whether the *Swallow* would do it at all. So they weighed, taking two days to do it, rigged every sound tackle that remained in the ship to help, and sailed on.

The ship passed by islands where every prospect was "the most beautiful and romantic that can be imagined." Again they sailed past the fruits they so urgently needed and could not obtain. Carteret and his lieutenant could scarcely crawl. They were the only officers left, and day after day, night after night, they shared the watches. Watch and watch, four hours on and four hours off, sick with scurvy and with fevers, weakened by the lack of all useful food, Carteret carried on. They were compelled to sail a wretched ship past endless islands which could have succored them if they had had strength enough on board to anchor and weigh again; the ship streamed grass from her leaky undersides. The rigging was rotten; the few skeletons who could still work were feverishly engaged in reducing good cables to junk, that they might weave sail twine to repair a hundred burst old seams. Carteret would, he wrote, have furnished better descriptions of the new lands he discovered "if I had not been so much enfeebled and dispirited by sickness, as almost to sink under the duty that for want of officers developed upon me."

In the meantime, Wallis, whose crew were still fat from the ample stocks they had obtained at Tahiti, was further refreshing himself at Tinian.

Carteret sighted the Admiralty Islands, but was too weak to examine them. He was still over 1,200 miles from the nearest civilized land. It was September 15, 1767, when he found the Admiralty group. It was not until November 3 that he came to anchor in a bay at Mindanao—seven weeks later. Seven weeks to sail 1,200 miles! Mindanao was hostile. The ship continued to Macassar, in the Celebes. By that time thirteen of the small crew had been buried, thirty more were dying, every petty officer aboard was sick or dead, the ship was leaking badly, and unless rest and refreshment were quickly found, the *Swallow* would drive up on some coral reef to rot there until all on board her died.

No British ship of war had visited Macassar, but Carteret did not doubt that his reception would be reasonable. On December 15, 1767, he anchored the *Swallow* before Macassar. To his request for shelter for his ship and permission to buy food for his crew, the governor made answer that the *Swallow* "should instantly depart from the port without coming any nearer to the town." So much for the humanity of the successors of the Portuguese.

Carteret's reply was forceful and immediate. If he was not permitted to refresh his crew, he said, he would get his ship under way and sail her into their walls, where they would sell their lives as dearly as they could. They had, he pointed out, nothing further to lose. He was under way to carry out this threat when at last the churlish governor relented.

In due course Carteret sailed the *Swallow* back to England via Batavia and the Cape. He had sailed over much of the area where *Terra Australis* was supposed to be. He had discovered Pitcairn, Gower, New Ireland, the Admiralty group, and some smaller islands. He had rediscovered the Solomons. Moreover, he had made a voyage which, for sheer guts, stands unequaled even in the story of Pacific exploration. Alone of the officers who had been sent out by England to prosecute discoveries in the South Seas up to that time, Carteret was of the stuff of which true discoverers are made. A lesser man, left by Wallis at the windy Pacific's southeastern corner, would promptly have gone home again. Indeed the *Swallow* had long been thought wrecked in the Strait of Magellan, and no man thought she had continued the voyage.

Carteret was promoted captain in 1771 and served on the West Indies station from 1777 to 1779. His experiences in the *Swallow* had broken his health and he lost his power of speech. Retiring from the navy in 1794, he died at Southampton in August, 1796.

Given half a chance, Carteret would have been the man to draw back the veil that shrouded the Coral Sea. Queiros, Torres, Dampier, and Tasman had flirted with corners of it. Carteret intended to lift it once and for all, but circumstances defeated him. But before he was back in England, James Cook sailed on his first voyage. There were to be no more Wallises and Byrons fooling in the South Seas.

CHAPTER THIRTEEN

THE ENGLISH—II

A MAN from the lower deck came to the forefront, purely upon his own merits, and at the eleventh hour—when one more poor voyage of the Byron–Wallis class would have finished England's hope of important discoveries—showed how great voyages of discovery should be made.

The career and achievements of Captain James Cook are too well known to need detailed description here. As seaman, discoverer, hydrographer, navigator, disciplinarian, and humanitarian, the six-foot Yorkshireman was outstanding. His is one of the few cases in the story of Pacific discovery where the right man turned up at the right time and did magnificently.

Yet, at the time of his appointment to command his first expedition, his name was quite unknown to the general pub-

lic and not much known, except among specialists, in the
navy. He was not then a commissioned officer. His only command had been a small schooner, which he used to survey the
coasts of Newfoundland. His whole sea career had been spent
in two restricted spheres—the North Sea in Whitby colliers
and the North Atlantic station of the Royal Navy. It was not
customary for Admiralty to seek its higher officers from among
those whose service had been almost entirely in colliers, and it
was a great tribute to him that he was selected. He had never
been across the equator. As far as is known, he was not particularly interested in the South Seas. He was without influence, save such as his merits earned for him. In the navy of
his day, this did not ordinarily amount to much. At a time
when most men were either forced into it or born into it,
James Cook had deliberately chosen the navy as a career. At the
age of twenty-seven, his way already made in the merchant
navy, and a command in a good Whitby fleet being his for the
taking, he volunteered for active service as an able seaman.
Rapidly he became a master's mate and then a master. These
were warrant ranks.

Cook had been master of an important king's ship commanded by a Captain Hugh Palliser, who afterward became
an admiral and a knight. Admiral Palliser knew a man when
he saw one, and Cook's thorough efficiency, excellent character, and unusual qualities of natural leadership impressed him
greatly. His name was noted, and he again came to favorable
attention when he distinguished himself by the courage and
skill with which he marked a channel in the St. Lawrence for
the combined operation to capture Quebec. His job there was
to make such running survey as was necessary and practicable,
and to establish marks by which the large vessels carrying the
military could be brought up the river. There were many de-
fenders whose job it was to remove the marks and shoot those
who tried to place them. Cook was not a surveyor at the time.

But he was a man accustomed to intricate coastal work, not afraid of shoals, and of considerable practical mathematical skill. He was that rarity, a seaman born; as such, all those things which had to do with the sea came easily to him, or he made them do so. To mark a passage for the big ships, to look after the rigging of a three-decker, to sail the awkward bulk of a 60-gunner under the critical eye of an experienced post captain or even an admiral, to prepare a chart of an ill-surveyed piece of coast, to superintend the cutting of a suit of sails or the heaving down of a ship, or to look after the administration of some hundreds of the ill-used seamen of his day—all these things Cook took in his capable stride.

When he was offered command of the expedition, ostensibly to observe the transit of the planet Venus in the South Seas, Cook jumped at the chance. He was given a commission as a lieutenant; he was given, too, what none of his predecessors had even dared hope for, a voice in the selection of his ship and in the organization of the voyage generally. He did not at that time know quite what manner of voyage was proposed, except that he would have to beat his ship to windward round Cape Horn and perhaps be absent more than two years. His choice of a Whitby collier, named *Endeavour,* is history. Anyone else would have taken a smart frigate or a comfortable East Indiaman. Cook was against both these.

> *A ship of this kind must not be of a great draught of water* [he wrote], *yet of a sufficient burthen and capacity to carry a proper quantity of provisions and necessaries for her complement of men, and for the term requisite to perform the voyage. She must also be of a construction that will bear to take the ground, and of a size which, in case of necessity, may be safely and conveniently laid on shore to repair any accidental damage or defect. These properties are not to be found in ships of war of 40 guns,*

*or frigates, nor in East India Company's ships, nor in
large three-decked West India ships, nor indeed in any
other but North-country ships such as are built for the
coal trade. . . ."*

How right he was, became obvious many months afterward when the *Endeavour* struck a reef in the Coral Sea. Any
other vessel would probably have been a total loss.

His sail up the coast of what he called New South Wales; his
discovery of Botany Bay; his sailing past Sydney [he saw the
entrance; but he had no time to make detailed surveys]; his
discovery of the Great Barrier Reef, and his conquest of the
Coral Sea—all these are stories which have often been told.
But it is not generally realized how close Cook came to the
loss of his ship in the Coral Sea. The whole of his passage up
the Queensland coast must have been a nightmare. To this
day, great powered vessels equipped with every modern navigational and safety device proceed with caution here and are
accustomed to employ skilled reef pilots. Cook did not even
know how far the reefs extended, nor how he would find a
way out of them. He had no idea that the Barrier Reef was
really a vast zone of coral rather than the ordinary lines of
defined reefs.

In the middle of June, 1770, thinking he was past the worst
of it—having already sailed more than 1,000 miles with the
lead going the whole time, and the ship proceeding with the
utmost caution—he was under quiet way early on a moon-
lit night when suddenly, without warning, the *Endeavour*
struck. The last sounding had been seventeen fathoms, which
is more than enough to float the *Queen Elizabeth*: suddenly
a peak of the coral reached up from the sea bed and impaled
the bark. In such a place it is astonishing that the accident had
not happened before.

The situation when she struck was soon desperate. The

night had been calm and she was under easy sail, making little more than a knot. Nonetheless, as soon as she was impaled, the sea began to rise, and the swell surged her bluff bows against the reef. They could hear the coral grinding her stout planks, and the sea gushed into her. By the grace of God there was no pounding, which would have ended her. Immediately, under the energetic leadership of Cook, there were well coordinated efforts to get the ship off.

When such an accident happens, there is only one course available to the sailing-ship. She may throw her sails aback and hope to slip off if the tide be rising or if a swell works her *off*— not on—the reef. This failing, the only way off is to kedge off —to carry out an anchor and hope that the ship may be hove off to it, on the top of high water. To do this means infinite work, but the *Endeavour* was well manned. They lightened the ship to the best of their ability, throwing overboard all the guns they could get at, and other heavy stores. They sent down the lighter masts and yards and lashed them alongside. They carried out anchors, to which stout hawsers were secured. This in itself was backbreaking work, but they had also to keep the pumps manned to prevent the ship sinking. As soon as they could, they passed a collision mat under the most damaged part of the hull, liberally covering the mat with oakum, bits of rope yarn, and sheep dung, and anything else which they thought the rush of water might wash in to stop the lesser leaks. This "fothering," as they called the maneuver in those days, immediately lessened the leak so that it could be kept under control. When daylight came they saw how thankful they should be for the selection of a North Country ship that was built to take the ground. They had struck the reef on the top of high water, and with a four-foot fall of tide, most ships would have capsized.

The situation was still critical. The morning tide did not rise as high as had the night tide, when she struck, and they

had to wait under the broiling sun all day. Meanwhile, the
boats were away, trying to find a place to beach the ship if she
came off afloat. By the grace of God there was such a place, a
narrow river on the mainland some thirty miles away. There
was only enough water to float the *Endeavour* in, deep as she
was, with her hold full of water. On the next night's tide, with
all hands straining at the capstans and heaving her off to the
carried-out anchors, she floated again. Cook let her stay at her
best anchor through the night, until daylight would show him
the way to the river. She was leaking badly, but she was afloat.
In the daylight he began to sail her toward the mouth of the
river. It took a week of heavy work to get the damaged ship
that far. Once inside, she was further lightened and her bows
driven up as far as they would go. The damage was for'ard,
and they were able to dry out the fore part of the ship suffi-
ciently to carry out temporary repairs. But they were not able
to examine the whole ship. When the bows dried, they saw how
providential had been their escape, for the worst hole was
jammed with a piece of coral broken from the reef.

It took almost two months to get the ship fit for sea again,
and even then she still leaked. Cook tried at once to get outside the reefs and find a way north toward the New Guinea
coast, intending then to make to the westward off that coast.
But he bargained without the reefs of the Coral Sea. He was
too far in to get out so easily. Some of the leaks opened up when
the heavier seas outside the coastal reefs caused the ship to
labor. Cook tried to sail into the inner passage again, but before he could do that the ship was nearly lost. He was caught
by the combination of circumstances which led to the wreck
of so many sailing-ships in those waters—the sea and current
setting on to a steep reef, and no wind to blow the ship off. In
such circumstances there is nothing to be done. Arm power
will not pull ships off reefs toward which the sea is setting
them; but arm power was all Cook had. The *Endeavour* could

not anchor, for the reef rose steeply from the sea bed, and no cable she had would reach the deep floor of the sea there, to hold her. There had been a light easterly air, but this died away and left calm. The little ship drifted until she was only the trough of the sea away from a horrible reef, over which the surf boiled and the great Southern Ocean rollers smashed in fury. A few yards more, and not a soul aboard nor an un-damaged plank of the ship would have survived.

> *The same sea* [wrote Cook] *that washed the side of the ship rose in a breaker prodigiously high the very next time it did arise, so that between us and destruction was only a dismal valley, the breadth of one wave; and even now no ground could be felt with 120 fathoms. Messrs Green, Clerke, and Forwood were engaged in taking a lunar for the longitude.*

Messrs. Green, Clerke, and Forwood continued taking a lunar for the longitude, despite the peril of their ship. There is no finer tribute to Cook's leadership and discipline anywhere than this. For three of the most important officers in the ship calmly to proceed with the accumulation of precise data to work out laboriously some reasonable approximation of the longitude of the ship, when that same ship was five minutes from one of the nastiest pieces of reef in the Coral Sea, and when the great swell was edging them to their deaths—this is on a level with the great moments of the sea. Messrs. Green, Clerke, and Forwood were perfectly aware of the danger the ship was in, because, before they had the data for their sights, the foam from the reef was making a fine spray on their instruments.

God was on the side of men like this; when all seemed beyond hope, a way opened in the reef, a slight air sprang up again so that the sails gave some flaps of hope, and the sturdy mariners in the boats put their broad backs into it once more. Slowly, slowly, the *Endeavour* came clear. Cook saw a crack in the reef and sailed through. He dropped the anchor inside as soon as he could, and all hands breathed a great sigh of relief, while Messrs. Green, Clerke, and Forwood, with sundry assistants, continued to work out their lunar.

After that experience Cook stayed within the reefs. Gradually he edged his way to the north, working the ship only in the daylight hours, with the boats ahead sounding and himself often at the mastheads, searching for a way through the coral. Through many a long and tiring day the *Endeavour* crept slowly to the north, while the Australian coast trended to the northwestward, and they were come almost to within sight of New Guinea. On August 21, 1770, the *Endeavour* reached the end of the Australian coast. Cook found a passage through the reefs to the west—not Torres's way, for the Portuguese had coasted through on the New Guinea side. The passage Cook found is now called Endeavor Strait.

Once they were through this labyrinth, Cook's great work of discovery was done, at any rate for this first voyage. He continued westward, passed south of Timor and Java, and sailed through the Straits of Sunda to Batavia, and thence by the Cape to England.

Cook returned to the Pacific several times, and he always went to New Zealand and to Tahiti. He did not sail again to the Australian mainland, and he kept his ships a long way from the Barrier Reef. On a subsequent voyage he discovered Tanna and Erromanga in the group of islands to which he gave the collective name of New Hebrides, and he charted Queiros's Espiritu Santo. He found the eastern coasts of New Caledonia, and Norfolk Island. But he took great care not to get to leeward in the Coral Sea, and the Solomon Islands and New Guinea remained almost the only large groups in the vast Pacific which he did not visit.

After Cook, it remained merely to follow up, send out ships and people, and develop and exploit. Trained in the hard school of the North Sea and the British east coast in merchant ships; his established prowess fostered by naval officers who saw his worth; himself both a merchant-service and a naval officer, yet not so firmly cast in either mold as to restrain his true genius or distort his immense abilities, Cook was indeed a man of destiny. He was the first man with courage enough to approach New Holland boldly from the Pacific side and to sail right through the Coral Sea. His reward was immortality. He succeeded where others failed because he knew ships, was a truly great sailor, and had in abundance those Yorkshire qualities of character, courage, and integrity.

James Cook's body was hacked to pieces on a beach in the Hawaiian Islands toward the end of his third Pacific voyage. His old ship drove ashore at Newport, Rhode Island, not long after. She had been there with a cargo of whale oil. When she grounded on the American coast, she was not so fortunate as she had been in the Coral Sea twenty years earlier: she was so badly damaged that she was left to rot where she lay. For many years her bare ribs and ancient timbers lay forlornly in the Rhode Island mud. Some of them may still be there.

CHAPTER FOURTEEN

THE FRENCH

JAMES COOK had made his three great voyages in the Pacific by 1780, but it was not until 1788 that the first of the English arrived to colonize Botany Bay, on the coast of his New South Wales. The American Revolution had something to do with the new colony, for a fresh repository had to be found for the wretched surplus population from England's overflowing jails. There was another reason, however, and that was anxiety about the French, who seemed particularly interested in the islands of the Coral Sea.

The first French circumnavigator, and the first of that country's many able explorers in the southwest Pacific, was an aristocrat named Louis Antoine de Bougainville, who was not a sailor at all. He was a soldier who had taken part in the de-

fense of Quebec while Cook was buoying the St. Lawrence for
the assault on that city. After that, he took a shipload of
French colonists to the Falkland Islands, which were to be a
base for French shipping bound round Cape Horn, but this
scheme came to nothing. Apparently taking a liking to the sea
life, Bougainville then made a voyage round the world in the
frigate *La Boudeuse,* with the transport *L'Étoile* in company.
His voyage occupied two and a half years: he followed Wallis
to Tahiti and Carteret to the Solomons, and he nearly fore-
stalled Cook on the Queensland coast.

Bougainville might not have been a sailor, but he made an
excellent voyage. The officer who actually sailed *La Boudeuse*
is entitled to great credit; but the leadership was Bougainville's.
The two French ships began their voyage of discovery from
Rio de Janeiro—they had previously been to the Falklands—
in the middle of 1767 and reached the Pacific by way of the
Strait of Magellan. The frigate *La Boudeuse* was well fitted
out and exceptionally well manned. Bougainville was a scientist
as well as a soldier, and it was his intention that the utmost
scientific use should be made of the voyage. A botanist and an
astronomer of note took passage, and the volunteers included
the prince of Nassau, aged twenty-one. The ship's company
was more than two hundred. At least one of these was a young
woman, though this discovery was not made until the ships
were at Tahiti, where the Tahitians danced around her, shouting *Wahine! Wahine!* * and making the most indelicate ad-
vances. The young woman was valet to the expedition's
naturalist, one M. de Commerson, whose shipmates had
thought it rather strange that valet and master shared the same
cabin. This valet was probably the first woman to circum-
navigate the modern world.

From Tahiti, Bougainville stood westward. Sailor or not—
perhaps, indeed, because he was *not* a sailor—he did what

* *Wahine* is the Polynesian word for woman.

many of his predecessors feared to do, for he had his ships
sailed boldly toward the Coral Sea. Going that way, he could
not help but make discoveries. He sighted the Samoan group,
which he called the Isles of the Navigators because of the excellence of the native's canoes. Next, he found himself among
the islands of the New Hebrides, where he was not impressed.
He sailed through the channel which separates Espiritu Santo
from Malekula. Bougainville noted that there was excuse for
Queiros's thinking these islands to be a continuous mainland,
for they looked much like it. The French remained long
enough to dispel this illusion. They might have remained
longer had the natives been welcoming. The weather was poor,
the natives fierce and warlike, the land uninviting. "The Ne-
groes howled exceedingly in the woods, where they had retired,
and we could hear their drums beating," the French reported.
There seemed to be a state of perpetual war.

Since he had chanced upon the land which was undoubtedly
Queiros's Austrialia del Espiritu Santo, Bougainville decided to
investigate whether there really was a continent close by. The
island itself and the others of the group soon dropped astern:
but what else might he discover? At the time of his voyage
Torres's letters of proceedings had not yet been made public;
they had indeed been unearthed only a few years previously.
It was as obvious to Bougainville as it was later to James Cook
that the land of New Holland must have an east coast somewhere, and there was no better place to seek it than the unknown seas to the westward of Queiros's discovery. By that
stage of their voyage the French ships were seriously short of
food. They were extremely foul, and their hempen rigging was
in very bad order. Ahead of them was the Coral Sea, with its
appalling maze of dangerous reefs: after he had sighted a
sandy cay and a coral reef, Bougainville had had enough of
it and altered course. But he was too late then. He was embayed.

It was June 6, 1768, when Bougainville turned away from the Coral Sea reef which now bears his name. He was less than 100 miles from Australia, 80 miles from the Great Barrier Reef, and—strangely enough—exactly 90 miles from the spot where Cook was to sail the *Endeavour* on a reef a year or two later. He was close to a great discovery; but it was prudent to turn away. At that stage of the voyage he was running under all sail during the daylight hours and under reefed tops'ls at night. To run on toward the Barrier Reef would have been to court disaster.

Bougainville had other worries besides those of sailing. Scurvy was seriously affecting his ships' efficiency. Food was so short that even a rat was a delicacy: not for the first time, nor the last, many a rat went to the making of a sea pie. The food situation was so bad that Bougainville had to take strong measures to prevent the removal of the leather chafing gear from the yards. In a square-rigged ship with hempen rigging, chafing gear was all-important, for it preserved the cordage and made long voyages possible. The sailors wanted the leather for making soup.

Just what it means to be embayed is little appreciated today, in the middle of the twentieth century, when all European ships are powered and safe navigation is, in the main, a matter of following well-defined routes. The situation in which Bougainville found himself was a nasty one. In ships which depended for their motive power entirely on the wind, he was caught to leeward in the dangerous corner of what was to him an unknown sea. The wind and the current were alike forcing him further and further into that sea, and the only way he could get out was to beat out, to bring his ships up to the wind, and under a press of sail to thrash them to windward. But they were so dirty they would scarcely sail; the manner in which they went to leeward was appalling; their rigging was poor, and their sails all but worn out; their people were hungry, sick, and tired. He could not hold a press of sail; sometimes the ships drove bodily to leeward. He headed toward the north and found more reefs barring his path. There were reefs everywhere except to the east, and the wind blew from there, so that he could not sail that way. Yet get out that way he *must*, somehow. He had no knowledge of Torres's Strait or China Strait. There might be a passage that way, and there might not. If he tried to find what was not there, then surely his ships would be lost, and all aboard would drown or die of starvation.

He himself had strong views on the probable existence of some passage between New Holland and New Guinea: but opinions were one thing, lives another. He sighted the reefs of the islands to the east of New Guinea and kept on sighting them. The weather deteriorated; no longer was there a succession of sunlit days, with the great winged ships skimming gracefully over a blue sea. The sea was gray and all too often a shallow green: it rained and blew, always from ahead. Sometimes the very sea threw sand and coral fragments aboard as it broke over the weather bulwarks, and the sound of breakers roaring was ominous and all too frequent. It speaks well for Bougainville's qualities of leadership that his mixed ship's company were behind him, in this extremity, to a man. He had few crew troubles.

Day after day, whenever it cleared, the grim mountains of the high islands eastward of New Guinea blocked the way north, and in the nearer waters the breakers roared on countless miles of coral reef. Bougainville pressed his ships to windward past Ushant Island [which he named; it is 50 miles from Samarai], past the Long Reef, past Bramble Haven and the barrier reef of all Sudest. The masts began to work, so that the crew had still further to reduce the amount of sail set on them. Yet without sufficient sail, the force of the wind on those crude airfoils would not drive the sluggish hulls to windward. It was

June 20 before there was at last an end to breakers and reefs. Sunrise of that day showed what looked at last like the end of land: all day they sailed toward the northeast—which was a course the ships could make—eight points from the southeast wind. By the grace of God the end of land was no illusion. The beat was over: they had weathered all the islands.

Bougainville called the archipelago past which he beat, the Louisiades: the weather cape he called, with a great sigh of relief, Cape Deliverance, and he took good care to steer clear of its fringing reef.

Now he was in waters which no European had sailed. All the long-lost Isles of Solomon were before him, and at last the southeast trade was a fair wind. The weather continued bad, but within a few days he was among the northern Solomons. He named Choiseul, Buka, and Bougainville, but stayed to examine none of them. The food and general health situation was still appalling, and he had to find a port of refreshment quickly or lose half his men. A boat trying to land for wood and water was skillfully attacked by canoes off Choiseul. Some of the canoes were taken. In one was the underdone jaw of a recently killed man.

From Buka to New Ireland is an easy sail, and the way from there to the East Indies was a beaten track. Bougainville tarried a while in a bay on New Britain not far from today's port of Rabaul; by chance he had hit almost upon the precise anchorage of Carteret, who had been there with the *Swallow* a few months before him. New Britain, though praised by Dampier, offered almost nothing save wood and water, but at least the rigging could be repaired. Shells and sea food were of some value, but there was nothing else. The ships were got under way again as soon as possible and sailed for the Dutch East Indies. At Batavia, Bougainville learned of Carteret's voyage. Since his call at New Britain he had known that someone was before him, but more than that he

did not know. He hurried on from Batavia as soon as his ships
were cleaned and his crews refreshed, anxious to overtake the
Englishman and find out what he knew.

At the Cape he was only three days behind the *Swallow*:
in the South Atlantic, a week or two later, he finally caught
up with that poor sailer and—from Carteret's account, at any
rate—was oversharp in his endeavors to prize out her intelligence. He sent aboard an officer dressed in rough clothes who
said the French ships had been to India. He was so curious about
the *Swallow's* movements that Carteret gave him an arrow
from Santa Cruz and told him to be off. It was not until the
boat had gone that the Englishman learned the truth from a
French Canadian in his crew who had conversed freely with
the French boat's people. Carteret and Bougainville did not
meet, which was a pity. *La Boudeuse* sailed off across the horizon and in due course was back in France where, though Bougainville was hailed as the greatest of French navigators, many
Frenchmen refused to believe that he had been around the
world, as he had not visited China.

Bougainville died in 1811, honored even in a France which
had by then summarily executed many of his kind. He was
buried in the Pantheon: today, outside France, he is best remembered by the flamboyant creeper which his lecherous
naturalist saw at Tahiti and gave the name of *Bougainvillea,*
and by the great island in the Solomons which also bears his
name.

The next Frenchman in the Coral Sea was Jean François
Galoup de la Pérouse, whose two frigates actually put in at
Botany Bay while the English transports there were picking
up their anchors to pass on to Sydney. Indeed, the naval captain in command of the fleet was worried, at first, when he
saw the tricolor on two approaching frigates. But he had no
cause for alarm. La Pérouse was on a voyage of exploration,

which in many ways was one of the most remarkable made in
the Pacific, or any ocean. He had already been over three
years on the way when he touched at Botany Bay. The unfortunate commander had been charged by an optimistic government virtually with the task of dispelling every obscurity
which still remained in maritime geography. He was to examine the island of South Georgia in the South Atlantic, and
the South Shetland Islands, south of Cape Horn, as well as
whatever of Graham's Land the ice might allow him to approach; after beating round the Horn, he was to seek *Terra
Australis,* or whatever islands might be discovered in the place
of that dim continent; he was then to unravel every knot that
still remained about the islands of the whole South Sea. After
that he was to examine Australia, more particularly in the
Coral Sea area and the Gulf of Carpentaria.

This done, he was to chart the coasts of Japan and the adjacent Asiatic mainland and continue the voyage through the
northwest passage. He was also, as occasion offered, to complete the survey of New Caledonia, to seek the islands of Mendaña and Queiros and to investigate further his countryman
Bougainville's land of Louisiade off the east of New Guinea.
When not doing anything else, he was to have a thorough look
in high southern latitudes for another countryman's lost Cape
Circumcision. The extraordinary thing is that La Pérouse
came near to doing all these things, or as many of them as
were practicable.

The immediate object of his visit to Botany Bay was to
assemble a couple of longboats to replace two lost at the islands. La Pérouse was received hospitably by the English and
throughout his stay was given every assistance. He remarked
ruefully to Phillip that Cook had left him little to do, save
admire his work. When his longboats were completed and his
men refreshed as well as the scanty resources of the new settlement would allow, he sailed. This was on March 10, 1788.

La Pérouse sailed off into mystery from that day for thirty-eight years, and neither he nor any member of his crews ever reached civilization again.

While at Botany Bay the French navigator took the opportunity of sending dispatches to France, bringing the story of his voyage up to date, and detailing something of his future plans. "I shall proceed to the Friendly Islands," he informed the French authorities, "and do everything enjoined in my instructions relative to the southern part of New Caledonia, to the island of Santa Cruz of Mendaña, the southern coast of the land of the Aracides of Surville, and the land of Louisiade of Bougainville, and shall endeavor to ascertain whether the latter constitutes a part of New Guinea or is separated from it by a strait. Toward the end of July, 1788, I shall pass between New Guinea and New Holland by another channel than Endeavour Strait, if any such exist; and during the month of September and part of October I shall visit the Gulf of Carpentaria, and all the coast of New Holland as far as van Diemen's Land. . . ." This was an ambitious program, even for La Pérouse.

He did not get far. The dangerous islands of the Coral Sea wrecked his two ships in a cyclonic storm on a reef off Vanikoro, between the Solomons and the main group of the New Hebrides. Though two searching ships—one British, one French—passed within sight of his signal fires during the time he might still have been alive, neither stopped to investigate what by then were familiar signals. Since the natives of most islands communicated with one another frequently by means of smoke signals, there was no way of distinguishing fires which were begun by Europeans. One of these searchers was Admiral Bruni d'Entrecasteaux, sent by France to find La Pérouse. The other was Captain Edward Edwards in His Britannic Majesty's frigate *Pandora*. Captain Edwards's quest was the mutineers of the *Bounty*: by the time he sighted Vani-

koro, he had had more than enough of searching the South
Seas and seems to have been little interested in either the
Bounty or discovery.

The mystery surrounding La Pérouse's fate was cleared up
by a sea captain named Peter Dillon. Captain Dillon was one
of those adventurous mariners with whose picturesque careers
the early story of the South Seas abound. At one time a master
in the East India Company's employ (which would seem to
establish him as a competent and reliable master mariner), he
had a habit of turning up mysteriously in odd islands of the
western Pacific without always being able to give a very clear
account of what he was doing. Some time in 1813 Captain
Dillon was at Norfolk Island, on the southern fringes of the
Coral Sea. While he was there, a ship named the *Hunter,* bound
on a wandering voyage after sandalwood, called to get some
spars. Dillon shipped as third mate. For a while he helped in
the gathering of sandalwood from islands in the Coral Sea,
graduating in this process from third mate of the *Hunter* to
master of a small Sydney cutter known as the *Elizabeth,* whose
former master had been eaten by cannibals.

In the *Elizabeth,* Dillon was able to assist some white beach-
combers who were established ashore on a precarious footing
in the sandalwood and allied trades. Among these was a Prussian named Martin Bushart, with whom, as well as several
Fijian women, was a Lascar whose name is given as Achowlia,
a deserter from a ship. Dillon took this party to the island of
Tikopia, or Tucopia, a lonely volcano top in the New Hebrides. Here Martin the Prussian and his friends settled, while
Dillon sailed away. He turned up again in Tikopia, apparently
by chance, in 1825, when he was sailing a ship called the *St.
Patrick* from Valparaiso westward over the Pacific toward
India. A call at the island, in those leisured days, was not much
out of his way. He did not expect that the Prussian would have
remained so long on so small an island, but to his surprise, Mar-

tin Bushart himself was the first person he saw as the *St. Patrick's* boat touched the beach.

In the course of a yarn, Bushart showed him a spoon of French manufacture, and the Lascar meanwhile sold a silver sword guard to one of the crew. On this, Dillon thought he could make out the initials of La Pérouse. Bushart told him that, when he first came to Tikopia, articles of French manufacture were abundant, though there had been no French trader or ship there. When he learned the local language, he was told that these things came from an island two days' sail by canoe to the west, and on this island there was a native tradition that two European ships had been lost there many years before. The crew of one had lost their lives, according to this tradition; most of the others sailed away subsequently in a small vessel with two masts, which they constructed out of the wreckage of the big ship. A few elected to stay behind and had been killed in local warfare, in which they had been useful. Achowlia had actually seen two of these men.

On a subsequent voyage Dillon was able to visit Vanikoro, where he quickly uncovered evidence enough to establish the scene of La Pérouse's wreck. There were brass guns of French manufacture still on the reef. The natives produced the remnants of an instrument that looked like a theodolite, and the backboard of a boat decorated with the fleur-de-lis. They also had a ship's bell inscribed in French, quantities of iron bolts and other ship's fastenings, and some fragments of glass and china. Ashore were the remains of a stockade which the French had considered it necessary to build.

According to one informant (not a native of Vanikoro), a party of natives had attacked the French and killed the crew of one vessel. It was said that the skulls of the sailors were in a local spirit house, though Dillon could not find them. There was a general native denial that the French had ever been attacked, though it was admitted that their visit was not welcomed. They were thought to be sailing gods, and visitors from the spirit world were not wanted at Vanikoro.

In 1828 Captain Dillon reported to Paris the results of his voyage, and the guns and other things were determined to be from La Pérouse's ship. Some armorial bearings on a silver candlestick from Vanikoro were recognized as being those of the expedition's botanist.

What happened to the small vessel with two masts which the French built at Vanikoro has never been established with certainty, though it is generally thought that the wreck of a vessel found in 1861 at Temple Island, about 150 miles from Mackay on the north Queensland coast, was probably this ship. The wreckage was from a ship of European design, built largely of unseasoned native wood cut from trees of the same type as those growing on Vanikoro. It was likely that La Pérouse would have tried to make for Koepang in the Dutch East Indies, and the place, then, to look for the bones of his little ship was the length of the Great Barrier Reef, whither the set of the sea might be expected to fetch them. A sharp lookout was kept for years, but the wreckage on Temple Island remains the nearest approach to identification.

The mystery of La Pérouse led to another important French expedition. In 1791 Admiral Bruni d'Entrecasteaux was sent with two ships, his orders being to search for traces of La Pérouse. He did a great deal of useful work in the Coral Sea. By inexplicable mischance, almost the only island which he sighted and did not examine was Vanikoro. At that time, survivors were actually watching his ships and were making smoke signals furiously on the beach. The admiral himself was sick at the time, and perhaps the officer of the watch was a reef-shy individual. The fringing reef of Vanikoro is a nasty one.

D'Entrecasteaux died at sea, and his ships were seized by the

Dutch in the East Indies, where they arrived to find that the French Revolution had deprived the officers of their commissions and their careers.

Other Frenchmen had been in the area. While Cook was examining the coasts of New Zealand, a Frenchman named de Surville touched there. M. de Surville was in command of a private expedition of two ships fitted out by a French firm in Bengal for what was described as a trading voyage toward Peru. According to one account, while the ships were fitting out, a garbled story of the English discovery of Tahiti reached their owners. This was to the effect that an island "exceedingly rich and inhabited by Jews" had been discovered some 700 leagues to the west of Peru, in latitude 27 degrees south. De Surville was instructed to examine this discovery and to establish trade with the Jews.

It was generally imagined that, if one of the lost tribes of Israel had found a South Sea island worth the settling, the trade offering there ought to be worth while. [Perhaps Messrs. Law and Chevalier, the sponsors of the expedition, or M. de Surville himself, had been studying Rabbi Aaron Levi's *Muckwa Israel,* wherein is put forward the idea that the Polynesians are descended from some of the dispersed tribes of Israel.] But de Surville found no Jews and little trade. He visited the Solomons on his way through the Coral Sea and formed no high opinion of them. He fought briefly with the Maoris of New Zealand and passed on to South America, where he was drowned from an overturned boat in the surf at Valparaiso.

The next Frenchman to sail for the Coral Sea fared no better. This was Captain Nicolas Marion-Dufresne, who sailed from Mauritius in 1771 to wander toward Tahiti and find what he might in the tracks of Bougainville. Marion-Dufresne was a rich man, who financed his own expedition. The reason given out for the voyage was to return a Tahitian whom Bougain-

ville had given passage to France. This Tahitian, who became
a connoisseur of the Paris opera (among other things), seems
to have become disheartened at the prospect of returning to
his native "paradise," and died. This, however, did not delay
the sailing of the new expedition. It was a pity, for the Maoris
killed the captain at the Bay of Islands and ate him.

Early in the nineteenth century, yet other distinguished
French navigators visited the Coral Sea. Duperré, in 1822, and
Dumont d'Urville, in 1825, paid particular attention to the
eastern end of New Guinea and the Melanesian islands. D'Urville made several additions to knowledge of these, as D'Entrecasteaux had done before him. Many French names in the
area remain as evidence of their work.

But the great work of exploration, even in that remote area,
was all but completed. Details remained, and the interiors of all
the large islands were still unknown. Two other navigators of
note passed through the Coral Sea. These were Bligh, of *Bounty*
fame and the so-called Rum Rebellion in New South Wales,
and Matthew Flinders. Bligh was there twice, first with the
Bounty's boat on that classic voyage, after the mutiny, from
Tofua to Timor (even in the crowded boat he continued to
survey new islands and made a useful running survey of parts
of the Fijis, and a new channel through the Great Barrier
Reef), and again on his second breadfruit voyage. He sailed
the *Providence* and *Assistant,* via the Coral Sea and Torres
Straits, from Tahiti toward the West Indies, but this was
purely a voyage to bring breadfruit to the West Indies and
was not meant for discovery. Flinders was wrecked in the
Coral Sea and gave his name to some reefs there. He did excellent work charting the waters of Torres Straits, but his
main work was outside this area.

The great figures of the Coral Sea are Mendaña; Queiros,
that thwarted visionary; the shadowy Torres; the reef-shy

Tasman, who might have done so much more; Bougainville, Carteret, and James Cook. These were the true pioneers, who blazed the paths for others to follow.

CHAPTER FIFTEEN

THE NINETEENTH CENTURY

ONE RAPID result of the founding of Australia was the entry of free shipping, not only into the waters of the Coral Sea but throughout the Pacific. Many transports employed to bring convicts to New South Wales were either East India Company's ships or English whalers. At that time, and for many years afterward, the East India Company claimed monopoly over the whole of the trade of the Pacific and Indian oceans, and no other British shipowners could send ships there. Even the whalemen had to have the company's permission if they flew the English flag. American ships, thanks to the Revolution, were under no such restriction.

Many East Indiamen, sailing from Sydney to China to load, made interesting discoveries in the Coral Sea. The early Australia offered no homeward cargoes, and there was a good deal of shipping between New South Wales and Canton. The transports in the so-called First Fleet, in 1788, included the ships *Lady Penryn* (Captain Watts), *Charlotte* (Captain Gilbert), and *Scarborough* (Captain Marshall). All three added to Pacific discovery. Theirs was, as far as is known, the first more or less direct passage between Sydney and China, and the three captains could please themselves how they made it. Watts, in the *Lady Penryn*, sailed well to the east and put into Tahiti, which was somewhat off his course. He had heard of the attractions of that island and perhaps had no stomach for sailing the Coral Sea, but since the visit added something like 5,000 unnecessary miles to the passage between Sydney and Canton, he probably had to explain himself rather thoroughly to the marine superintendent of the company, later. The *Lady Penryn's* name was given to a small island which Watts discovered. It was said that Watts had visited Tahiti as an officer in one of Cook's ships and had women there.

Sailing in company, captains Gilbert and Marshall went a more intelligent and scarcely less interesting way. Details of their leisurely voyage are to be found in an appendix to a book entitled *The Voyage of Governor Phillip to Botany Bay*, published in London in 1789, and in an account which Gilbert wrote.* The two captains sailed northward through the Coral Sea, giving a wide berth to all representations on their charts of the Solomon Islands. Shortly after sailing across the equator, not far from what is now the international date line, they came upon two large groups of atolls, which had probably not been seen since Queiros was forced to pass that way when returning from his abortive settlement at Espiritu Santo in 1606.

These groups, each of which lies in a rough north-south line across the trade wind, have been known ever since as the Mar-

* The voyage was the subject of an interesting article by Professor S. E. Morison in the "American Neptune" of April, 1944.

shalls and Gilberts, though in the intervening years many of their atolls have had a dozen other names. Captain Gilbert had given some thought to the making of his passage and did not wish to miss any chance of refreshing his ship. He had painted the old *Charlotte* a brilliant crimson, as "some of the *Voyages* I had perused pointed out that colour as the most pleasing to the natives of these climates." He found the natives somewhat "facetious"; possibly the marvelous apparition of a lumbering blood-red East Indiaman under a cloud of sun-bleached sails may have amused or astonished them.

British—or at any rate Australian—interest in New Guinea was more or less continuous from the time that Cook's survey of Torres Straits indicated the strategic importance of the great island. Before long there were optimists who declared that the place was destined to become another Ceylon or another Java. As early as 1793 two East India traders named Chesterfield and Kormuzin took possession of New Guinea and all the islands in Torres Straits, but their act was immediately disclaimed, and for almost a century afterward there was great reluctance on the part of the British to annex either that area or any other group in the western Pacific. Again in 1846 Yule took possession of the southern coast of New Guinea; but officialdom in England refused to confirm his action.

By 1867 the government of New South Wales was urging the occupation of New Guinea, to protect the vital approaches to the colony through Torres and China straits, but the official view, expressed by Lord Derby, was that England had already "black subjects enough." By 1853 France had annexed rich New Caledonia, which lies close to New South Wales—as distances are reckoned in the Pacific. Within a year or two the French were making a convict settlement out of the place, to the consternation of the citizens of Sydney. Having but recently emerged from such an undesired state themselves, they did not want another power to set down a horde of desperate men on an island within a few hundred miles of them.

In 1842 Captain Blackwood, in the *Fly,* charted the Gulf of Papua and discovered the Fly River, the mud from whose mighty waters adds greatly to the difficulty of navigating in those coral-strewn seas. Yule was doing some surveying in the *Bramble* farther to the east in 1846. H.M.S. *Bramble,* then and later, surveyed a considerable area of the Coral Sea, and her name has been liberally bestowed there. Both on her own account and as tender to Captain Owen Stanley's *Rattlesnake* she did good work. She was a shapely little topsail schooner with plenty of sail area and a big crew—the ideal ship for those waters before the days of engines. Stanley, in the *Rattlesnake,* with the *Bramble* in company, did some further surveying of the east coast of New Guinea in 1849, when the artist Oswald Brierly did some excellent illustrations of the area. In 1873 Moresby discovered the harbor which bears his name. Beagle Bay, Blanche Harbor, Goodenough Bay, and other names in eastern New Guinea and its islands bear testimony to the work of British ships and naval officers. But Albion, perfidious or not, refused to accept any part of New Guinea into the Empire.

By 1871 the London Missionary Society had a station at Daru on an island close to the coast, by the mouth of the Fly River. Prospectors were beginning to find gold. The pearl and *bêche-de-mer* fishers of Queensland had extended their activities as far as the eastern Louisiades, and Torres Straits was becoming of more and more importance to shipping. Meantime, not only French, but Italian, Russian, and above all German explorers were turning their attention to the possibilities of New Guinea.

In 1875 the New South Wales government, under John Robertson, put forward an annexation scheme which included not only all New Guinea not then Dutch, but the adjacent islands, all the Solomons, the New Hebrides, and the Marshall, Gilbert, and Ellice islands of Micronesia, as well. This was far-sighted and intelligent, but the British government turned down the scheme. In 1878 the Queensland government ex-tended its own boundaries to include Torres Straits and the islands there as far as the coast of New Guinea, and placed a station on Thursday Island to control shipping. Having suc-ceeded in this, and knowing that the German government was interested in the area, the Queenslanders next sent the magis-trate of Thursday Island to annex all non-Dutch New Guinea, without prior approval from the British government.

This more or less forced the reluctant hand of a Whitehall somewhat out of touch with events in Europe as well as in New South Wales: within a year or two the Germans had an-nexed the whole of northern New Guinea, the Bismarck Archipelago, and half the Solomons. A British protectorate was declared over southern New Guinea and the D'Entre-casteaux, Louisiade, and Trobriand islands; but it was a little late. By then, not only New Caledonia but most of the New Hebrides were under French influence, if not the French flag. The Australians were incensed at what they regarded as the unnecessary encroachment of a foreign power into north-eastern New Guinea, but at the time the British government was more worried about possible German actions in the Middle East. There was trouble in Egypt, and German friendship there was bought, for the time being, by an acceptance of her claims in New Guinea.

As for the New Hebrides, an Anglo-French naval commis-sion was set up there in 1887, but it worked poorly. This was in the days before the Entente Cordiale, and there was con-siderable Anglo-French friction in Egypt, southeast Asia, and elsewhere. The Australian colonists were violently opposed to the French convict settlement in New Caledonia, which per-sisted until 1898, and they took the view that not only were the New Hebrides of considerable strategic importance to themselves, but Australian trade interests were extensive there and ought to be paramount. It was not until 1906 that a condominium was set up, under which both Britain and France are represented by a resident commissioner in Vila, and every district has a British and a French district agent, with parallel authority, and a joint court for the administration of justice. This arrangement has not worked well, and every few years there is an upsurge of Australian agitation for its abolition. However, in 1949 it still persists.

A British protectorate was declared over the southern Solomons in 1893; Santa Cruz, Tikopia, Vanikoro, and other islands in the vicinity were added just before the turn of the century. In return for a British agreement to give up western Samoa, the Germans transferred Ysabel, Choiseul, Ontong Java, and other lesser groups to the British protectorate in 1900. In the Solomons, as elsewhere in Melanesia, the flag followed the trade; there were white traders living ashore there well before 1860, though planting and trading on a large scale were not developed in the Solomons before the twentieth century.

The Fiji Islands were annexed as a British colony in 1874 at the persistent request of some of the chiefs. The Gilbert and Ellice islands, in the outer ring of Micronesian atolls which extends round so much of Oceania, did not acquire the same status until 1915, though both groups had been included in a protectorate since 1892. The Carolines and Marshalls, comprising most of the remainder of Micronesia, were German until the 1914–1918 war.

Part of the British government's reluctance to assume responsibility for Pacific islands was the cost of administering them. They were a long way from Whitehall, and so was all Australia. Though some guano had been discovered here, a little gold there, and other minerals in another place, most of them did not seem to be worth much. The British government was occupied in maintaining the status quo in Europe and its own expansion elsewhere: the southwest Pacific had to wait.

America, which sent the large and not very happy Wilkes expedition into the Pacific in the 1830's, sought no colonies in the Coral Sea, though American sailing-ships were among the more important traders in that area. Between 1792 and 1812, fifty-five American vessels entered the new port of Sydney. Many others were whaling and sandalwooding in Melanesian waters. A good many captains, even of English whalers, were men from Nantucket, and Yankee runaways settled many an island.

Despite the slow acquisition of a few protectorates and colonies, the story of the nineteenth century in Melanesia, on the whole, is one of uncontrolled and often ruthless exploitation. This was for the most part conscienceless, and frequently also murderous. The rich harvests offering *bêche-de-mer*, sandalwood, and pearls; the hopelessness of policing a sea so vast; the reluctance of officialdom to accept responsibility for maintaining law and order, and the comparative freedom with which profligates could roam and pillage at will—these conditions bred that disreputable figure of romance and adventure, the sailing trader of the South Seas. The Coral Sea was for years a haven for any renegade who could get a ship. Seen from the perspective of the mid-twentieth century, the era now may seem a colorful one. But it was an evil time for the people of the coral islands. While great powers pigeonholed schemes for the colonization of their islands, and evil men exploited, corrupted, and dispersed them almost as they wished, no one thought to ask the Melanesians what their views were of this new invasion.

By no means all the sailing traders of the Coral Sea were villainous, though as a bishop of Melanesia once remarked, it was

practically impossible for a just man to engage in its more
profitable callings. The whole Pacific lent its winds, its currents, its islands, and its climate to the small sailing-ship. This
was man's really mobile means of transport, in which he could
roam among the lovely islands so long as he could maintain his
ship and avoid the cannibals. The winds and currents of the
Pacific Ocean, once understood, are peculiarly suited to the
making of passages in sailing-ships which use them and do not
try to sail against them. The general trends of the wind from
east to west in the tropic zone, and from west to east in the
temperate zones, make ambulatory passages under sail comparatively simple, provided the cyclone and the hurricane
seasons are avoided. The abundance of good weather is easy on
rigging. In the northeast trade wind, the sailing-ship may
wander from Mexico to the Philippines with a favorable wind
the whole way, and not have to worry about much save calms,
reefs, and provisions. For much of the year south of the equator, the southeast trade will blow a ship from Peru to Queensland.

For the greater part of the nineteenth century, might was
right in the islands. They had no international status. Beach-
combers from the seven seas, desperadoes who had escaped
from Australia, runaway whalemen and the like, might set up
domain on almost any atoll or small island. Nor were large
and expensive vessels required for the navigation of such
waters. A schooner sixty feet long would do nicely. Such vessels
could be cheaply built of local woods in Tasmania, New South
Wales, Queensland, and New Zealand. Schooners, small brigs,
and fast ketches were turned out by the dozen in Tasmania.
Less than two thousand pounds would equip the usual expedition with everything, including the ship. If the unscrupulous
seeker after trade could not afford to buy a ship, he could
charter one and forget about the charter. Better still, he could
steal a ship with what seems now to have been remarkable ease.

This kind of lawless wandering went on until the twentieth century and did not cease entirely even after all the islands had been divided among the Powers. The end of "recruiting" on a slave basis, radio, control of shipping and trade, and the growth of missionary influence put an end to the chances of the odd marauder. He died hard; but he died. He had done a great deal of harm, the repercussions of which have not yet all died away, and his ranks included no true pioneers. No Rajah Brooke, no Stamford Raffles, no Cecil Rhodes, ever sailed the Coral Sea or settled in its islands, though for over half a century picturesque adventurers flourished there, and the field was great.

If there have been none like these to personify and dramatize development, much of the area has been well served by a succession of able administrators, painstaking, patient, and thorough. Men such as Sir William Macgregor and Sir Hubert Murray in New Guinea, who between them guided the fortunes of Papua almost continuously from 1888 to 1940, have done splendid work. Besides being an unusual pacifier and administrator, Sir William Macgregor was an explorer in his own right. He twice crossed the wild hinterland of New Guinea, then almost completely unknown. He ascended the Fly River for 600 miles. He examined the territory behind Milne Bay. A man of indefatigable energy, both he and the farsighted Sir Hubert Murray did their best to see that the impact of the white man on the primitive Papuan was not only for the white man's good. It was not their fault that their start was late and they had to make up so much leeway.

Sir Hubert Murray died in 1940. Had he lived only a year or two longer, he would have had the satisfaction of observing the magnificent resistance of so many of the Stone Age natives, both in New Guinea and the Solomons, to the invaders from Japan.

CHAPTER SIXTEEN

FIVE KNOTS IN A PALM FROND

THE CLOUDS were clear around Traitor's Head, behind Dillon's Bay on Erromanga, on the bright morning in November, 1839, when a pretty brig hove in sight and made for the anchorage. There was nothing especially to distinguish the brig from any sandalwooder or adventurer in quest of fortune. As far as could be seen, she was not armed, but many another brig looked unarmed, only to spit death at the islanders and plunder their villages. A few days earlier, just such a brig—the Erromangans thought it was the same one—came into Dillon's Bay and dropped a boatload of white scum on the beach by the pretty river. They foraged inshore, plundered gardens, raped young women, murdered all who stood in their way. From many a grass hut and vantage point in the fertile woods, Erromangans looked darkly on the approaching brig. Did the white murderers never have surfeit of their infamies? Why come here to plunder yet again? The gardens were still spoiled: no grass had grown above the graves of their last victims.

The brig, shortening to topsails and fore-topmast staysail, stood in to anchor with the quiet morning wind making her a picture of loveliness. At a shouted command, the watching natives saw her round into the wind. Her backed sails took off her way; an anchor dropped from the port cathead, its splash disturbing a shoal of gay-colored fish sporting below. Figures clambered into the rigging, laying aloft to furl the sails. She meant to stay, then. The natives knew that, even before they saw a boat swung out and, well manned, pull in toward a landing place on the beach. The boat headed for the very spot where the sandalwooders had landed a few days earlier.

The chief, Kauiau, rushed from his hiding place, brandished some warning arms, signaled the boat to be off! The Erromangans wanted no more white plunderers. This time they intended armed resistance.

The people in the boat paid no attention to the warning. The boat came on steadily: now Kauiau and the warriors hidden in the bush all round him could hear the converse of the figures aft.

Kauiau slipped back into the bush. He would wait. If the white men landed, perhaps they would be off again soon. They must know there was little left to steal. But if they tried to go along the track beside the river, they must be attacked and driven back into the sea. Kauiau knew the chances. The white men still gave no sign of being armed, but their guns might lie in the bottom or along the sides of the boat. The islanders could be covered by other men, or by the big guns of their brig. Kauiau knew about big guns.

The boat grounded. Not an Erromangan was to be seen.

A large man, stout, full faced, benign of countenance, got

out and looked around him. With him was a smaller man. The
smaller man walked toward the track beside the river.

Kauiau raised his club.

Instantly the silent bush became a bedlam of noise. Natives
sprang from all directions, and their blood-curdling screams
and shouts filled the air. Kauiau was a brave man. As the senior
chief present, he fell upon the large white man, and his great
club rose and fell. But the white man was strong. He parried
the first blow, shouting something. He turned toward the sea.
But Kauiau was upon him. The white man staggered a few
steps before pitching full length into the quiet water; blows
rained upon him. Accursed sandalwooders! This was a lesson.
The white man shouted only once. In a matter of seconds he
was dead, and his companion was struck down by the banks
of the stream.

The boat lay off. No firing came from it. No burst of gun-
fire broke from either boat or brig. Kauiau thought that
strange. In the boat, a white man stood aft, crying: the boat
pulled in, the man aft saying something. But the blood of all
the warriors was up, though already Kauiau sensed that something was not quite as it should be. The warriors danced along
the water's edge, screaming defiance against the men in the
boat. Some dragged the body of the big man ashore and carried it off to the ovens. Others saw to similar preparations for
the second man, meanwhile shouting imprecations at the boat's
crew.

When they saw that they could do nothing, the boat's
crew pulled away, the figure aft wringing his hands and
crying.

Kauiau watched him, wondering. What sort of white man
was this? He had not seen a white man cry before, nor heard
of it. Was this a great chief he had killed? He remembered
the benevolence of the features, even as he clubbed the man.
He looked again at the dead big man and examined his counte-

nance. Despite the wreckage caused by his club, he gazed upon the face of a man who knew power and peace.

Though he did not know it then, Kauiau was the murderer of the missionary John Williams and his assistant Mr. Harris. The brig in Dillon's Bay that morning was no sandalwooder, but the missionary brig *Camden,* up from Sydney via Samoa and the islands, bound upon a voyage of good will to bring the word of God among the heathen. It was the missionaries' great misfortune that they had been preceded by the marauders. No Erromangan could distinguish one brig from another, nor one European from another. So John Williams died, not the first or the last brave missionary to lose his life in Melanesia.

Twenty years afterward, Kauiau, now long a Christian, stood in the saloon of the mission barque *John Williams,* anchored in Dillon's Bay. The *Camden* had gone the way of all good brigs, and the *John Williams* had taken her place as a mission cruiser among the islands. Kauiau looked at the portrait of John Williams. This time it was he who wrung his hands and showed deep grief, as he asked forgiveness for having killed a man of God.

It was the sandalwooders who killed John Williams, not Kauiau, who was left to live out his days in his native island. John Williams was dead, but his work lived on.

Missionaries were early in Melanesia, though a less promising field for their endeavors it would be hard to find. "No authentic record remains that even the Apostles went into a situation like that of these islands," one of the early missionaries laments in a book published in London in 1810.* The ship *Duff* carried missionaries from England into the Pacific in 1796. In 1845 the French Mission of the Society of Mary landed a party of twelve at San Cristoval, in the Solomons, but

* *An Authentic Narrative of Four Years' Residence at Tongataboo,* Longman, Hurst, Rees, and Orme, London, 1810.

Bishop Epalle, the leader of the group, was murdered by the natives shortly afterward. The murder of three other members a little later and the death of another from malaria caused the withdrawal of this mission. Many other missionaries and teachers lost their lives in the New Hebrides or in New Guinea.

Despite these setbacks, the missions persevered. They were the pioneers of European influence and authority, and as such the missionaries' lives were hazardous and their labors endless, often with scant reward. They were the first teachers and the first medical men. Often their greatest enemies were their fellow whites, who, intent upon gathering quick fortunes by any means they could, did not care for the propagation of the idea that the native had a soul. The runaway sailors and beach-combers of the South Seas were godless human beings whose state was often lower than any heathen's. Some of the traders were little better. With their example it was difficult for the missionary to convince the simple Melanesian that the European was the better way of life.

Some of the early missionaries had to flee for their lives, so great was the opposition of the local priesthood and sorcerers. The wild New Hebrides were among the worst islands. The day before he was murdered at Erromanga, John Williams had landed at Tanna to arrange to leave some Samoan teachers there, for the mission's plan was to found colleges and training centers for the peoples of the Pacific and prepare them to spread the gospel among their kind, as there were few Europeans to carry on the work. His reception at Tanna seemed good, but it was deceptive. Williams was murdered on the Erromanga beach on November 20, 1839; within less than a year the first party of white missionaries was on its way to the New Hebrides. These were the Reverends G. Turner and H. Nisbet, of the London Missionary Society. They spent some time in Samoa to become acclimatized and to learn the Samoan language; in early 1842 they landed at Tanna, among natives who went about habitually armed to the teeth and who were, to a man, the world's most expert and callous thieves. When the women of every household went to their gardens, they did so with all the family possessions on their backs, even to the brood of chickens, to prevent their loss.

The whole island was in a state of constant warfare, and the natives were in the control of an avaricious and cunning priesthood of sorcerers. These were the real enemies, determined to rid themselves of the missionaries.

Mission attempts to start schooling at Tanna came to nothing. So did the first church. The Tannese would not hear of giving up every seventh day to the new deity, pointing out that their old gods had required special offerings and prayers only once or twice a year. It was of little value to learn the dialect of the natives among whom the missionaries were living, for it was unintelligible four miles away. There was not the slightest pretext of real government, and little discipline. Law was the law of the club. When an outbreak of dysentery followed soon after the missionaries set up their house, the priesthood declared that the missionaries were to blame and raised the countryside against them. Though there were men among the natives who upheld the missionaries, the position of the latter was untenable, and after a few months they had to run for their lives. The Hobart whaler *Highlander* (Captain Lucas) stood into Port Resolution just as the Tannese were pressing in on the mission house to kill its occupants: the missionaries were fortunate to escape. Within a year or so they were back again at Tanna, but for a while at least, their visits were confined to the cruises of the mission barque *John Williams,* first in a long line of mission ships of that name, which arrived in Samoa from England early in 1845 and began almost at once to cruise through the New Hebrides and to New Caledonia.

The experiences of Messrs. Turner and Nisbet were unusual only in the fact of their own survival. As they were escaping

from Tanna, a mission family at nearby Futuna was being
murdered. A long succession of courageous men and women
—by no means all of them white—continued the effort to
bring Christianity to these dark islands, in some of which there
survive to this day the least lovable natives of all the South
Seas. Parts of the interior of Malekula are considered dangerous, even in the middle of the twentieth century, and much
remains for the missionaries to do.

When Missionary Turner came back to Tanna, the natives
met him on the beach with a queer story that Satan was with
them, staying in the mission house. Satan, they said, was a
white man, very sick. They had tried to induce him to leave,
having heard more than enough of the evil he could do, but he
refused to do so. Mr. Turner hurried to his house to find a
curious stranger there.

*He reclined on a sort of bedstead made of some sticks
lashed together, and raised a little off the ground* [he
wrote].* *A mat and a blanket formed his scanty bedding.
A loaded gun lay at his right side, another stood up in the
corner at his left. He had an old number of the* Times
*newspaper in his hand, and a little fire smouldered in a hole
in the earth at the foot of the bed. There he lay, with a
long black beard, pale, pensive, and emaciated. As we
appeared at the door of the little place, he raised himself,
bowed, and spoke most politely: "Have I the honour of
addressing either Mr. Nisbet or Mr. Turner?"*

His name was Sutton. He was from Essex, England, the
scion of a good family. He had tried his luck in New Zealand
and was sandalwooding among the islands when fever laid
him out. He was, it appeared, grateful to the missionaries for
having made the name of Satan so respected; but within a few

* *Nineteen Years in Polynesia*, John Snow, London, 1861.

months he had gone to another island, where the natives knew neither of Satan nor of God, and he was murdered.

Mr. Sutton, *alias* Satan, might have been a reasonable man in the sandalwood business. If so, he was a rarity. The misdeeds of the sandalwooders and of the blackbirders led directly to the death of many missionaries, among them at least one bishop. This was Bishop Patteson—John Coleridge Patteson—who, after a distinguished career at Eton and Oxford, served under Bishop Selwyn in the southwest Pacific. His principal job was to "rove about the Melanesian department," as he described it himself. He had a sixty-ton schooner, the first of many mission ships named *Southern Cross,* and his "beat" was the Solomons, Santa Cruz, the Banks, and the New Hebrides. Life in the schooner was pleasant and she did much good work. Unfortunately, there were other schooners of similar appearance which cruised the same islands, doing far from good work. To the natives, all white men's schooners looked alike. They could distinguish one canoe from a thousand others, for there were peculiarities of build about them, and rig: but to them, one schooner was like another.

The *Southern Cross,* with Bishop Patteson aboard, became one of the most popular vessels in the Coral Sea—so popular, indeed, that natives flocked aboard her at every anchorage and in every roadstead. The blackbirders heard of it, and one of them pretended to be the bishop, in order to entice natives aboard. When there was a good crowd, he clapped them under hatches and sailed off, to sell them for twelve pounds a head in the Fijis. This sort of thing might be successful once, but the bush telegraph works fast in the islands. The news spread. In isolated islands, suspicious natives began to watch for any schooner which looked like the *Southern Cross.*

On a bright morning in September, 1871, the *Southern*

Cross sailed slowly in toward Nukapu, a pretty island in the
Santa Cruz group. The bishop had had charge of the Melanesian see then for just over ten years; as ever, he was happily busy
aboard with his native students, who had been enlisted from
the islands to learn the Christian faith and, after a course at
the mission's college at Norfolk Island, to return among their
kind. The bishop's lesson that morning was from the Acts of
the Apostles and concerned the martyrdom of Stephen: "And
they stoned Stephen, calling upon God and saying, 'Lord Jesus,
receive my spirit.' And he knelt down and cried with a loud
voice, 'Lord, lay not this sin to their charge'; and when he had
said this, he fell asleep."

With these words the lesson ended. Soon afterward, the
emerald-green island being close aboard, the bishop went away
in a boat to visit the natives. He had been in Nukapu before.
The natives, in whom there is a considerable Polynesian strain
—the bishop noted that they understood many Maori words—
were always friendly. "They are all Man Fridays, if you know
how to treat them," he had said. But he was reckoning without
the blackbirders.

The tide was out as the boat approached the lagoon. The
reef was bare, and the boat could not find passage. The bishop,
who was always prepared for such emergencies, leaped overboard and made his way ashore, with the assistance of some
natives in a canoe. He was seen to land, and then he disappeared.
He had told his boat to wait until there was water enough to
use the passage over the reef. He would wave his handkerchief
to them when he wished to be taken off.

For a while all was quiet and seemingly peaceful. The island
was a paradise to outward view. It was one of those perfect
Pacific days when all the world seems gentle and filled with
loveliness and peace. A solitary cloud, drifting slowly, passed
across the sun. And then, without warning, some canoes came
toward the mission boat, their paddles striking the water in

hurried unison. They paused; the natives in them stood and loosed a flight of arrows. Several of the boat's crew fell, badly wounded, and the boat had to retire to the *Southern Cross*. Among those badly hurt was the bishop's secretary, but he insisted on returning in the boat as soon as the arrows were drawn from his body.

Not long after, two canoes were seen to leave the beach at Nukapu. One was towing the other, which appeared to be empty. The tide had risen now, and there was a way into the lagoon. Freshly manned, the boat from the *Southern Cross* returned and pulled in. The towing canoe stopped and set the towed canoe adrift. It came on slowly, drifting gently toward the sea. As it approached, the people in the boat saw a figure in it, lying motionless, covered with native matting. Nothing else. They pulled alongside in profound silence. They turned back a corner of the matting and gazed upon the dead face of Bishop Patteson.

"The sweet face smiled as of old: there was not the slightest trace of terror or of agony," wrote one of the boat's crew, afterward. The body had five wounds—two from clubs, three from arrows. On the breast was a palm leaf, with five knots tied carefully into its fronds.

They learned afterward that the blackbirders had recently been to Nukapu, and with violence and treachery had forcibly kidnaped five young men.

By the beach a simple memorial was raised in after years. On it one may read:

In memory of
JOHN COLERIDGE PATTESON
Missionary Bishop
Whose life was here taken by men for
Whose sake he would willingly have given it
September 20, 1871

Missionaries of the Coral Sea have been blamed for much. They were early regarded as bad influences among the natives. They were often blamed for spreading white men's diseases. In an area where even today it is considered necessary to have "closed districts" to protect the islanders from such simple things as common colds and so-called influenza, any white man could be the innocent cause of the decimation of whole islands. The peoples of the remoter atolls and small islands, like Tikopia, Ontong Java, Sikiana, Rennell, and Bellona, were particularly at the mercy of white men's ills. They had no chance of developing immunity to them. At Ontong Java the population declined from more than 6,000 in 1900 to less than a tenth of that number a few years later. Yet it was to just such islands that mission efforts were directed, though no missionary knowingly brought ill to his dark flocks. The golden-maned Tikopians—graceful, tall, slender men, light in skin, cheerful in disposition—and the other atoll dwellers of the Polynesian fringe were ideal converts. Today, access to them all is strictly controlled, and even government officers, when they visit them at all, must go under virtual quarantine conditions.

In such islands many died. It was sometimes easy to blame the missionaries, particularly those who had been implacable opponents of the nefarious blackbirding, and who had sought to restrain the worse instincts of their fellow whites. True, there were early mistakes in some of the missions. The haste to get clothes upon dark skins not used to them, the smug acceptance of a Mother Hubbard neck-to-ankle gown as evidence of true conversion; the rigorous condemnation of much of native life without real effort to comprehend its meaning or its value; the breaking down of cultures which could, far more intelligently, have been slowly blended to a more modern and beneficial way of life; the introduction of sectarianism, here and there, among peoples still groping painfully from primitive mythologies—something of these charges stands.

But the missions of the Coral Sea have been well and abundantly served throughout their long and useful careers by men such as John Williams and Bishop Patteson. Men and women of many denominations and many countries have brought not only Christianity, but education, medicines, and a wider and a better life to the peoples of Melanesia. Their work is not yet finished. Much of it has been of the greatest value, and their activities and their influence have been, and remain, one of the chief factors in the development of the islands.

CHAPTER SEVENTEEN

SHIPWRECK AND BOAT VOYAGES

MANY ADVENTUROUS seamen have passed through the Coral Sea, and some of them died there. Of them all, no name is better known to maritime history than that of Bligh.

Over a century and a half after it was made, despite the occurrence of two wars, both of which abounded in astonishing voyages and escapes at sea, the voyage of Lieutenant—later Vice-Admiral—William Bligh in the longboat of the *Bounty* from Tofua across the Coral Sea, through Torres Straits and the Arafura Sea to Timor, remains one of the most extraordinary boat voyages made. Whatever might have been his faults, Bligh was a man. Said to be a bully, overbearing, incapable of appreciating the feelings of those more sensitive than himself, or even of imagining that such feelings had existence, mean enough to omit important passages from his narrative of the *Bounty* mutiny when innocent young men were brought to trial—of all these Bligh has been accused. Yet he was, above all else, a splendid seaman and a fearless leader. It took later generations to make a sort of hero out of Fletcher Christian, the leader of the mutiny.

The manner of that mutiny, the forcing of Bligh and eighteen others into the ship's launch, the *Bounty's* sailing away to leave them to their fate—all these are incidents in a story which has often been told, and almost as often misrepresented. The island of Tofua was in sight when the launch pushed off, and the *Bounty* hauled the wind to return to the eastward. In the boat were 19 men, 150 pounds of biscuit, 32 pounds of salt pork, 6 quarts of rum, 6 bottles and 28 gallons of water, and 4 empty barricoes.

Bligh made at once for Tofua to seek fresh water and food. But the natives, who had seen the ship sail away, wondered why so crowded a boat approached their island when the ship was out of sight. They were seamen themselves, and they knew the boat was overloaded. Showing, for once, bad judgment— perhaps his view of all South Sea islands was still colored by his pleasurable stay at Tahiti—Bligh told the natives that the ship was lost and they were the survivors.

When they heard this, the Tofuans immediately "began knocking stones together," which was a signal for attack. Bligh knew the signs and hastily organized a retreat, since he had no firearms. They were not quick enough. One of the quartermasters, a man named Norton, was stoned to death in the surf. Every man in the boat was hit and injured by the stones. Their only method of defense was to throw the stones back again, but the natives were too good for them at this kind of warfare. Bligh got the boat away as quickly as he could; after that they dared not touch at islands.

A survey of all the food and drink aboard showed that they could survive perhaps two months—time enough, Bligh thought, to reach Timor.

We bore away [he wrote] *across a sea where the navigation is but little known, in a small boat twenty-three feet long from stem to stern, deeply laden with eighteen men. I was happy, however, to see that every one seemed better satisfied with our situation than myself. It was about eight o'clock at night on the 2nd of May when we bore away under a reefed lug-foresail; and having divided the people into watches, and got the boat into a little order, we returned thanks to God for our miraculous preservation, and, in full confidence of His gracious support, I found my mind more at ease than it had been for some time past.*

Next morning the sun rose fiery red, for May was in the cyclone season. The wind got up as the day grew, and the sea rose until the boat's sail was becalmed between the crests of the seas as she sank in the troughs. Yet they dared not lower the sail. They must keep the boat before the wind, lest she broach to and roll over. They jettisoned all they could, except food, to lighten her, but the sea broke over the square transom, and every moment of that long and dreadful day Bligh expected to founder. Only by consummate skill at the tiller and in his handling of the boat was he able to bring her through.

Next day the same conditions held, and the seamen went through purgatory. Throughout that day and night and all the following day Bligh stayed at the tiller, and never once did his great spirit falter. He knew the bread was spoiled and the sea had got at their fresh water, and he was well aware that any of those great seas was enough to make that small boat founder, to roll her over while they drowned. He served all hands with a teaspoonful of rum.

A few days later they came among the Fiji Islands. The natives at that time were treacherous cannibals. Two large sailing canoes were launched from the beach of an atoll and came after them, their great sails lovely in the wind, with streamers flying. There was nothing lovely about those canoes in the eyes of Bligh and his men, armed only with a few blunt cutlasses. Bligh pressed the boat with all the sail he could and drove her along until he had the satisfaction of watching the canoes put about and return to their atoll. This part of the Fijis had not been seen by Europeans before, and Bligh did his best to record what he could and make some sort of chart of the islands.

The days were cold and the nights wet and bitter to men whose resistance was running down, cramped as they were in a tumbling boat. Five hundred miles to the west they ran, and came within sight of the outer New Hebrides. Again they dared not land, for of what use were a few cutlasses against the ferocious savages of Malekula? A thousand miles—fifteen hundred miles—two thousand miles—still they ran on, and the boat's ribs were bleached and the men's buttocks chafed on the thwarts so that it was hellish to sit down. They could not stand up, and there was not room for all to lie down.

Through all this, Bligh kept up the morale of his men, always doing his best to see that their minds and bodies had some occupation. Like all naval officers, he was a past master at devising routine, the planning of duties, necessary or unnecessary, which could be regularly carried out at the same time each hour or each watch or each day, so providing some sort of occupation for his too-large crew. They had some fishing lines, and he made a log which was hove every hour. The watches were religiously kept and punctually relieved. The boat was kept as tidy as circumstances would allow.

Day followed day, and the little boat drove before the trade wind steadily toward the west. They had grown used to the miracle of the curling seas which followed the tiny transom constantly yet never broke with fatal weight aboard. The sea flung its salt in their eyes, and its spume drenched the boat. When the wind was fresh, the salt in the air almost blinded them. Salt rimmed their eyes and stuck to their faces, clotting in their beards. Bligh wrote in his log:

> During the whole of the afternoon of the 21st we were so covered with rain and salt water that we could scarcely see. We suffered extreme cold, and everyone dreaded the approach of night. Sleep, though we longed for it, afforded no comfort; for my own part, I almost lived without it. On the 22nd, our situation was extremely calamitous. We were obliged to take the course of the sea, running right before it, and watching with the utmost care, as the least error in the helm would in a moment have been our destruction. It continued through the day to blow very hard, and the foam of the sea kept running over our stern and quarters. The misery we suffered this night exceeded the preceding. The sea flew over us with great force, and kept us baling with horror and anxiety. At dawn of day I found everyone in a most distressed condition, and I began to fear that another such night would put an end to the lives of several. . . .

If the wind and the sea gave them no rest, at least they were being driven to the west at a famous rate. On May 28 they saw the breakers of the Great Barrier Reef. Bligh had to find a channel through the coral while his people had strength enough to work the boat. As far as they could see, the water broke violently over the reef, which seemed to stretch interminably to both horizons, a wall of deathly coral in their path. The wind and the sea were driving them down upon it. They could not beat back against the trade wind; they had no strength to row. Anxiously, Bligh coasted along, while his much-tried men could see, as the boat was flung up on the crests of the driving seas, the peacefully calm water of the long lagoon beyond the reef, mocking them. At last Bligh found a break in the reef about a quarter of a mile across, and the sea boiled through at such a rate that the boat was almost upset. Once through, they were in calm water. Compared with the conditions they had survived during the previous three weeks and more, they were in heaven.

Bligh headed for a small island, while they thanked God for their deliverance. They had come over 2,000 miles. There was now less than 1,500 to go. He grounded the boat in the calm lee of a sandy point on an island which he named Restoration Island, for here, he said, they were restored to life and to their right minds. Here, the master and the carpenter, disgruntled men who had always been against him and were in the boat only because Christian would not leave them in the *Bounty,* turned on him, and he had to challenge them to a cutlass duel. Both cravens refused to fight, but Bligh felt he had to watch them closely. He rested the sailors a day or two, while they restored their strength, replenished their water, and took a stock of oysters and birds. Then they steered to the northward along the Queensland coast, inside the Barrier Reef. For a week, conditions were good, though the carpenter still brooded, and the master, who had been threatened with death if he tried to start a mutiny, glowered on his thwart.

Round the head of Cape York Peninsula, in the extreme north of Australia, they found a way through the reefs, still called Bligh Entrance. Bligh continued making careful note of the boat's position, both for the sake of his own navigation and the benefit of any who might come after him. Once they were past Cape York, the way was clear. They were free of the cyclone area, and the weather was good. Some of the men had cadaver countenances and great swollen limbs, like skeletons with elephantiasis. But the worst was past. On June 11, 1789, they were within sight of Timor. On the 14th, a Sunday, they brought the boat into Koepang Bay. It was six weeks and two days since they had left Tofua, and Bligh's reckoning of the distance covered was 3,618 nautical miles. Not a man had died.

"It was Bligh's misfortune not to have been educated in the cockpit of a man-of-war, among young gentlemen, which is to the navy what a public school is to those who are to move in civil society," wrote Sir John Barrow, permanent secretary to the Admiralty, at the time of the *Bounty* incident. If that were Bligh's only misfortune, it was one he shared with Cook and other distinguished officers. His greater misfortune was in too many of his biographers. Bligh was a member of an old Cornish family which gave at least one other admiral to the king's navy, though his own early service was largely in merchant ships. His merits gained him selection as master of Cook's *Resolution* by Cook himself, and the great navigator always spoke highly of him. He earned the good opinion of Sir Joseph Banks and of the Royal Society, which in neither case was given lightly. He earned the personal congratulations of Lord Nelson for his conduct at Copenhagen. He was commended for his "intrepidity and address" at the mutiny at the Nore. He was selected as governor of New South Wales at a time when that appointment called urgently for an able man: there, the measure of his good intentions is to be found in the story of those who opposed him. Home again from New South Wales, he was promoted rear admiral of the Blue. By June, 1814, he was a vice-admiral. He lived at Farningham, Kent, and died in London in December, 1817. He left six daughters, and a great story.

The real villain of the *Bounty* story was the captain of the frigate *Pandora,* which was sent by Admiralty to capture the mutineers and bring them to trial. The captain was Edward Edwards, a man with a reputation as a strict disciplinarian. He sailed the *Pandora* to Tahiti, found some of the *Bounty* people there—by no means all of them were mutineers, for Bligh's boat would not accommodate all who wished to go in her—clapped them in irons, and imprisoned them in a foul box built on the *Pandora's* poop. At Tahiti he also found a small schooner, which some of the *Bounty's* people had recently completed. This he used as a tender until parting company somewhere near the Friendly Islands.

After sailing past several islands, including Vanikoro, and narrowly avoiding shipwreck on some reefs not far from the Louisiades, Edwards lost the *Pandora* on a spur of the Great Barrier, in the Coral Sea.

It was a ghastly incident, not for the wreck itself but for the inhumanity of the commander afterward. While the ship was breaking up and in imminent danger of foundering, the prisoners were kept ironed in their cage, under armed guard. Though the *Pandora* was in danger for some time before she struck, and after striking took several hours to sink, Captain Edwards refused to allow the prisoners to be freed from their irons. As far as he was concerned, they were guilty of mutiny and they could drown. Somehow, three of them got out and lent a hand at the pumps. Edwards saw them there and ordered them to be ironed again.

As the *Pandora* heeled to take her last plunge, Captain Edwards climbed over the prison on his way to safety. The men inside implored him for God's sake to have mercy on them and to give them at least the chance to swim. Edwards seemed not to hear. Some senior members of the *Pandora's* crew were with their captain, and these had greater humanity. The master-at-arms opened the scuttle and dropped the keys of

their irons to the men inside. William Moulter, the boatswain's mate, seeing this, leaped inside to help loose the irons.
It was too late. The *Pandora* was already going. With a series
of dreadful lurches she slipped from the reef and disappeared,
taking four of the *Bounty* men down with her. These included
Midshipman Stewart, who was not guilty of mutiny. The last
out was Midshipman Heywood, who afterward became a captain in the Royal Navy.

Inside the reef was a small sandy cay, and here the survivors were assembled. Even here, Edwards refused shelter
and aid to the *Bounty* survivors. Though there were sails to
spare and it would have been easy to contrive a shelter, and
though all the *Pandora's* people were properly cared for, he
forced the *Bounty* men to stand all day in the sun. They dug
themselves up to their necks in sand, and this was their only
shelter. The sand wore their skins—already softened by long
confinement in "Pandora's box"—almost from their bodies,
so that they peeled and looked like scalded persons. In this
condition they were herded into the boats, and Edwards, like
Bligh before him, set off from the Barrier Reef to make for
Koepang, which he reached in fourteen days.

This was a different boat voyage, however, from that made
by Bligh. Edwards's boats had ample arms and were adequately
provided with provisions. They had a comparatively short distance to sail and a reasonable expectation of good weather.
Moreover, Edwards had lost the *Pandora* largely through his
own neglect of seamanlike precautions, for he had been running on blindly through the nights. To do so in that corner
of the Coral Sea was to ask for shipwreck. Even after narrowly
avoiding disaster once, Edwards continued to run blindly
toward the Barrier Reef.

When the *Pandora's* people, after their safe arrival at Koepang, came later to the port of Semarang on the north coast
of Java, they were astonished to find the little schooner from

Tahiti. I have found no record of the voyage she made. Edwards barely mentions it. To sail from near Samoa to Semarang in a little schooner built by amateurs out of local woods and without benefit of European fastenings, without charts or proper instruments and with little food, is a feat that should rank the petty officer in command not far below Bligh.

In the course of the voyage the schooner fought off a determined attack by the Samoans, off Upolu, and survived an attempt to seize the vessel by the same natives who had attacked Bligh at Tofua. She spent five weeks at one of the islands in the outer Fijis, possibly Matuku. The petty officer in command (whose name was Oliver) could find no clear way through Torres Straits and got through the labyrinth of reefs there by Tasman's method of finding the place where the water broke with least viciousness, and boldly sailing over. This exploit is one which few mariners have cared to attempt, and fewer survived.

When they arrived in Dutch waters, Oliver and his crew were nearly imprisoned, on suspicion of being pirates. The Hollanders had had unfortunate experiences with more than one boatload of odd persons who had blown in from the sea with vague accounts of themselves. They asked Oliver for his commission. As a petty officer he had none, and the Dutch would not believe that an English frigate would send a tender so far without a commissioned officer in command. They noticed, further, that the schooner was built of strange native woods. It is understandable that the Dutchmen found Oliver's story difficult to believe. They probably thought he was one of the *Bounty* mutineers, for whom by that time there was a hue and cry all round the known world.

Dutch suspicions might have been strengthened by a recent experience, when a boat's crew came in from the sea to Koepang with a story that the eight men, one woman, and two children aboard were the sole survivors of an English merchantman. They were somewhat vague about this merchantman, and they had no papers. The Dutch thought it strange that their boat should be an obvious fishing boat, not the normal type carried aboard ocean-going ships. However, the presence of the woman and the two babies added some support to the story. If they had not come from a wreck, where and what had they come from? How far could that little fishing boat have sailed? They had, as a matter of fact, come almost 3,000 miles. Far from being survivors of a nearby wreck, they were runaway convicts from New South Wales, and they had brought that fishing boat from inside Sydney Heads.

This party was led by William Bryant, an ex-smuggler from Devon who had been transported to New South Wales. With him were his wife, Mary, and their two small children, Emmanuel and Charlotte. Being a handy man with a boat, Bryant was employed at Sydney as a fisherman for the governor's table. He was given a boat, but it was not the type in which any but the desperate would attempt a sea voyage of 100 miles, let alone 3,000. An obliging Dutchman, in command of the snow *Waaksambeid*, gave Bryant, for reasons of his own, a rough chart, an old quadrant, and an older compass. Possibly Bryant bought these things with fish, for food was scarce in Sydney at that time. Bryant assembled a crew from his trusted friends. His wife and babies had been allowed to live with him. His friends were seven fellow convicts: William Allen, James Cox, Nathaniel Lilley (all "lifers"), Samuel Bird, *alias* John Simms, James Martin, George Morton, and Samuel Broom, *alias* John Butcher. Though the shortest sentence any of these was serving was seven years, the most serious crime of which any had been convicted was stealing three pigs. Mary Broad, Bryant's wife, had also been transported after being sentenced to death for stealing a cloak.

In the boat, along with the presents from the *Waaksamheid*, they took a fishing net, plenty of lines and hooks, a ten-gallon keg of water, and a little rice, pork, and flour. Mrs. Bryant had the children's clothes and bedding, but there was no adequate food. A pair of scales was found lying on the path to the place where the boat had been, hurriedly dropped as the party fled. This was evidence of Bryant's thorough organization: he knew it would often be necessary to apportion their supplies with strict accuracy.

No serious attempt was made to pursue the party, partly because of lack of means but more because the possibility of successful escape by sea was not taken seriously by the authorities in Sydney. The idea that Bryant's frail fishing boat, freighted with his wife, babies, and seven inexperienced men, could get clear away was not entertained. The authorities, however, were not aware of the constancy of Mary Bryant or of the power and capabilities of her husband.

It was the night of March 9, 1791, when the boat voyage was begun. On June 4 the party arrived safely at Timor. They had been under way for sixty-nine days and had sailed by way of the passage inside the Great Barrier Reef. Their most alarming adventure was a chase by Celebes *proas* when they were crossing the Arafura Sea. The babies were thriving and were of great assistance in helping the party to pass themselves as survivors from a brig which they declared had been lost at sea while on passage from Sydney toward India.

All went well until Captain Edward Edwards came along. Even then they might have escaped if they had kept their heads. The captain of a Dutch East Indiaman who had been moved by their story and was eager to tell the Bryants the news of the arrival of another party of castaways hastened to tell them that their captain had come.

"What captain? Damme, we have no captain!" exclaimed one of the lifers, starting up, caught off his guard.

When Captain Edwards heard of this it was the end of freedom. The party was carried off, babies and all, to Batavia, to await passage to England as felons. At Batavia the unfortunate Bryant sickened of a fever and died. He was followed shortly afterward by his infant son. In the Straits of Sunda one of the lifers jumped overboard from the ship which was taking him home, and two of the other convicts did not survive this voyage.

Mary Bryant, with her small daughter, was sent to England in a ship called the *Gorgon*. Her daughter died in the South Atlantic: Mary Bryant went alone into the dock at London. Yet she was not quite without friends: an officer of marines who had also traveled in the *Gorgon,* much taken with her quiet courage and her beauty, still youthful despite jails and prison ships and sentences of death and 3,000-mile voyages in open boats, was also in the court. On the day after the trial a cloaked stranger drove in a hansom cab to the city jail where she was being held, and informed the jailer that a pardon would shortly arrive. Apparently, the pardon did arrive; the last that was seen of Mary Bryant was in a four-wheeled cab with the officer of marines from the *Gorgon*, driving away from the jail.

The Bryants were the first to organize a successful escape by boat from New South Wales. They were by no means the last. Before the port of Sydney was a quarter of a century old, its less desirable citizens were scattered from Erromanga to Batavia and from Tahiti to Tongatabu. New Guinea was a favored place for escapees to make for, because once they had arrived there, recapture was almost impossible. A disadvantage was that, among those wild cannibals, survival was almost equally impossible; but each escapee had to learn that for himself. Those who most thoroughly learned the lesson did not pass it on to new arrivals.

Their peculiar flair for adapting themselves to savage society stood more than one Irishman in good stead after he escaped from New South Wales. There was, for instance, the remarkable Terence Connel, who became a chief among the Horaforas, in New Guinea. His story is given in a little-known book * written by John Coulter, M.D., and published in London in the 1840's. Coulter made a voyage in a South Seas trader called the *Hound,* with a man named Trainer. In the course of the voyage Trainer took the *Hound* into New Guinea waters, looking for trade. One day Trainer and Coulter were ashore at the head of a large bay, when they were surprised to see a strange-looking native making boldly toward them, a large spear in his right hand, a loincloth as his only garment, and a great dog trotting at each side of him.

It was unusual for dogs to show much affection for their native masters, and it was almost equally unusual for a native of those parts to advance toward Europeans. He was a tall, athletic man, and Trainer and Coulter noticed that the long hair falling to his waist was curiously light in color. As many natives bleached their hair, they attached no particular significance to this, but as the man came closer to them they saw that he was white.

They kept a wary eye on the loinclothed king. It was a favorite trick of renegade whites in the islands to approach people from visiting ships and lull them into a sense of security, while the cannibals with whom they were in league carried out an attack. The king of the Horaforas, however, was not of that breed.

When he had eaten, which he did with considerable zest, he told his story. He came from County Kerry, he said, via New South Wales: his name was Terence Connel, and he was an outlaw in Ireland. He had been transported to Botany Bay

* Adventures on the West Coast of South America and the Interior of California, including a Narrative of Incidents at the Kingsmill Islands, New Ireland, New Britain, New Guinea, and Other Islands in the Pacific Ocean, Etc., Etc.

for the term of his natural life. As a dangerous man, he went ironed and worked in the chain gang. As soon as a period of good conduct freed him from this, he joined a band organizing an escape by sea. They stole a "large boat with mast and sail"—which is all Connel says about her—and eleven of them started in her.

They got clear away and worked to the north, close inshore. Night and day they worked at the oars, setting the sail when there was a favoring wind by night but fearful to set it by day, lest pursuers see them. Their stock of food was small, and a storm nearly made an end of them. But at length they reached the sanctuary of the Barrier Reef. They rested for several months at an island which was probably one of the Northumberland group, not far from the Swain Reefs.

This was a lovely place, and they considered settling there. But they still felt insecure. They were within the area of New South Wales and dreaded recapture, so they launched the boat again and continued toward the north. They passed Cape York and crossed Torres Straits with difficulty, arriving at last at New Guinea. Some of them thought this was China, and they ran the boat into a river mouth to look for Chinese. No sooner did they nose the boat into a bank than an ambush of ferocious savages fell upon them, though there had been no previous sign of life. In a few moments nine of the convicts were dead. Only Connel and a fellow countryman named Jim Hutton survived. They were bound hand and foot and carried into the interior.

According to Connel's story—which there is no reason to doubt—they were cruelly treated by this tribe. At last they managed to escape, and after trekking for months in the interior, sick with fevers, eating wild berries and roots and whatever else the jungle offered, they had the luck to fall into the hands of the "Horaforas." As the Horaforas saw no sign of boats in which these mysterious white men might have sailed to their land, they thought them gods and took care of them. Reckless of their lives but glad to be alive, Hutton and Connel showed their gratitude by joining in the native wars, for which there was plenty of opportunity. They served with distinction and soon became lesser chiefs. After several years Hutton was killed by arrows in a big battle. Connel was alone. His good services in war and his general adaptability gained him the confidence of the tribe, and he was now the acknowledged chief. He did not remember when he escaped from New South Wales—twelve or fifteen years earlier, he thought.

Captain Trainer offered Connel a place on board, with an eventual passage back to Ireland. But the Irishman would not go. In that decision he was probably wise.

CHAPTER EIGHTEEN

THE SANDALWOODERS

THERE WAS a grim saying in the Sydney trade that every stick of sandalwood from the South Seas had blood on it. Dealers in that sweet-smelling wood made enormous fortunes—when they escaped the roasting ovens of the cannibals or murder at the hands of rival traders. For sandalwood was wrested from the natives, log by log, at a cost that ran high in human life and was attended by unspeakable butchery on the part of the white man no less than the native.

When the colonial schooner *Francis* sailed from Sydney to rescue Flinders's people, cast away from an East Indiaman in 1803 on Wreck Reef in the Coral Sea, the master was an enterprising mariner with an eye on the main chance. His name was James Aicken, or Aiken, and he had arrived in Sydney as a master's mate in H.M.S. *Supply* in 1794. He noted that *bêche-de-mer*, a sea slug much in demand in China as a delicacy in aphrodisiac soups, was abundant on Wreck Reef. Aicken had been to Canton, and he knew that he could get space in the East Indiamen sailing empty from Sydney to China, if he could supply the market with dried *bêche-de-mer*.

As soon as he could, he left the *Francis*, a government vessel, and got hold of the schooner *Marcia*, twenty-six tons, a Sydney-built vessel manned by five men. In the *Marcia* he returned to Wreck Reef, eager to profit from his discovery. But something had happened to the succulent slugs. Most of them had gone. Aicken had a large and increasing family, and he had to look round quickly for some other employment for his schooner.

He found this other employment in the sandalwood trade. Interested in the *Marcia* at the time was Simeon Lord, as hard-headed and as shrewd a businessman as was to be found in New South Wales, then or later, which is saying a great deal. Simeon Lord had heard whispers of the existence of sandalwood in abundance on the islands of the Coral Sea. Sandalwood was in even greater demand on the Chinese market than was *bêche-de-mer*. The farsighted Mr. Lord perceived that, if he could establish this trade on a sound footing, he might open up a permanent source of profit.

Simeon Lord, merchant venturer of the Coral Sea, was an enterprising and unusual man. He reached New South Wales in 1791 as a convict, on what charge is not known. (Perhaps he removed the records himself, as was done by more than one citizen both there and in Tasmania, after they had risen in the world.) At any rate his offense was trivial and not such as to brand a man a felon, either then or now. Before long he set himself up as a shipping agent, having either worked out his time, gained a remission, or induced the employer to whom he was assigned to finance his enterprise. He was an astute man, and he knew how to dispose of ships' business efficiently and profitably in a port which was not then, and has never become, an easy one for the shipmaster compelled to do his own business.

Lord soon earned a name as the man to employ for the quick transaction of ships' affairs, particularly if, as so often was the case, some irregularity had to be arranged or hidden. He was frequently employed by American captains, who began early to visit the port. The first American ship at Sydney was the brigantine *Philadelphia*, Thos. Patrickson master. She arrived in 1792 with a cargo of rum, gin, tobacco, pitch, tar, and salt beef, all of which were highly salable commodities in the port. Lord was perhaps too recent an arrival then to profit much from the visit of the *Philadelphia*, but before the turn of the century he had done so well out of similar vessels that he was a shipowner. An early venture was in the sealing business, with the American ships *Union* and *Fair American*, which was highly profitable to Lord and the masters of the ships, if not to the owners in America.

In those days, shipmasters of most American deep-sea ships were their own business managers and made long voyages buying and selling, far beyond the effective control of their owners. It was not the shipowners alone who profited from these voyages. The new and somewhat lawless port of Sydney offered infinite opportunities, and Lord built up his business by throwing these opportunities the way of the shipmasters who employed him. The sealing voyage over, he suggested to the *Union* that she might go after sandalwood, which she could either bring back to Sydney for transshipment to China by East Indiaman, or take to Canton herself. This venture failed, however, when the master and two boats' crews were massacred at the Friendly Islands.

The *Union* was a brig of less than a hundred tons, belonging to Fanning and Company of New York. She touched first

at the Friendly Islands to look for sandalwood. The mate, a
seaman named Wright, was somewhat worried when the master did not return from a trip ashore, and more worried
when two boats also failed to come back to the ship. His mind
was not set at ease when a canoe paddled out from the native
village with an English-speaking Malay on board, who passed
a message to him that the captain wanted him to come ashore.
The mate of the *Union* was suspicious. On the following day
the Malay returned, bringing with him a young white woman.
This girl added her entreaties to those of the Malay that the
mate should come ashore, but she was obviously acting under
duress. When the Malay was not looking, she shook her head
and indicated to the *Union's* people that they should not believe what she said and should on no account send any more
boats inshore.

Next day, out came the Malay with the young woman again.
This time she induced the Malay to come a little closer to the
Union; she suddenly jumped up in the boat, shouted that the
captain and the two boats' crews had been killed, and leaped
overboard. The mate lowered a boat at once to her assistance,
drove the natives off, took the young woman inboard, cut his
cable, sheeted home the topsails, and sailed away.

The name of this young woman was Elizabeth Morey. She
had reached the islands in the American ship *Duke of Portland*,
of which she was then the sole survivor, for the *Duke of Portland* was cut out and all hands massacred.

The *Union* returned to Sydney and abandoned the sandalwood voyage, at any rate for the time being. The arrival of a
young woman from a sojourn alone among South Sea natives
appears to have been accepted as almost commonplace. Miss
Morey left no account of her experience, which is a pity. Lord
thought of some other employment for the *Union* and called
in the impecunious Aicken, with the *Marcia*, to prospect the
sandalwood islands. The *Marcia* went to the Fijis. Aicken was

a careful seaman, and he managed to avoid both the reefs and the cannibals. Sandalwood was plentiful, and the Fijians had no idea of its value. They collected it readily for Aicken and received pieces of old iron in return. The *Marcia* loaded thirty tons. It would sell at nearly seventy pounds sterling a ton to the Chinese merchants on the Sydney market. Simeon Lord was pleased. The total initial cost of the schooner, fitted for sea, was less than fifteen hundred pounds and here she had brought in a cargo worth two thousand pounds. Lord soon afterward began to build himself brigs of over a hundred tons, which were big ships in those waters.

Lord's and Aicken's success was too good to be kept to themselves. Before long, anyone who could get hold of a vessel, no matter how small, sailed for the Fiji Islands and scoured the nearer groups of the Coral Sea looking for the scented wood. American ships, hearing of the profits to be made, added the quest of sandalwood to their activities. Shipbuilding at Sydney went ahead. White runaways, escaped convicts, deserters from ships, and human flotsam of all descriptions made for the Fiji Islands and spread from there to the Loyalties, New Caledonia, the Solomons, and the New Hebrides. On all these islands sandalwood was found. The natural result of the influx of drifters and ne'er-do-wells, the lack of regulation in the trade, and the fierce rivalries of the unprincipled scoundrels who sought profit by it, was savage warfare. The white-sailed schooners in quest of sandalwood often left death in their wakes, for both white man and native.

From Erromanga in the New Hebrides alone, the Sydney sandalwooders took wood worth seventy thousand pounds. It was not easy to take sandalwood, or anything else, from Erromanga. The natives had no idea of the value of this wood, but they were resolute and able warriors who knew the whites they met for their true worth. A minor armada was organized against the Erromangans in one of the big sandalwood raids.

This was led by the Sydney brig *Sophia* and included a number of smaller vessels and a party of "recruited" native warriors from other islands, said to be 500 strong. This fleet landed on the beaches of Erromanga in 1830, drove the natives inland, set up a stockade, and cut all the sandalwood they wanted. Any Erromangan who got in the way was killed. Many were driven into a cave and suffocated by smoke. The invaders did not have things all their own way. Poisoned arrows, poisoned water, and the fevers of the place decimated them. Only a handful of those who organized the raid survived it, but the profits were enormous.

The natives took fierce vengeance for the slaughter. For many years afterward it was dangerous for any vessel not heavily armed and provided with at least a double crew of fighting men to approach Erromanga. Within ten years the natives had cut out ten ships and massacred all on board. The Erromangans declared bloody war on the white man. Every boat that landed was attacked, and when the boats began to lie off and wait for sandalwood to be brought to them, the natives devised a daring scheme for upsetting them. They used to swim off with a tomahawk hidden under the upper arm, pushing a log of sandalwood in the other. While the log was being hauled into the boat, they would dive at the keel and capsize it. Then a crowd of swimming natives would be among the white men with their tomahawks and kill all they could. Seeing this, the people in the vessel which had sent the boat would open fire on the nearest village and kill more natives. So the bloodshed went on, year after year. Survivors from wrecked ships, whalers, missionaries—all were the same to the Erromangans. They killed and ate all they could get at.

One Friday afternoon in April, 1847, a boat drifted in toward the beach at Erromanga with two survivors from the wreck of the barque *British Sovereign*. They were killed and eaten at once. Soon afterward, another boatload of survivors from the same ship came in. There were twenty-nine men in this boat, all armed. The natives determined to kill them, but strategy was necessary. Some treated them with coconuts and sugar cane, while others sped through the countryside assembling warriors for the coming massacre. Under pretense of taking the white men to join the other survivors, a party was formed to walk through the bush. They set off in single file, a native between every two whites and others guarding the sides. A chief took the lead. At a prearranged signal from this chief, each native suddenly wheeled round and struck his man dead with a blow from a club. They cooked and ate ten men on the spot; others were divided among the villages which contributed warriors.

But it was the white men themselves who were nearly always the aggressors. A few days before the *British Sovereign* massacre, a sandalwooder had shot fourteen Erromangans in cold blood. It was common practice for sandalwooders to kidnap natives from one place and sell them to cannibals at another, either for their heads or as food. While the mission barque *John Williams* was at Tanna in 1848, for instance, an Erromangan was taken ashore from a Sydney sandalwooding schooner as part payment for some wood. At the time, the Tannese were at war with the Erromangans, and the unfortunate native was butchered and eaten as soon as he was landed. Sandalwooders tried to kidnap chiefs, who were then offered for ransom; the ransom being collected, they would sail away, still with the chief aboard, to sell him somewhere else as a slave or for roasting at the next meal. The sandalwood schooners went about armed with swivel guns and well manned. Trade was carried on from armed boats, the captain buying from natives assembled on the beach, a pistol ready loaded in one hand and his beads or fishhooks in the other.

When there was no one else to fight, the sandalwooders fought for trade among themselves. There is a record of an

incident when two schooners were lying off an island in the
New Hebrides, seeking sandalwood. A canoe laden with wood
put off to sell its cargo to one of the schooners. Immediately,
both schooners lowered boats and raced for the canoe. One
boat was much faster and was obviously winning the race.
Thereupon those in the slower boat lay on their oars and
opened fire on the canoe, sinking it and killing all the natives.

"Neither of us shall have it!" shouted the glowering sub-
human in charge. If such persons ended their careers in a
roasting oven on an island in the Coral Sea, the natives were not
to be blamed.

The natives of the Loyalty Islands, between the southern
New Hebrides and New Caledonia, carried on war against the
white marauders as relentlessly as did the Erromangans. There
was, for instance, the Sydney brig *Star*, which was seized by
the people of the Isle of Pines in 1842 by a cunning piece of
treachery. Thirty selected warriors paddled off to the brig
with a good load of sandalwood. As weapons, they took only
the adzes which they used for dressing the wood, in order to
allay suspicion. The sandalwood pleased the people of the *Star*,
and a request from the natives to sharpen their adzes, the
better to cut more wood, was at once acceded to. Up came
the thirty warriors, grinning. One of the brig's crew turned
the grindstone for them. The captain ventured nearby. Seizing a favorable moment, one of the warriors swung his adze
and hit the captain between the eyes. This was the signal for
instant attack. In a matter of seconds, seventeen of the crew
were killed.

The warriors had come from New Caledonia, Mare, and
Lifu, and each party received a share of the bodies. The *Star*
was looted and then burned. When the fire reached her magazine, there was a tremendous explosion, which pleased the
warriors watching from the beach. It was an additional diversion they had not been expecting.

The Loyalty Islanders who cut out the *Sisters* did not fare so well, for they made the mistake of taking her powder kegs ashore. Some sparks reached the powder. Up it went, and many of them were killed and wounded. Among those killed was a respected chief, and the survivors swore vengeance on all white men. They thought the explosion was an act of the white men's gods.

They had not long to wait. Shortly afterward, a boat full of escaping convicts from Norfolk Island chanced to land at the village. Norfolk Island was then used as a prison for the worst offenders from New South Wales and was peopled with desperate characters. The natives fell immediately upon the boat and clubbed five of its occupants to death. Two escaped and were taken under the protection of a humane chief, by name Ieui, though the rest of the islanders were out for their blood. Ieui was a man who had come under mission influence, which was fortunate for the two convicts. But they were typical of their kind. One dark night they robbed the old chief of his most prized possessions, stole a canoe, and made off.

Their subsequent behavior and treatment throw light on the mentalities both of native and of too many white men of that era. In the morning Ieui missed his possessions and canoe. Since the convicts had taken all his hatchets and other tools, which were the property of the community, and since he knew that they could not handle a canoe as dexterously as the most childish Loyalty Islander, he gave chase. An hour's paddling brought them up on the convicts, who fired on them with stolen muskets. Nothing daunted, the natives came on. The convicts threw all the tools into the sea, thinking perhaps that, seeing their possessions lost, the natives would give up pursuit. But the canoe followed them the faster. Then, thinking drowning better than a clubbing, they leaped overboard. But the natives rescued them.

By this time the sea was running high, and the outrigger of

the native canoe came adrift. All then had to jump out and swim along, with the canoe supporting them, while they propelled it in the direction of the island they had left. The two convicts, who were in a bad state, lay in the bottom of the canoe. Some of the Mare people were for killing them or leaving them, but the chief would not hear of it.

"The current is with us," he said. "Let us try it a little longer."

The whole party eventually came to the beach. The two miscreants were tried and ordered to be disgraced. This was done by stripping them naked and smearing them with mud and ashes. Then they were allowed to go; eventually, they got away in a whaler which touched at the island. They were fortunate men.

The wanton, senseless exploitation of sandalwood, wherever it could be found, had the natural result of bringing the trade to an early end, leaving the natives of New Caledonia, the New Hebrides, and other affected islands sullen, implacable enemies of the white man. But the white man was not finished with them yet—not by any means.

CHAPTER NINETEEN

THE BLACKBIRDERS

SANDALWOODING LED directly to raiding for slaves. As the precious wood grew scarcer, it had to be sought with greater thoroughness. It was no longer sufficient to ply among the islands and accept what the natives brought. The islands themselves had to be combed. The Erromangans would not do that sort of thing and could not be made to. So natives were forced to come from adjacent islands, compounds were set up, and a system of slavery was begun. People from Lifu and Tanna were taken forcibly to Erromanga, in fear of their lives from both the white men and the Erromangans. It was an easy step from this to running cargoes of Melanesians into the Fiji Islands and as far away as Tahiti, and even Peru, where they were sold for labor.

The further they were taken, the less hope there was of getting back. Few returned from either the Fijis or Tahiti, and none at all from Peru. Four young Lifu men, who had been kidnaped by a Sydney sandalwooder, succeeded after years of wandering in getting back to their own island; but they were fortunate. When the sandalwooders were finished with them, they sold them in the Caroline Islands. Here, they escaped to Hongkong by an American vessel. Thence they managed to get to Honolulu, where the American missionaries took care of them. Eventually they reached Rarotonga in the Cook Islands, and there the mission barque *John Williams*, learning of their story, took them aboard. On her next Melanesian voyage she landed them at Lifu.

"It was affecting to see how the people clung to them," states the mission record, "listening to their tale, and following them wherever they went." They had been given up for dead.

Lifu and the other islands of the Loyalty group were unfortunate in the blackbirding days. The first Melanesians ever shipped to Australia came from Lifu and Uea. They were imported into New South Wales in 1847 by an enterprising and ambitious capitalist named Benjamin Boyd, a pioneer in the Simeon Lord tradition who, if fate had treated him more kindly, might well have become known to fame as Rajah Boyd of the Solomon Islands.

Ben Boyd was a man with big ideas. In the early 1840's he tried to build himself a pastoral empire in a large section of the then undeveloped New South Wales, and the ruins of his "cities" at Boydtown and East Boyd still stand by Twofold Bay. Boydtown was to rival Sydney, and Ben Boyd's empire was to stretch from the Pacific westward across most of Australia. The success of his scheme depended on labor. In 1841 the flow of cheap labor from English jails came to an end. So Boyd turned to the nearby islands of the Coral Sea for his shepherds and cattlemen. If the sandalwooders could put them to work, why couldn't he? There were plenty of them. In 1847 he sent two schooners to the Loyalties and the New Hebrides for recruits. Captain Kirsopp, in command of the little expedition, got his men the same way the sandalwooders did. He bought them from the chiefs, whose influence was gained by paltry gifts which seemed great wealth to them. There was an understanding that the men would be returned to their native islands after serving their terms of employment. Kirsopp was a man already wise in the ways of blackbirding: he took care to accept only a few men from each chief. Each party was then afraid of all the others and unable to converse or form plans for rising against the vessels. All went well, and in a few weeks the two schooners were back at Twofold Bay with their human cargoes. Others joined the trade, and further cargoes were brought.

But the idea was a failure. The natives were indentured, but once they landed in New South Wales they could not be slaves. When they ran away (which they frequently did), they could not be brought back by force. Some of them were excellent workers. Others were not. They could not be induced to take any interest in sheep, which they regarded as inherently foolish animals. Worse than that, there was an uproar against them conducted, largely, by the former convicts of the colony, who foresaw a wage war which the employers, aided by their dark laborers, would win. Many of these convicts were employed on stations and big ranches, and they sometimes used force against the unfortunate islanders. Ben Boyd owned ships as well as sheep stations, and when he used a party of his Loyalty Islanders to break up an attempt at job control aboard the steamer *Juno,* in Sydney, there were ugly scenes. Even in the 1840's Sydney seamen were already gaining considerable power.

Ben Boyd had a brother named Mark, who wrote a long letter to the London *Times* * about Ben's labor scheme.

> *After having actively and usefully assisted in the washing of ten thousand sheep* [he wrote], *they were summarily driven out by those colonially termed the old hands and who, anxious to maintain the exorbitant wages then exacted for pastoral labour, regarded the newcomers with jealousy. Some of them, however, I am informed, have been allowed to remain in the interior, and are every day exhibiting increased usefulness and affording, in their peaceful demeanour and activity as shepherds and labourers, a striking contrast to the turbulence and idleness which characterized some of the civilised whites previously to their arrival. . . .*

Mark Boyd added that some of the islanders had gained work as seamen, whalers, wharf laborers, and lifesavers in Sydney harbor. Whether they were run off the stations or chose to leave of their own accord, they were certainly not the answer then to the labor problem in New South Wales. It has been said by other witnesses that they strenuously objected to assisting "actively and usefully" in the washing of 10,000 sheep, taking the view that there were far too many sheep, and that washing any of them was quite unnecessary.

Within a year or two the lucky ones were on their way back to the islands. One of the survivors, asked a few years later, what he thought of the experience, tersely remarked in pidgin English: "No plurry good. All time fella work, no catchem *kaikai!*" which means too much work, too little to eat.

By 1849 Ben Boyd's grandiose schemes collapsed. Boyd's

* Quoted by Thomas Dunbabin in *Slavers of the South Seas*, Angus and Robertson, Sydney, 1935.

Bank, which had provided the funds, was bankrupt, and the whole Boyd edifice came down with it. Of all his "empire," only a yacht remained. This was the year of the great California gold strike. As enterprising as ever, Boyd sailed his yacht to San Francisco to try his luck on the diggings. He had none: a year or two later he left San Francisco, still sailing his little *Wanderer,* and made his way back to the Coral Sea. Those islands had already produced much wealth, and Boyd still had schemes for getting more out of them. If he could not use the islanders in New South Wales, perhaps he could put them to work in the Solomons and Papua. He was working on a grand scheme which would put even his "empire" in Australia to shame. He proposed to take over personally the development and the government of the Solomon Islands. His idea was to found a state similar to Sarawak in Borneo.

He might have done it. The opportunity was there, and Ben Boyd might well have been the man. But he foolishly went ashore alone at a bay on the west coast of Guadalcanal, one day in October, 1851, and the wild Solomon Islanders fell on him, clubbed him, and ate him. They were unaware of his schemes or of his pioneer efforts in blackbirding, for to them he was just another roast.

The importation of Melanesians into Australia ceased for a while with the end of the Boyd schemes. A war for the suppression of slavery 8,000 miles away led directly to its successful resumption. The American Civil War, by temporarily interfering with the production of cotton, tobacco, and other commodities in world-wide demand, led to attempts to produce these things in tropical Australia and the islands of the South Seas. Not all such attempts were successful, but they all required labor. The Australian aborigine was unsuited to such work. With training, he develops into a good stockrider, but the dull monotony of agricultural labor is not for him. The softer Polynesian of the eastern and central Pacific also was unsuitable for continuous effort, but the tough head-hunters and cannibals of Melanesia, once tamed, could be made into excellent workers. The natives of the New Hebrides, much of the Solomons, and coastal New Guinea and its nearby islands were of good physique and made first-class slaves. They soon became hunted men.

In Queensland the trade was begun by Robert Towns, an English North Country master mariner who became a leading Australian merchant and gave his name to Townsville, an important port on the Queensland coast. Captain Towns was a merchant adventurer in the Simeon Lord and Benjamin Boyd tradition, though he prospered better than either of these. He was no stranger to the Coral Sea. He had been wrecked there at least once, and he had a sandalwood depot on the Isle of Pines when that horrible trade was in its prime. His agent there, one John Lewis, roused the anger of the missionaries and was brought to trial for murdering natives. Though Bishop Selwyn himself took an active interest in the case and the Royal Navy supplied evidence enough, Lewis was found "not guilty" in his trial at Sydney in 1851. Captain Towns—whose wife was the sister of William Charles Wentworth, often rightly called the Father of Australia—was a powerful man. It was openly said that at the time that his influence extended to the judiciary. By 1853 he was a director of the Bank of New South Wales and a member of the legislative council. As such, he was a respected member of the Sydney business world; but the full story of his activities is yet to be told.

The American Civil War did more than one good turn to empire-builder Towns. When he saw it coming, he bought heavy stocks of Virginia tobacco at the market prices, and saw them quadrupled within a year. When the Lancashire cotton mills ran short of American cotton, he started a cotton plantation on the banks of the Logan River in Queensland.

The climate there was trying for the ordinary Australian laborer. Towns first tried to import coolies from India, but this presented difficulties and was expensive. He therefore turned to his well-known New Hebrides. His letter commissioning his toughest skipper, an ex-navy man named Ross Lewin who was a notorious brute in the Coral Sea, was a model of how such instructions should be prepared. Indeed, there were investigators at the man-hunting activities of the same Lewin who, shortly afterward, declared that the instructions were meant to be only a model. They were for posterity and not for Ross Lewin, who in any event, was unable to read. A nice letter telling him to be kind to the natives would have its uses when shown to inquisitive missionaries, curious naval officers, and others who might suspect that a new slave trade was building in the isles of Melanesia.

The document Lewin carried in his schooner bound Towns to engage each Kanaka laborer whom the schooner landed in Queensland, for a payment to the Kanaka of ten shillings a month, with food, lodging, and necessary clothing. The food was to include rice, pumpkins, meat, and yams. They were to be returned to their own islands after a year's engagement, if they so wished, or they could give instructions for their wives to join them on the Queensland plantations. It is fair to add that Towns sent a covering letter to the missionaries, describing briefly what he proposed to do and undertaking to look after the spiritual and physical well-being of recruited Kanakas, to the best of his ability. If they were good laborers, perhaps he intended to do what he could on these lines. But the hope of getting Kanaka wives to ship with a man like Lewin or anyone else from the dreadful sandalwood trade was nil, and the only real way of inducing natives to ship with him would be to kidnap them or willfully deceive them in some way.

Towns knew the real conditions of the Coral Sea. He was

aware of the limitations of his servant Lewin. It seems likely that, when he drew up those first instructions and wrote his letters to the missionaries, he foresaw something of the grief and bloodshed which must follow the man-hunting voyages he was instigating, and he was washing his hands in public before it all began.

At any rate, on August 14, 1863, Lewin was back from the New Hebrides with sixty-seven natives, few if any of whom knew what they had undertaken. There were some angry protests from planters who lacked the foresight of Captain Towns, and from labor interests. But the government promptly quashed them. The natives proved good workers in Queensland's tropical conditions: within a year or two Blackbirder Lewin advertised in the Brisbane newspapers, offering to bring for all takers "the best and most serviceable natives to be had amongst the islands," at seven pounds a head. In 1872 Commander Markham described Lewin as the worst man-stealer in the Coral Sea, where by that time he had plenty of competition.

Towns's cotton ventures did not prosper as well as he hoped they would. He planted coffee and sugar and continued to recruit the "blackbirds" for labor. Within five years of his first shipment there were more than 2,000 Kanakas living in Queensland, and many others had died there and on the way. By 1885 there were 11,000, and the death rate was 250 per 1,000.

Towns himself lived to a hale old age in a mansion overlooking Sydney harbor, where he died in 1873. He made no blackbirding voyages himself. Others did the dirty work. But on him rests much of the responsibility for a dreadful trade which led directly to the deaths of thousands, depopulated whole islands, and left a dark stain across the Coral Sea that is not yet quite gone. Compared with blackbirding, even sandalwooding was a gentle picnic.

There was no recognized market for the Coral Sea slave trade, which was unfortunate for the slaves. The existence of a market might have shocked the governments concerned into putting an end to it. The slave trade in the southwest Pacific consisted in seeking healthy natives wherever they could be found, and filling small schooners with them for delivery to some Queensland port on "contract," or selling them direct to planters in Fiji, where no questions were asked, as there was no settled government. The natives were frequently picked up from beaches or kidnaped from their villages in any manner possible, and the horrible ingenuity and bloody enterprise shown in this industry led to many retaliatory murders.

All means of kidnaping were fair. Some blackbirders strutted about the decks of their schooners with sheets draped over them as surplices, while they gave out torn pages of old books as tracts. One blackbirder carried his own harmonium, the better to ape missionary ways. When he arrived at a remote island, the natives crowded aboard; his crew would suddenly descend upon them with clubs and belaying pins and force them into the hold. Then the hatches would be clapped on and the schooner sail away, to repeat the performance elsewhere until some other dodge had to be thought of.

Those who were inhuman enough to do this sort of thing did not scruple to throw children and the elderly overboard, as of no market value. If they could not entice the natives aboard, they ran down their canoes at sea and scooped them from the water or lassoed them. Until they learned to distrust the white man, the display of a few trade goods would often bring a crowd of the less sophisticated islanders aboard.

The natives, naturally, reacted to this sort of thing with violence whenever they had the chance. Unscrupulous traders began to run arms to them, and before long the price of the better blackbirds was a rifle a head. The blackbirders went heavily armed and their ships were well manned, but many were cut out and all hands eaten. No one wasted much sympathy on them. The blackbirder, in the main, was an unscrupulous scoundrel whose least misdeed was kidnaping. He was an enemy of society for whom the only thing that could be said was that he knew the risks he ran, which were considerable, and he accepted them. Seen now in retrospect, against the romantic background of the islands of the Coral Sea, the doings of these schooners, manned by scum, may even seem somewhat adventurous. A few blackbirders were picturesque rascals. Many who sailed out of Queensland were merely accepting Coral Sea conditions as they found them, and tried to observe a code which set at least some bounds to the infamy of the trade. But upon the whole, the most romantic things in the business were the ships, pretty little schooners, brigantines, and brigs built from Tasmanian, Australian, and New Zealand woods. They were excellent vessels, fast and weatherly, as they had to be to survive under Coral Sea conditions.

The dearest wish of the natives was to see a schooner wrecked and to make a cannibal feast of the crew, if edible. Some connoisseurs avoided joints made from blackbirders on the grounds that they were spoiled by the pickling in rum they had received while in use. "Man belong bush goodoh. Kaikai [eats] plurry good. Man belonga Sydney no good, too much plurry salt," as a cannibal of the Duke of York Islands told Captain Wawn of the schooner *Stanley*.

Captain William Wawn wrote a book * about his experiences. As a recruiter always scrupulous (he says) to observe the Queensland government's regulations for the trade, he stoutly defends his calling. His defense of blackbirding is not the usual one that, by bringing the natives in contact with the benefits of European civilization, they had greater op-

---

* *The South Sea Islanders and the Queensland Labour Trade*, London, 1893.

portunities for conversion to the Christian faith. Wawn took
a more practical view. He pointed out that Queensland and all
the other governments of the then unfederated Australian
states spent a good deal of their citizens' money sending agents
to England to induce the English to migrate to Australia,
while he brought cheaper migrants from near at hand, at no
public cost at all. Moreover, he knew his migrants were excellent laborers, and they were already acclimatized. A tropical Australia which badly needed population and would go on
needing people for at least a century to come was foolish, in
Wawn's view, to neglect the rich fields of Melanesia right on
its own doorstep.

It is, at this stage, a little difficult to see much resemblance
between the free migrant from Europe and the indentured—
or kidnaped—Kanaka from the Coral Sea. Wawn also held
that "wealth, freedom, and civilization"—he puts them in that
order—awaited the blackbird on the plantations of Queensland. Perhaps they did: but the islander rarely found any of
them. Wawn blamed most of the evils of blackbirding on ships
holding French or Samoan licenses which, he said, were granted
to anyone.

Another favorite means of ensnaring blackbirds was to
carry a decoy. This was a native who pretended that he was a
prosperous ex-plantation worker. It was his duty to tell tales, to
all who would listen, about the delights of working in Queensland and the easy fortunes which awaited the Melanesian
there or in Fiji. One such traitor was a Tongan who had far too
much sense ever to have been a blackbird. He used to be dressed
in fancy costume as the "governor of Sydney," going ashore
in a regular procession and receiving—sometimes—the hom-
age of the chiefs. This kind of trick usually sufficed only once,
no matter how well done. News moved fast by the bush telegraph, and still does so. The blackbirder had to think of some
new scheme almost every voyage. It was simplest, in the long

run, to concentrate on plain kidnaping, or pay a strong chief to provide the bodies.

To do this, there was no infamy to which some blackbirders did not sink. One way was to assist head-hunting expeditions. In many New Guinea and Solomon Islands tribes, a young man had to bring home the head of a warrior—or any head—before he was admitted to the full status of a warrior or could take a wife. An early blackbirder thought of the idea of taking young men to lonely islands, where the inhabitants, unaccustomed to such practices, fell easy victims. He then took the new-fledged warriors back to their own islands, where they paid for the services rendered by providing a number of strong slaves.

It has frequently been alleged that several blackbirders helped the head-hunters by active work in the field, but this—though probable—has never been proved. There is plenty of evidence that they did carry head-hunters, and there is at least one record which strongly supports the charge that they were not above collecting heads themselves. A blackbird landed alive in Queensland was worth at least eight pounds, and anything up to ten or twelve pounds in the Fiji Islands. A cargo of 100-odd would yield high profits in a schooner, the original cost of which was about £1,000. She might make twenty or thirty voyages before the reefs or the cannibals got her. But it seems extraordinary, even in this brutal trade, that—except perhaps to get the good will of a powerful chief—it paid to remove the heads from any prospective customers. In the Coral Sea islands, a really powerful chief was rare.

The Rev. Charles Hyde Brook, of the Melanesian Mission, who was stationed for a time on the island of Florida in the Solomons during 1871, has left evidence on record of having seen a blackbirder in a black brig actually engaged in the murder of natives from that island, for the sake of taking away their heads. The brig, at the time, was about a mile and a half from the beach. She showed no flag. She was a sinister vessel, heavily armed. Her lines were unusually fast; she looked as if she might have been an ex-opium clipper from the China trade. The chief of the island gave orders that no one was to approach her or have any dealings with the white men aboard her. But a canoe disobeyed his instructions. Two boats left the brig as the canoe came alongside, and cut it off from retreat ashore. The missionary's statement goes on:

> *Anticipating what was about to happen, I could not look steadfastly at what took place, but I have not the least doubt that my companions saw everything plainly. At each successive act in the murder of their fellow-islanders, they raised a loud cry, and at length launched a war fleet and put off either to save their friends or to have revenge. . . . The heads were taken as before. . . .*

It is probable that the sinister black brig was commanded by the notorious Bully Hayes, of Cleveland, Ohio, a man whose lawless but colorful career is in itself almost an epitome of the achievements of too many white men in the Coral Sea. Any quest of the facts of Hayes's career now is made difficult by the legends that have grown around him, by the remarkable ease with which other scoundrels, not so keen on publicity, had their misdeeds attributed to this most publicized of them all, and by his habit of disappearing every now and again and spreading the report—accepted with profound relief all round the Pacific and Indian oceans—that he was dead. When at last a blow from a meat ax, or some such implement, used upon him by an angry sea cook goaded to madness, put an end to his career, even the cook hesitated to believe the monster dead and hove the carcass overboard at once, in case he was not.

It was a good riddance. Hayes has been much written about.

The notion that his was a romantic figure ought to be scotched. Head-hunting, wife stealing, kidnaping, blackbirding at its worst, fraud, barratry, piracy—of all these he was guilty. He was a villain of extraordinary plausibility, who found it as easy, apparently, to "marry" a wealthy widow as to steal a ship, and he did both these things all round the Coral Sea and the whole Pacific, besides. He stole at least five ships, the custodians of which must have been extremely careless, and he married at least three widows.

In an ocean where white men, murderers of natives, and known slave traders could carry on as they liked, the few naval vessels on patrol could scarcely be expected to cope with all evils. Even when they caught slavers red-handed, it was almost impossible to secure a conviction against them in the courts of New South Wales. The fact that the slave trade was more or less regulated by Queensland laws often gave the lawless the semblance of legality, for they pretended to comply with those laws, and a little pretense was sufficient. All they had to do was to fit out as legitimate recruiters and then turn slaver. A license from the government as a "recruiter," and a clearance from a colonial port for Tanna or Erromanga or any other island in the Coral Sea was equipment enough. It was easy to forget to inform the government agent when they were sailing, or to get rid of him on some pretext. There was no need to bring blackbirds to Queensland when there was a more profitable market for them in Fiji.

The Queensland regulations insisted on the provision of sleeping room for all natives, which limited the numbers carried and so interfered with profits. The government agent, living aboard with the recruiter, was supposed to see that no one was kidnaped, that all natives embarked freely and understood what they were doing, and that a proper form of contract was explained to them and legally made. In the Fijis there were no contracts and there was no pretense that the plantation labor was anything other than slaves.

On several occasions British men-o'-war brought recruiters and their ships into Sydney and forced notorious slavers to stand trial. There are few records of successful prosecution. "I would like to be informed what constitutes the definition of a slave in these waters," said Commander Palmer of H.M.S. *Rosario* when the desperadoes of the hellship *Daphne* walked smiling out of the Sydney courts, after facing charges which almost anywhere else would have hanged them. Commander Palmer added that, if the African slave trade had been conducted in accordance with the precepts of the courts of New South Wales, it would still be a flourishing industry.

The *Daphne* was a schooner of less than fifty tons, registered in Melbourne, and commanded by one Daggett, said to be a native of Boston, Massachusetts. The schooner was licensed as a recruiting vessel in accordance with the laws of the colony of Queensland and was authorized to carry not more than fifty-eight native laborers. One day in 1869 Daggett sailed into Levuka Roads in the Fijis with more than a hundred Banks Islanders clapped down below. His only papers were a clearance from Australia toward the New Hebrides. At anchor off Levuka was H.M.S. *Rosario*. Investigation showed the naval captain, who was no novice in these matters, that the *Daphne* was fitted out in precisely the manner of a West African slaver, except that she had no leg irons; no interpreter was provided for the natives, who had no idea where they were or for what purpose they had been forcibly removed from their own islands; and the only person who could speak the language of the Banks Islands had been deliberately left behind at Tanna. There was not even a pretense of any contractual obligation toward the islanders. The case was one of barefaced slavery.

The *Rosario* packed the *Daphne* forthwith back to Sydney,

where the case was dismissed "for lack of evidence." The court held that there was no evidence that the natives did not go abroad voluntarily, though it was brought out clearly that a decoy named Charlie had enticed them to the ship with lying stories about life as a plantation hand in Queensland. No one called the islanders. Nine of them were dead by the time the trial was held; no interpreter was provided for the others. The survivors were shipped back to their own islands in due course, where most of them were promptly kidnaped again.

The captain of the *Rosario* remarked later, in a book which he entitled *Kidnapping in the South Seas*, that the interests of several powerful Sydney merchants in Queensland's plantations and their influence with the government made it impossible for blackbirding cases to be heard fairly in the courts of New South Wales. It was, he said, the Australian view that the proper function of the king's ships was to protect the blackbirders and all other white men, no matter what they did, and not to seek to control their wrongdoing. The king's ships were expected to exact a bloody revenge whenever a blackbirder's or a trader's schooner was cut out and the crew eaten, and not to waste time inquiring into the prior acts of the white men.

On a few occasions the islanders got something of their own back. A cunning old chief of one of the outer islands in the New Hebrides is alleged to have provided his own son as a decoy for the blackbirders, in a deep plot to seize a schooner. The son was, in fact, an agent for his father, though he pretended to be a decoy to get slaves for the small schooner *Mary Ida,* which belonged to two adventurers named Unthank and Percy. Neither Mr. Unthank nor Mr. Percy could navigate, and the schooner carried a seaman named Collins to do this. In due course, without having aroused any suspicion, the son of the chief guided the schooner to his father's island. Here the chief brought down ten large and apparently docile

natives for Messrs. Unthank's and Percy's inspection. A sale
was made on the spot, and the chief received some muskets
and ammunition. Some of these arms were smuggled back
aboard. The "docile" natives, led by the decoy, rose, murdered
the two owners, and compelled Collins to sail the vessel ashore.
There he, too, was murdered, and the schooner was stripped
and burned.

Incidents of deep-laid schemes such as this are rare, though
from first to last many a blackbirding schooner and brig was
seized by the islanders and all on board massacred. Neither ships
nor men grew old in the blackbird trade, but the profits were
good while they lasted.

It is impossible now to reconstruct statistics of blackbirding. The regulated trade from and to Queensland ports, which
lasted from 1863 to 1904, was only part of it—and not the
worst part. Nearly 60,000 Coral Sea islanders were landed in
Queensland during that time. More than a fourth of them died
there, though comparatively few settled. They came from the
New Hebrides, the Solomons, the Louisiades, New Ireland,
New Britain, the Torres Straits islands—wherever sturdy
Melanesians were to be found. So many were kidnaped from
the Bismarck Archipelago that the Germans put a stop to the
trade there, and those islands were thereafter restricted as a
source of labor for German planters only.

There were many apologists for blackbirding, particularly
among those who profited most from it. "It is no offence to go
to islands inhabited by savage and barbarous people, and bring
those people within the protection of British law," argued
counsel for the defense of a callous kidnaper and a white head-
hunter at Brisbane in 1871. According to this counsel, as soon
as any native was received into a British ship, he was "free."
Among other things, he had the right of *habeas corpus*. But
no one ever told the native of these "rights."

A royal commission which inquired into blackbirding in 1885 considered the cases of 630 islanders who had been brought to Queensland. One hundred and sixty-seven of them had died in the first twelve months, though the official death rate for blackbirds was said then to be between 70 and 110 per 1,000. The commission found that fraud was used in engaging every native it examined, every single man having been secured either by kidnaping or by false statements, and that the methods used throughout the trade were not only cruelly deceptive, but quite illegal.

Blackbirding into Queensland had been going on for twenty years then and was to continue for twenty more. What happened there was mild compared with the fate of the unfortunate Melanesians who were shipped to the Fijis. There, Sir William Macgregor found death rates of 500 and even 750 per 1,000 on some plantations. On the guano islands off Peru, *all* the natives died, and they were shipped there by the thousand. In Fiji, as a writer in the Melbourne "Argus" stated early in 1869, it was "quite a common thing to flog natives with nettles; sometimes they used the cat and then applied the juice of the chili pepper plant. They also chopped off the ears and toes of the unfortunate wretches."

Women and children did not escape the attention of the blackbirders. On some of the islands, as soon as the natives saw a schooner—any schooner—in the offing, they buried all the young women and girls in the sand, leaving only slight apertures for their mouths and nostrils. There they remained until the schooner was gone.

From first to last, blackbirding was a fearful business. It was one of the most important factors in depopulating many islands. So many natives were taken from the New Hebrides that Tonkinese later had to be imported to work on the French plantations there. Fiji's European planters brought coolies

from India when the supply of Melanesians threatened to dry
up. Today there are more Indians than Fijians in the islands,
and the number is increasing, while the Tonkinese in the New
Hebrides and the Chinese in the phosphate islands thrive. In
places such as Tanna, Malaita, Erromanga, Efate, and many
other Coral Sea islands the memory of blackbirding has not
yet died away. Blackbirding continued to flourish in remote
corners long after the system was abolished in Queensland,
though the ocean telegraph and, later, radio, were severe
blows to the later emulators of Ross Lewin and Bully Hayes. It
took a long, long time for the Lewin–Hayes tradition to die
out from the odd corners of the Coral Sea and the lovely
atolls of Micronesia.

Today the pendulum has swung the other way. An Australian law in 1946 proposed to abolish the professional recruiter from the waters of New Guinea, though he had been
doing useful and well-regulated work there for over quarter
of a century. Henceforth, Papuan and New Guinea planters
had to find their labor for themselves, and strict regulations
controlled the manner in which they could do this, and their
treatment of the native when he had signed on.

CHAPTER TWENTY

THE FORTY QUIET YEARS

THE TWENTIETH century, until 1941, was in general a period
of steady progress and development throughout the islands of
the Coral Sea and in much of New Guinea. But the reef-
littered waters of the southwest Pacific were still among the
loneliest in the ocean world. The opening of the Suez Canal
and, over half a century later, of Panama, made little difference to that remote corner. Coastwise shipping inside the
Barrier Reef; a few islands traders carrying passengers [very
few] and cargoes between the ports of the Solomons and
New Guinea, and Brisbane and Sydney in Australia; an odd
freighter to the phosphate islands of Nauru and Ocean Island;
ships bound to and from China and Japan—these used the
Coral Sea and kept to its well-defined, safe tracks. Slowly, the

ports of Nouméa in New Caledonia, Vila in the New Hebrides,
Tulagi on its small island off Florida in the central Solomons, Port Moresby in Papua, and Rabaul in New Britain
grew as trade increased.

The shipping firms of Burns Philp and Company, established in Sydney, did much to develop the islands. The great
copra combine of Unilever developed large-scale plantations
in the Solomons. Traders spread among the islands, and soon
there were few which were not under some trader's influence. Fleets of picturesque but often smelly little ketches and
schooners maintained communications, for it was a long time
before there were real roads. These small sailing-vessels, which
had to be hauled out and repainted twice a year against the
ravages of the teredo worm, brought copra and other products
to the main ports. They carried recruiters who procured labor
for plantations; they fished for trochus shell (used in Japan
for making buttons and ornaments) and *bêche-de-mer;* they
carried missionaries, medical men, district officers. Every
trader needed his vessel, and most district officers could not
hope to keep in touch with their territories without at least
a launch.

By the beginning of the twentieth century all the islands
were under European or Australian control: for the greater
part, they enjoyed orderly administration and good government from Germans, French, British, and Australians alike.
The Germans were developing their territories in northern
New Guinea, the Bismarcks, and the northern Solomons—
as well as in much of Micronesia, north of the equator—still
on much the same lines as the old British and Dutch East India
companies. But they were painstaking, thorough, and capable.
Gone were the days of picturesque characters such as the well-
known "Queen Emma," that extraordinary half-American,
half-Samoan young woman who carved out a colony for herself and relatives at the northeastern end of New Britain.

Queen Emma's real name for much of her adult life was Mrs. Forsaythe, though Mr. Forsaythe died young. She was one of the daughters of Jonas Coe, American consul in Samoa in the middle years of the last century. With a confederate named Thomas Farrell, she pioneered in the Duke of York Islands and round Blanche Bay, and was soon so successful that hordes of her relatives came from Samoa and proceeded to establish flourishing plantations and trade throughout a large area. In the nineties, prospering greatly, she married a German named Kolbe; the Germans established themselves at Kokopo, in her territory, and in 1910 they founded Rabaul, a few miles to the north. Madame Kolbe's wealth was tremendous and her power autocratic. She sold out in 1912 and died a year or two afterward at Monte Carlo. Emma Coe, later Forsaythe, later Kolbe, *alias* Queen Emma was a powerful figure, and not only in New Britain. She stood no nonsense, and she had a remarkably astute understanding of business ways. At a time when most traders were set down on beaches with a box of trade goods, some provisions, and a rifle and were left to shift for themselves in a terrible isolation, Queen Emma established a successful colony despite the most difficult conditions.

At that time, and for years afterward, many traders were killed simply because the natives took a dislike to them or to their methods.

Queen Emma's colony, and all the German territories, went for nothing in the 1914–1918 war. The Germans were in no position to defend themselves in Melanesia. A small Australian force occupied Kokopo and Rabaul early in September, 1914. Within a few days the Germans had surrendered; in 1920, what had been German New Guinea and the German Solomons was mandated to Australia and became the Mandated Territory of New Guinea, including New Britain, New Ireland, the Admiralty group, and Buka and Bougainville of the Solomons. At the same time the Japanese, whose power and infiltration in the western Pacific had been steadily increasing, assumed control of the Caroline, Marianas, and Marshall islands in German Micronesia. These were mandated to Japan, but when in 1935 Japan withdrew from the League of Nations, it was announced that all three groups were henceforth part of the Japanese Empire. With ever-increasing thoroughness and some truculence the Japanese exploited the marine wealth of the western Pacific, while they quietly and systematically set to work converting suitable islands in the Micronesian groups into bases for future military operations. These were to be their "unsinkable aircraft carriers," from which, in due course, they intended to mount their well-planned attempt at Pacific domination.

But the Japanese were not yet established in Melanesia, though their long-range diesel sampans poached trochus and *bêche-de-mer* there almost at will. It was easy to take advantage of the inadequate policing in the Coral Sea. Japanese businessmen and traders ashore, and Japanese fishermen, pearl divers, and sailors afloat, spread far and wide through the waters and islands of the southwest Pacific. In this, there was a deep-laid scheme.

In the meantime, slow, steady progress continued in the islands. The seemingly hopeless task of bringing most of the natives under control had been accomplished successfully by the 1930's. The twenty years between 1919 and 1939 were years of steady improvement, economically, socially, and in health, among most of the Melanesians. Populations which had been dangerously on the downgrade took a slow upswing as various administrations put a stop to tribal warfare and controlled the spread of disease. The long, difficult work of the missionaries was bearing good fruit. There was scarcely an important village on the coasts of any of the islands which was not served, in some way, by the white man. The more im-

portant centers had their district officers—or resident magistrates—their missionaries, and their traders. Even the remotest
islands were visited.

Where Europeans could not be spared, natives were taught
to be medical dressers, mission teachers, administrative assistants. They did well, and their people had much to be grateful for. A head tax of a few shillings yearly, submission to
inoculation against yaws (that curse of the Solomons and
so much of Melanesia), and the annual or semiannual visits
of the district officer—these were a low price to pay for the
end of warfare, which had been wretched at its best, carried
on in a state of constant fear and treachery. The sorcerers took
longer to defeat, and many of them still retain some influence.
In the remoter areas of New Guinea, head-hunting and cannibalism died out slowly and might not yet be quite gone. As
late as the 1920's both were still practiced in parts of Papua.
A government publication * had to admit that "beyond the
sphere of government influence, no part of Papua can be regarded as safe." Most of the natives still carried arms as a neces-
sity of daily life. Yet they accepted quietly and—as far as
could be discovered—even with considerable gratitude the
coming of law and order. If it was the trader's view that every
native who changed his skirt of plaited grass for a piece of
printed calico, his stone adze for a tomahawk, his *poi* and fish
for a tin of bully beef, became a welcome new consumer of
European goods, the administration had visions of greater
things.

There has been a central medical school for native islanders
in Fiji since the 1880's, whence a strong and devoted corps of
native medical practitioners has spread through much of the
western and central Pacific, doing excellent work. A school
for native nurses was also established in Fiji, and the famous

* *British New Guinea (Papua)*, H. M. Stationery Office, 1920.

leper station at Makongai, in the same group of islands, dis-
charged nearly 700 patients as cured during the twenty-five
years between 1918 and 1943—a creditable record.

As medical men, members of native constabularies, mission
teachers, lesser clerks, sailors, and plantation workers, the
Melanesian and the Papuan did well. A few, mainly from Fiji,
found their way to universities in New Zealand and Australia.
In the majority of the islands, during the period between the
two world wars, the native was making slow and sometimes
not obvious progress toward his goal of self-government. It
was a progress which did not please all the white men with
whom he came in contact, for, here and there, something of
the beachcombing spirit still survived. But progress it was,
measurable in terms of increasing populations, absence of
serious trouble, improved output, and ever-mounting trade.
Melanesia was no paradise and could not be made one. Compared with the softer folk and the lovelier isles of Polynesia, it
may sometimes seem a frowning, even a forbidding, zone.

Only a blinded optimist would seek to make a Java out of
New Guinea, or a Rio de Janeiro from Nouméa. Not for the
Malaita boy is the soft lilt of the alleged South Seas guitar and
the swing of well-trained skirts performing the hula for a
group of tourists. But he has attractions of his own which
are obvious to those who take time to know him—the merits
of solid worth and real ability.

The Coral Sea, in its long story, has known no queerer invasion than the procession of idle wanderers sailing there in
yachts. Joshua Slocum, in the sloop *Spray,* was the first. His
voyage took from 1895 to 1898. A retired master mariner
who had tired of the idle life he found ashore, Slocum
rebuilt a tiny vessel not thirty feet on the water line but beamy
and (when he had done with her) staunch. In this, he sailed
alone around the world for no reason other than that the

idea appealed to him. His success started a fashion which is still popular. After beating through the Strait of Magellan in the classic manner—a thing few of his emulators cared to do— he sailed westward over the Pacific, touching at islands as the spirit moved him. Like a wise old salt, he visited few islands in the Coral Sea, though reefs did not alarm him. After a call at Melbourne and a visit to Tasmania, he passed to the north, inside the Barrier Reef, and made westing by way of Torres Straits, perhaps the smallest vessel to engage in that passage since the days of the runaway convicts from New South Wales. Slocum's ship was little larger than Bligh's open boat, though she was a very different proposition. The *Spray* drew only a few feet of water, but the passage inside the Reef was worrying even to Slocum, who had sailed her, by then, nearly twenty thousand miles.

"The sea itself might be called smooth indeed," he wrote about that part of his voyage, "but coral rocks are always rough, sharp, and dangerous. I trusted to the Maker of all reefs, keeping a good lookout at the same time for perils on every hand."

Slocum sailed through Whitsunday Pass, in the Barrier Reef, and called at Cooktown, where he speaks of seeing "physical wrecks of miners from New Guinea, destitute and dying." Here he met Judge Chester, who, as magistrate of the northernmost Queensland settlement, had annexed New Guinea. "While I was about it," he told the wanderer, "I annexed the blooming lot of it."

Leaving many friends in his wake, and always managing to keep his little vessel out of trouble—though he touched on a reef or two in his time—Joshua Slocum passed on, to continue westward through the Arafura and Timor seas and through the whole Indian Ocean, round the Cape, and back to Boston again. Here he was acclaimed the modest hero he was; some years afterward, on another voyage, both he and the *Spray* disappeared. Probably some blundering steamer knocked him down.

After Slocum, odd wanderers of all sorts set out by the score from the ports of the United States and Europe. The old seaman started a fashion which has not yet passed, though the less venturesome navigators stayed out of the Coral Sea. A large proportion, indeed, never succeeded in getting far from their starting points. But at least two other great circumnavigators passed that way after Slocum. First was Captain J. C. Voss, who sailed his curious *Tilikum* from the New Hebrides over the Coral Sea and through Torres Straits, on his way from Vancouver round the world in the early years of the twentieth century. The *Tilikum* was nothing but a built-up canoe carved from a large cedar log. She had a water line of thirty feet and was five and a half feet beam. How Voss got such a vessel round the world has been a source of wonder ever since; but he managed, and this was not his only unusual voyage.

The second great circumnavigator after Slocum was the redoubtable Harry Pidgeon, with his yawl *Islander*. Pidgeon was an elderly farmer from California who, until he was nearly fifty, had never been at sea. He had always wished to sail in the South Seas. He therefore built his own vessel from plans he studied in an American yachting magazine—she was about the size of the *Spray*—studied seamanship and navigation as well as he could, and then, as a trial run, sailed singlehanded from the California coast to Honolulu. Having got that far, he thought he might as well sail round the world, which he accordingly did.

For the following sixteen years he lived alone in his little yawl, twice making lengthy and far from easy circumnavigations. The second grew out of the first—as he wished, he said, to "look up his friends in various parts of the world." One of the legs of this extraordinary voyage was from Hawaii direct to Port Moresby, in New Guinea. The Coral Sea meant nothing to Harry Pidgeon. It was not until he married and set out, at the age of seventy-eight, on his third circumnavigation—still in the little *Islander*—that its reefs brought him to grief. Early in 1948 the brave *Islander* was wrecked during a bad blow in the New Hebrides, though both Mr. and Mrs. Pidgeon survived.

He is described as an "elderly, wiry little fellow, with snow-white hair, a badly burned face, and mild, tired, bluish eyes—a charming, unassuming old gentleman," who neither smoked nor drank but had a great craving for acid drops, and the latest report is that the *Islander* is to be replaced and the Pidgeon family intends to set out anew.

Not all wanderers in small yachts have fared as well as Slocum, Voss, and Pidgeon. There was the mystery of a curious little man named Sparks, for example, and his sixteen-foot cutter *Dauntless*. Ira C. Sparks, mild mannered, soft of speech, always courteous, a carpenter by trade, hailing from Peru, Indiana, reached Honolulu in 1923 as a stowaway inside a large packing case in the hold of a Japanese steamer. He was, he said, on his way to the Holy Land, following a vision. In Hawaii he found work at his trade and built himself such a boat as he could afford. This was surely one of the most astonishing vessels ever to cross the Pacific, for she was ill balanced, badly rigged, and must have been a poor sailer even in a millpond. She was sixteen feet over all, with a beam of about five feet. There was no living accommodation—nothing but a sort of rough coach roof, with scuppers at the sides to catch rain water. Sparks sat in a canvas apron lashed to an iron hoop in a cockpit about two feet square. For a man accustomed to life in a packing case, this was perhaps satisfactory. At any rate it sufficed: in this tiny vessel, well named the *Dauntless*, he sailed from Hawaii on January 9, 1924, and passed across the ex-

panse of the Pacific, through all Micronesia, to fetch up in the
Philippines seventy-three days afterward. Sparks said he was
bound for the Marshall Islands and thence for Singapore, but he
had neither charts nor compass, nor even a timepiece, with
him. The sun, he said to those who questioned his disregard
for the elements of navigation, set in the west, which was compass enough: if he sailed far enough in that direction, he could
scarcely miss Asia.

After touching at a place called Tandag, in Mindanao, and
at Matimus Point, Sparks sailed for Zamboanga. From that day
he disappeared, though his boat was discovered weeks later,
beached in a bay on an island off Mindanao, stripped of what
little gear she had but still sound and watertight. She was
taken to Zamboanga to await Sparks's return, but he never
came and nothing was ever heard of him. After he had crossed
so much sea in safety, it was a pity to be lost on land. His
Dauntless was small and not the ideal vessel, even for singlehanded day sailing. But she had come a long way and could
have gone farther.

Some years later, a Sydney butcher named Fred Rebell, of
Latvian origin, sailed an eighteen-footer from Sydney across
the Pacific and through the Panama Canal to Windau, in
Latvia. His vessel was a half-decked centerboard cutter named
Elain. Like Ira Sparks, he knew nothing of navigation or of
sailing before he began. But he did take some copied charts
or maps, a boy-scout compass, and a sextant which he had
made for himself out of hoop iron. Being tired of a boat so
small as the *Elain,* Rebell exchanged her in Latvia for a twenty-
three-foot fishing boat named *Selga.* In this, he set off for
Australia again. But this time his luck was out, and the *Selga,*
with Rebell asleep in the cockpit, drifted upon the beach at
Aldeburgh, in England, a week or two after passing through
the Kiel Canal. A week's gale in the wild North Sea had worn
him out.

While the *Joseph Conrad* was in the Solomon Islands during 1935, a queer little converted lifeboat of American origin drifted ashore in the Kia Passage, by Ysabel Island. At first sight there seemed to be no one in the boat, but boarding natives found a very old man lying dead in the cabin. From his log, which had been kept meticulously until the day he died, it was discovered that his name was John Dow. He was an old master mariner, making a voyage in the Slocum manner. He had come from New York via Panama, but malaria attacked him in the Coral Sea. His lifeboat, which he had named the *Chance,* was too much for one man. Hard winds blew out his sails. When he knew that he could carry on little longer, he secured the helm and lay down. With his last strength he wrote a letter to whoever should find the boat. Then he lashed the United States ensign at half-mast, and died.

While these strange adventurers in their little ships were drifting about the Coral Sea and all the Pacific, other men no less adventurous were combing the New Guinea mountains and searching the mountain streams for gold. This was no new quest. The Spaniard Alvaro de Saavedra had found traces of gold on New Guinea's coast in 1528. Stories of an "island of gold" persisted through centuries, but though good workings were established in the islands of Sudest, Misima, and Woodlark in the late nineteenth century, it was not until the 1920's that the real "strike" was made. This was on the fabulous Morobe field, in what had been the German territory of northeast New Guinea. Lone Australian prospectors had, it seems, known something of this field in earlier days, but since the area was then German, they had kept all knowledge to themselves. "Sharkeye" Park, Arthur Darling, and Matthew Crowe were almost inhabitants of the Morobe ranges, where they advertised themselves as hunters of the bird of paradise. At least one of them knew about Morobe gold before 1913.

In 1921, when the territory had been mandated to Australia, Park was taking twenty ounces a day from Koranga Creek. A find so rich, not even the tight-lipped Sharkeye could keep to himself, though the dreadful terrain and the risk of fatal fevers kept away all but the most hardy. But the whisper started that "Sharkeye was on to something rich." By the end of 1923 there were nearly a score of tough Australian prospectors washing out gold from Koranga Creek and the Bulolo River and making fortunes which they did not always survive to spend. Had the climate of the Morobe area been as cold as it was humid, the place would have developed rapidly into another Yukon. But the wet, steamy jungles, the savage mountains, the endless morass of coastal swamps which characterize so much of New Guinea, deterred many and killed some. Dysentery and fevers killed more. Treacherous natives attacked the lines of communication. Although the gold field was only thirty miles or so from the coast, the terrain was so rough that it could be reached by the most expert, knowing the best tracks, only after a severe trek of ten days. The pioneers of the Bulolo, the Koranga, and Edie Creek earned their fortunes hard.

Later a man named Levien, who had been a district officer in the administration's employ, left the government service and organized a company known as Guinea Gold. With dredges flown in by sections across the mountains, and with regular air transport to serve the field, Guinea Gold's prosperity was soon fantastic. From 1931 to 1941 the Morobe gold field produced gold worth twenty million pounds, though it took five years to get the first dredge going, and even aviation enthusiasts were skeptical, at first, of the success of air transport in that wild region without workshops, landing fields, or aids to navigation and, in the mountains, with some of the worst weather in the world. The early pilots were pioneers in the true tradition, though their aerial voyages lasted minutes instead of months, and they rarely died of scurvy.

The "island of gold" had been found at last, not so far from the position where the Portuguese and the Spaniards had first sought it.

Though the airline flying between Salamau and the Morobe field quickly became the largest aerial freighting company in the world, the coming of the airplane had little effect in general upon the state of things in the Coral Sea. It was not until 1938 that W. R. Carpenter and Company inaugurated a regular service between Sydney and Rabaul, with three biplanes. Aircraft were used extensively inside New Guinea, where the gold business was rich enough to pay for it. But the growth of other trans-Pacific services touched only the southern fringe of the Coral Sea. In 1927, flying a sturdy three-motored monoplane of good performance for those days, Sir Charles Kingsford-Smith (who later was to leave his bones in East Indies waters, not far from the Coral Sea) pioneered trans-Pacific air travel with a great flight from San Francisco to Australia. But he touched Melanesia only at the Fijis, and it was to be nearly twenty years before his own countrymen could profit much from his great trail-blazing. Meantime, the American airwoman Amelia Earhart disappeared while trying to fly round the world in a Lockheed machine in 1937. She left Lae, in New Guinea, bound for Howland Island, close by the equator near the Phoenix group, and was never seen again. She had to cross or fly round the mountains of the Solomons and traverse a great stretch of the western Pacific at its loneliest. Her fate is a mystery: she may have been lost anywhere in the area.

What the Japanese might be doing in their new empire of Micronesia, no one but the Japanese knew before the 1940's. But in 1939 it was announced that there was an air-mail service

between Japan and the Carolines, via the Bonins and the Marianas. Between the Carolines and Melanesia, however, there was
then no link. The Japanese air-mail services had nothing to do
with the Coral Sea.

At least, not then. But by September, 1941, when a savage
war had been raging for two years in distant Europe, a retired
rear admiral of the Japanese navy—one Tanetsugu Sosa—
was having a frank discussion with an American correspond-
ent.* It was ten weeks before the attack on Pearl Harbor
ushered in the Pacific war. He said, "No matter how much the
United States or British navies may gnash their teeth in
chagrin, it is absolutely impossible for them to bring down the
line of fortresses built in the Pacific by the great hand of Nature. . . . The strategic position of Japan and the steel-
plated walls of defense scattered all over the seas of East Asia
enable our empire to attack or defend, in any direction."

Good use had been made, from the Japanese point of view,
of those "mandated" islands of Micronesia, the southernmost
of which were less than two hours' flight from northern
Melanesia. For the first time in its known history the Coral Sea
was assuming real strategic importance: the forty quiet years
were ending.

* Hallett Abend, quoted in *Ramparts of the Pacific*, Doubleday & Company, Inc., New
York, 1942.

CHAPTER TWENTY-ONE

WAR COMES TO THE CORAL SEA

THE ARC of Melanesian islands around the Coral Sea, and that sea itself, are of great strategic importance to Australia and New Zealand. But until December, 1941, the general view in both countries was that active warfare was the last thing that could reach that corner of the Pacific. Who could be the aggressor? Japan, of course, might be, if she could: but the Japanese were involved in a long-drawn and indecisive war in the great maw of China, where they could safely be left to dissipate their energies and expend their weapons. If the Japanese could not occupy China, how could they wage a general war in the Pacific? In any event, there were the British bases of Hongkong and Singapore, the United States bases of Guam and Wake Island, and the United States Pacific Fleet itself, based on

Hawaii, to stop them. Singapore was "impregnable"; the Philippines were strongly held; French Indo-China, British and Dutch Borneo, and all the Dutch East Indies stood between Japanese land forces and the Coral Sea.

True, there were persistent stories of fortifications in the Carolines and the Marshall Islands; true, too, Japanese "fishing" sampans had swarmed into the Coral Sea and around all the dark islands from the middle 1930's, and Japanese "business" infiltration ashore was increasingly thorough and widespread. The Japanese South Seas Development Company had its tentacles everywhere, and Japanese products were cutting into the lucrative markets. Naval men had been heard to say that they wished they had access to Japanese topographical information of the Pacific. But when the second World War broke out in 1939, both Australia and New Zealand sent their best troops out of the Pacific as soon as they could. The troops went to North Africa and Greece; it was unthinkable that they should be required nearer home. Wars were affairs to be fought far away, distant catastrophes to which heroes traveled a long way and from which, if they were fortunate, they returned with medals and honors, though perhaps not otherwise much improved.

Then suddenly, one day in late 1941, the Japanese, who had been bogged down in China, broke from their islands and flung the whole western Pacific into violent warfare almost at the twinkling of an eye. The slant-eyed men who "could not fly" roared across the American Pacific Fleet in Pearl Harbor and reduced it in a few moments to a state of temporary impotence. The undersized soldiers who could not defeat the Chinese leaped upon Malaya and all the Philippines and soon were sweeping all before them. Singapore, the "impregnable," fell in a matter of weeks; the Dutch East Indies followed. In eighty days of unbroken success, the long-feared "Yellow

Peril" had washed into the heart of the Coral Sea, three thousand miles from Japan.

The Japanese did everything they were not expected to do; the great amphibious war which erupted suddenly into the Pacific was something the world had not seen before and, with excellent coordination between land, sea, and air, the Japanese— the majority of the landing forces skilled, courageous, and highly trained marines—swept down as far as Guadalcanal, in the Solomon Islands. All northern and eastern New Guinea (but not the vital southeastern strip), the Bismarck Archipelago, the northern Solomons, the Gilberts, and the Ellice Islands were in Japanese hands. Worse than that, there was little available then to stop their further penetration. Northern Australia, New Caledonia, the New Hebrides, New Zealand itself—all these might fall, and fall quickly. The yellow men, in split-toed rubber shoes and mottled green uniforms, carrying their bags of rice and dried fish, and spitting death with their automatic weapons, might strike anywhere. Their navy had temporary superiority, and their air force, for the time being, was invincible.

Yet the Coral Sea stopped them, for all the speed of their initial, well-planned success. In the Coral Sea their hopes of Pacific conquest died; in its waters their defeat began, and on its lush and fever-ridden islands their picked troops met more than their match and died there in their foxholes by the thousand. No split-toed shoe touched any Australian or New Zealand beach, though Japanese bombs fell on a few North Australian ports, and Sydney once was shelled. The Japanese never occupied southeastern New Guinea or passed beyond the central Solomons. They had bitten off more than they could chew. In less than a year after they first reached Guadalcanal, they were flung out again after a bloody, violent campaign; though they reached the Kokoda Pass back of Port Moresby, they never quite crossed the Owen-Stanley mountains; though they held most of the vital Melanesian islands, they never controlled the Coral Sea.

In that failure, their ultimate defeat was certain. The long story of how that defeat was achieved must be sought in other books when there has been time for just appraisal of all the facts. Here is the story of the Coral Sea only, and its immediately adjacent waters. The battles there were vital.

As early as February 20, 1942—before the Japanese were in the Solomons—the re-formed United States Pacific Fleet was striking back at Japanese bases in New Britain. An attempted air and surface raid against Rabaul was temporarily frustrated when the task force was sighted and attacked by Japanese aircraft, but sixteen enemy bombers were shot down into the sea. Earlier than that, another task force had successfully raided strong points in the Marshall and Gilbert islands. On March 10, the carriers *Lexington* and *Yorktown*, with supporting ships, raided the New Guinea gold-field ports of Salamoa and Lae, where the Japanese had landed in force a few days earlier.

This raid was made entirely by aircraft flown from the two carriers which remained in the Coral Sea, with the mountain ranges of eastern New Guinea between them and the enemy. Twenty-nine bombers, twenty-four torpedo bombers, and fifty supporting fighters flew through a gap in the Owen-Stanley mountains 7,500 feet above sea level and, coming out of the New Guinea sky like a horde of savage eagles, found the Japanese below them before the yellow men, unprepared for an attack like this, had time to man their antiaircraft guns. In a matter of seconds the vicious *crumph, crumph* of high-explosive bombs was reverberating round the Huon Gulf hills. The explosions of a score of torpedoes shook the heavy, heated air, as ship after ship lying anchored off the beaches was struck down. Within a matter of seconds, five transports were in a sinking condition and several others were on fire and otherwise heavily damaged. At the moment the attacking aircraft swarmed through the mountain gap, a Japanese force of one cruiser, five destroyers, and six transports was on its way into the gulf to join a fleet already discharging there. Delighted to find this unexpected new target, the American pilots swooped upon it. Not a ship escaped severe damage, and many were sunk. Return antiaircraft fire was feeble, from both the attacked ships and the batteries ashore. The Japanese had thought themselves safe behind the 13,000-foot mountains.

This curious action may be reckoned as the beginning of the sea-air battle of the Coral Sea. There were three great campaigns in Melanesia and its waters—the battle for the Solomons, the campaign in New Guinea, and the sea-air battle of the Coral Sea. Of these, the last-named was the most important.

By the middle of April, 1942, the Japanese had established bases in the New Guinea–Bismarck Archipelago–Solomon Islands area, from which they threatened not only all Melanesia but Australia itself. They were rapidly extending their system of island airfields, from which each successive wave in their highly successful invasion had been launched. The next step would be to sever the life line between the United States and Australia. On May 3, 1942, the Japanese began to occupy Tulagi, the capital of the British Solomons Protectorate. It was high time to intervene. The United States forces, which had already shown what they could do in the surprise attack on shipping off New Guinea, went immediately into action. Admiral Frank Fletcher was cruising in the Coral Sea with the carrier *Yorktown* and supporting ships, looking for just such a target as the Japanese transports and naval shipping off Tulagi presented. Again with high mountains intervening between the ships, aircraft roared away from the *Yorktown*. Again achieving complete tactical surprise, the naval aircraft sank or damaged almost every ship off the beaches. Only one American aircraft was lost on that first raid: a repeat performance the same afternoon did a great deal more damage, for the loss of two of the attackers. Meanwhile, the *Yorktown* was more than a hundred miles away, southwest of Guadalcanal. This was a new kind of warfare, where aircraft became the guns and the torpedo tubes of ships of war, and battle was joined between fleets without ever a shot fired by the vessels themselves.

The *Yorktown's* attack on Tulagi began on May 4. Meanwhile, intelligence indicated that Japanese transports were being massed at Rabaul and elsewhere for yet another invasion. The check at the gold-field ports was only temporary, and all the southwest Pacific still was in jeopardy. It was known that three aircraft carriers—thought to be the *Shoho, Shokaku,* and *Zuikaku*—had left the Japanese base of Truk, in the Carolines, on May 1, bound toward the southeast. The assembly of troop-carrying transports at Rabaul was menacing. The Japanese were soon patrolling the northern waters of the Coral Sea with long-range seaplanes, on the lookout for American carriers and other naval forces.

By May 6, it looked as if the large Japanese forces in the Bismarck Archipelago–New Guinea area, covered by the aircraft carriers and a force of cruisers and destroyers, contemplating an assault upon Port Moresby, or upon the northeastern coast of Queensland further south. They had to be stopped. A force of three cruisers—two of them Australian—and two destroyers, under Admiral J. G. Grace, Royal Navy, took station south of the Louisiades to intercept any enemy who might try to break through the Jomard Passage or other channels through that labyrinth of islands. The remainder of the Allied forces—almost all American—moved north and east to bring battle to the Japanese covering forces and to sink the transports.

On the morning of May 7, 1942, Admiral Fletcher's force struck. Aircraft from his carriers *Yorktown* and *Lexington* found a large group of Japanese transports, two large cruisers, and the aircraft carrier *Shoho*. These were steaming at high speed and at a point north of Misima, northernmost of the larger Louisiade islands, about 175 miles from the American ships. The Americans attacked at once. They roared out of the sky down upon the *Shoho* as, maneuvering at great speed, she was turning into wind to launch a wave of aircraft. She was heavily struck before she completed the turn, and she was never fit to fly off aircraft again. Bombs tore up her flight deck, and her aircraft were splintered and burned. Three more heavy hits on her great flight deck opened her up, and orange flames billowed through. Flames and smoke belched from her as she continued to writhe and twist to avoid the hail of bombs. Torpedo bombers, sweeping in at wavetop height below the dive bombers, loosed their deadly weapons on her at fatal range. Exactly how many torpedoes struck the *Shoho* will probably never be known. Fifteen hits were claimed: there might have been more. Now belching smoke like an oil-well fire, she swung in uncontrolled circles three times and sank with most of her aircraft still on board.

The loss of the *Shoho* was a severe blow to the Japanese. Worse was to follow. One of the heavy cruisers followed her quickly to the bottom, and the loss of both these ships cost only one American dive bomber. The Japanese fought back violently. Aircraft from their two other carriers in the area— not with that force—joined in, as well as land-based aircraft from Rabaul. Shore-based Allied bombers from New Guinea and north Queensland also joined in, and the air-sea battle waged all day. The Japanese carrier forces dissipated a lot of energy, fuel, and munitions in an attack on the United States

fleet tanker *Neosho,* which they sank, with her attendant destroyer. Darkness broke off the action, but only for the time
being.

That night, Tokyo radio claimed the sinking of the United
States battleship *California* and the aircraft carrier *Saratoga,*
among other vessels not within five thousand miles of the
scene. Some false claims were undoubtedly made in good faith
by pilots whose ship recognition was not so good as it might
have been, but it was surely difficult to mistake a fleet tanker
for a battleship, and a destroyer for an aircraft carrier.

Next morning, May 8, battle was again joined, still in the
air. Waves of American aircraft sought out and attacked
Japanese carriers, while at the same time waves of Japanese
aircraft sought out and attacked the American carriers, so
that soon there was a real possibility that neither fleet of aircraft would have a carrier to return to. Both the *Lexington*
and one of the Japanese carriers were sunk, and later the *Yorktown* and the other Japanese carrier were too badly damaged
to land on. The *Lexington* was sunk when a severe explosion
shook her, hours after the main attack on her, and she was
damaged so severely that she was uncontrollable. The *Yorktown's* damage was less severe. The Allied forces emerged from
the Battle of the Coral Sea with actual losses of only one carrier, one destroyer, one tanker, and sixty-six aircraft. Japanese
losses were much heavier. They had failed in their objective
and had to flee the Coral Sea.

Whether their forces were intended to cover an attack on
Port Moresby or an actual invasion of Australia was not known,
for neither assault was ever made. The tide had turned, after
that strange week-long fight. Its first taste of war put the
Coral Sea, of which most people had never heard, in the head-
lines of the world. The Japanese tasted the humiliation of a
severe defeat, and their determined sweep toward the south
was checked permanently.

They landed on Guadalcanal after that, and it took six long, bloody months to drive them out again. They did not at once give up their plans for a southward drive: for two years afterward the Japanese still fought in Melanesia. But it was a losing struggle, and it could have only one end. The Coral Sea battle was followed by the defeat of a Japanese fleet off Midway, in the North Pacific; these two actions put an end to the long Japanese offensive and turned the balance of naval power against them, despite the heavy American losses at Pearl Harbor.

Japanese reaction to the severe mauling of their all-important aircraft carriers was to revert to building airfields ashore. They chose Guadalcanal. The United States forces had established themselves in the New Hebrides and New Caledonia. At last there was a great settlement on Queiros's Espiritu Santo, for at one time 300,000 Americans were based there, while Nouméa was an important naval base. The Japanese obviously contemplated an assault on both Espiritu Santo and New Caledonia, with the aim of cutting the life line to Australia. The assault was never made. Instead, the attack was carried home to them. On August 7, 1942, a force composed almost entirely of those splendid fighting men, the United States Marines, landed on Guadalcanal. The Japanese, to give them their due, had shown what well-trained and well-handled marines could do in amphibious warfare. The lesson had been learned, and now the tables were turned on them. The United States Marines were no newcomers to amphibious warfare or to tough, savage fighting: but even for them, the Battle of Guadalcanal was, and remains, one of the hardest and most bitter ever fought.

For eight weeks the issue hung in precarious balance. Though the original landing went well, the Japanese reacted swiftly and showed at no time an inclination to give up anything. As in New Guinea, so also in the Solomons: they were good fight-

ing men who knew how to die, and they were prepared to die
in their foxholes. Ordinary men tried to keep up at least some
of the decencies of living, even in the green, wet hell of
Guadalcanal. Not so, the Japanese. They fought from foxholes
out of which, once dug in, they never moved, or from coconut treetops where, once established, they remained until they
were shot down or burned down. They fought tenaciously,
savagely, and at first with great skill, and they never knew
when they were beaten. The only safe Japanese was a dead
Japanese, and it took some time to kill them on Guadalcanal.

There were two battles for Guadalcanal. The first was a
savage, deadly slogging match in the jungle and the steaming
swamps: the second was at sea, in the tortuous, reef-lined
channels of the central Solomons, off Savo, off Santa Cruz.
Over the long-lost bones of Alvaro de Mendaña, the throb of
powerful destroyer propellers raced, and lean cruisers, armed
to the gunwhale, steamed through the black tropic nights.
Sometimes Allied and Japanese forces found themselves suddenly opposed, and there were gun duels like those between
coastal forces and enemy convoys in the narrow seas of distant
England, though here the opponents were major war vessels
of vital importance to both sides, not motor torpedo boats and
gunboats.

One such battle burst suddenly in the black second night
after the American landing. An Allied force, caught off guard
when swinging round Savo Island, was decimated by accurate
and rapid Japanese fire. That night two Allied naval forces
stood guard in the central Solomons to prevent any attempt at
Japanese reinforcement. At 0145 hours both forces found
themselves suddenly illumined by flares dropped from aircraft.
Simultaneously, a devastating fire was opened up on them by
enemy cruisers and destroyers coming undetected from the
northwest. For a few moments pandemonium reigned: within
half an hour four important Allied cruisers had gone to the

bottom of the Coral Sea. The Japanese force swung round Savo Island and, without waiting to make sure what damage they had done, steamed off rapidly to the northeast. Apparently, they never did make a proper appraisal of the effects of that action, which was just as well. For some months after, Allied naval forces in the southwest Pacific were stretched to the limit. The loss soon afterward of two American aircraft carriers gave the Japanese the advantage there; but they did not know this, and they made no attempt to press their local superiority. The force which sank the *Quincy, Vincennes, Astoria,* and *Canberra* off Savo could have gone on to raise havoc on the American positions at Guadalcanal and could have interfered, perhaps fatally, with the passage of supplies and reinforcements over the beaches. But they steamed away.

Night after night, furious naval activity went on in the waters of the Solomons. Japanese attempts to bring up supplies and reinforcements by destroyer and by reef-hopping barge; intense Allied concentration to keep open the supply lines to Guadalcanal, and submarine and aircraft activity on both sides made the waters of the eastern Coral Sea the scene of almost nightly battles. By day most battles were between aircraft flown from the carriers: by night they were short, sudden, devastating gun duels between ships. Replacing the *Lexington* and the *Yorktown,* the carriers *Saratoga* and *Enterprise* were the hubs of new task forces. The Japanese flung more carriers into the fight; on August 23 they had lost yet another, when a powerfully supported transport group was intercepted north of Guadalcanal and decimated. Again, in the battle of Cape Esperance, on the night of October 11, a Japanese force of surface vessels was heavily attacked by a force under Admiral Scott, which included the cruisers *San Francisco* and *Salt Lake City.* Admiral Scott's force more than made amends for the earlier Allied losses off Savo. This time it was their turn to take the enemy unprepared, and there was no return fire for nearly

ten minutes. During that time most of the important enemy
targets disappeared beneath the sea.

The sea battle off Santa Cruz—which was never occupied by
the Japanese—was remarkable again for the successful use of
attacking aircraft by both sides; yet again American and
Japanese aircraft pressed home savage attacks on each others'
carriers, the attacks more or less canceling out. The *Hornet* was
sunk after being badly damaged by a suicide attack, and the
Enterprise was damaged. The two Japanese carriers were badly
damaged and had to limp away.

That night many a pilot in a tiny rubber dinghy surveyed
the dark waters of the Coral Sea and wondered what all the
fighting was about. Many American pilots had to make for
Japanese-held islands, but there was a remarkable behind-the-
lines air-sea rescue service, organized among the Solomon Islanders, which brought many of them back to safety, despite
great hazards. The fuzzy-headed savages, who had murdered
blackbirders, tax collectors, and missionaries with equal gusto
a few years earlier, now faced risks of death and torture for the
sake of men who had come ten thousand miles to fight in the
air above their islands. British district officers and administrators, working from hill hide-outs and the recesses of swamp-
infested, coral-filled lagoons far behind the Japanese lines, controlled the air-sea rescue service and kept up the morale of the
islanders. The peoples of the Solomons were not deserted when
the yellow hordes descended on them. A bishop of Melanesia,
in direct line of descent from Bishop Patteson, stuck to his
post on Malaita Island and did all he could to maintain mission
work. The British administration had gone underground; but
it was there, and the natives, to their own great credit and the
good repute of the twentieth-century white man among them,
were behind it to a man.

The grim, weary, soul-destroying battle for Guadalcanal, to
which all these naval fights were ancillary, meantime con-

tinued. The airfield the Japanese were building was captured early and renamed Henderson Field by the Americans, but its retention was costly. Before long, Henderson Field was—at any rate temporarily—the best-known air base in the whole Pacific. If any troops, Allied or Japanese, steamed toward those malarial and turgid beaches with visions of a tropic paradise, their illusions were savagely dispelled. By day, as one steamed through the long lines of the volcanic Solomons, the vista could be enchanting, with distant views of sunny lagoons and golden beaches, palm-fringed islets scattered on the blue-green sea, and, ashore, orchids of fabulous beauty, around which fluttered butterflies of gorgeous colorings and nearly a foot across. But this was no land of flowers and prettiness! The jungle which was silent by day became a bedlam of noise by night—noise the enemy exploited to cover his movements. Warfare was a sinister business of ferocious attacks, without quarter, without cessation. The coral in those pretty lagoons was poisonous; the very jungle was poisonous, so that the slightest wounds became gangrenous quickly. Disease struck indiscriminately. The wet wall of the dreadful jungle was the enemy on both sides. With uniforms a muddy, bloody covering of sweaty, irksome cloth; weapons requiring ten times the care of normal climates to be half the use; tropic diseases violent and often fatal, and existence itself a ghastly testing of physical and mental endurance, the only campaign which approached that of Guadalcanal and all the Coral Sea islands was that in Burma.

It took six months to throw the Japanese out of Guadalcanal, where twice they succeeded in landing whole new divisions. After that, they had still to be driven from the other islands of the central and northern Solomons. After Guadalcanal came Russell Island and New Georgia, Kolombangara and Vella Lavella, Choiseul and Bougainville. From the troops' point of view, the most romantic things about all these Pacific islands were their names. There was no fighting of quite the savagery of Guadalcanal; although it was February, 1944, before Allied forces had reached as far as the atoll of Nissan, between Buka and New Ireland. Many Japanese strong points remained to be reduced in their rear, but the real fighting in the Solomons and the sea-air battles of the Coral Sea were over.

Meanwhile, the campaign in New Guinea, largely fought, at first, by Australians, and then by Australians and Americans, was going well though slowly. The land fighting in New Guinea is a story by itself, and there is neither space nor place for it here. The dreadful disabilities of warfare in the Solomons applied just as much in all New Guinea, except that the terrain was even worse there and diseases more abundant. Step by step, after he had been within thirty miles of Port Moresby, the Japanese had to be driven painfully and slowly back. Place names such as Buna, Gona, Wewak, Hollandia—which even residents in the Coral Sea, if they knew them at all, knew only vaguely—became household words all round the world. Again the Japanese refused to accept defeat and died to the last man. But as the campaign went on, their morale flagged; it had been built upon the falsehood of assured victory and bolstered by too-easy overrunnings of Malaya and the East Indies, where false premises had led to poor defense. Against the dogged, determined, and skillful fighting of the Allied troops, unprepared as they had been at the war's beginning, even crack Japanese troops wilted and died.

Unlike the Solomons, which led nowhere strategically but did protect the Coral Sea, New Guinea aims directly at the Philippine Islands. In September, 1944, the Americans landed on Morotai, 300 miles from the Philippines. War moved out of Melanesia and into the western Pacific, and from there into the China Sea. Final victory was assured. Again the quick-growing jungle swept down upon the beaches of the Solomons, the Bismarcks, New Britain, and New Guinea. The war-winning amphibious fleets, no longer Japanese, moved on, and the

Trobriands canoe and Solomons gondola could be withdrawn from air-sea rescue. The great waves of steel landing ships, stemming from the United States of America, swept on to Iwo Jima, Okinawa, toward Japan itself. The British Pacific Fleet had an advanced base at Manus in the Admiralty Islands, and the fleet train of great cargo ships with breweries and repair facilities, supplies, and amenities of all kinds followed them.

Japanese submarines had operated briefly in the waters of the Coral Sea and off the coasts of Australia, sinking nineteen ships. A Japanese midget submarine once broke into Sydney Harbor: but by 1944 it was over in the Coral Sea. No enemy submarine was there after the middle of 1943. By the middle of 1945, it was over in the whole Pacific. In August of that year the Japanese surrendered. In 1946 the white man, his war over—at least for the time being—chose a lonely atoll named Bikini, north of the Coral Sea, for further experiments with his atom bomb. Here he evacuated the last of the islanders and assembled a strange fleet, whose function was to record the effects of this ghastly new weapon.

The Japanese war left more in its wake in the southwest Pacific than a site for experiments with the atom bomb. Native life and ways were interfered with grievously, and the white administration faced a test of its worth, the severity of which could not have been foreseen. Administrative machinery, built up painfully to a pitch of reasonable efficiency, came to a sudden stop. In all the Pacific capitals and in London and Washington, officials watched anxiously and with deep interest for signs of ill effects upon the Melanesian of the Pacific war. They were greatly encouraged by reports which began to reach them of devotion to duty and high heroism on the part of Solomon Islands chiefs and lesser men, and the Fuzzy-Wuzzies of New Guinea. They learned, for instance, of the case of the old police trooper, Sergeant Major Vouza, who, captured by the Japanese at a time when he knew vital military information, refused to speak under brutal interrogation and repeated tortures. Finally he was lashed to a coconut palm, bayoneted six times, and left for dead, silent to the last. Sergeant Major Vouza did not die; when the Japanese had gone, he staggered from his bonds and, weak from wounds and loss of blood, somehow reached the Allied lines and made an invaluable report on the Japanese positions, before collapsing.

For this, the old policeman received the George Medal and the American Silver Star. More important than these awards, he received the whole-hearted admiration of his own people, who stood behind that kind of conduct to a man. Bravery was no new quality in the Solomon Islands; they had a tradition of resistance to invaders. Asked afterward to say something of his thoughts while in the hands of the Japanese, Sergeant Major Vouza simply said, "I think I do something good for my king."

Then there was Seni, high chief of Mindi-Mindi Island, who formed a highly efficient battle force of his own against the Japanese, using the arms of ambushed invaders, and became a source of real Allied strength on the island of New Georgia— and Ngatu, the old blind chief who insisted upon fighting. His specialty was stealthy assaults by canoe on enemy beaches. He could not see to shoot, but his sensitive touch made him a remarkable stealer of automatic weapons. Ngatu and Seni were chiefs, but the common men were behind them. So were the Fiji commandos, trained units which, when the Japanese were held in the central Solomons, came from their own islands to join in the fight. Fijians, Tongans, Solomon Islanders, Papuans, bush boys of New Guinea—all these were willing and useful allies. The Japanese found little cooperation among even the most backward Melanesians. It is a remarkable tribute to the latter-day administrator that the opposition of the native to the invader remained whole-hearted while a Japanese was in the islands.

At long last the war was gone, and the surplus equipment and the surplus administrators were removed from the islands. In 1949 the jungle is fast taking over even the last remnants of the great base on Espiritu Santo. The blasted Guadalcanal plantations may thrive again. Milne Bay, Buna, Gona, Savo, rest again in their hot quietude, and the trade wind blows in the coconut palms. Here and there the twisted wrecks of oriental landing craft and the rusted hulks of bombed-out ships are grim reminders of the recent war. Again the European administrator, missionary, and medical man are at work among the Melanesians, their efforts strengthened, in many ways, by the unforeseen ordeal through which the peoples of the Coral Sea were made to pass.

During the long months of the Japanese war there was an opportunity for stock-taking of the good and evil the white man had done in all the islands. His was a mixed record in the Coral Sea. First came the mysterious Portuguese, leaving no discoverable records; then the Spaniards from Peru, in quest of gold and a great continent which is still lost and which, if it ever existed, must have been part of some forgotten Pacific civilization, whose traces survived in sixteenth-century Inca legends. Then silence, for more than a century and a half, while the Hollanders skimmed the further borders, knocking at the door of Torres Straits three times and never coming in, and once voyaging from New Zealand through Tonga and the Fijis and outside all the islands, back to Indonesia. Then the English, their buccaneers preceding them and their discoverers barely in front of the French—Carteret, Cook, Bligh in his open boat, Flinders in his worn-out surveying ship, which was fit only for the scrap heap. After them, the East Indiamen, the convict escapees from New South Wales, the whalemen from New England and old England, the *bêche-de-mer* fishermen, the sandalwooders, the murderous exploiting scum. Then blackbirders, spoilers, and depopulators, whose evil deeds would never have been done had not smug squatters, hundreds of safe miles away, required the labor that they brought, for their own enrichment. Here and there, in that black record of the nineteenth century, a ray of light from some noble missionary fell upon the dark islands, but the story, on the whole, was one of conscienceless exploitation and utter debauchery.

Then all that changed: not overnight, sometimes not even immediately for the better. But the coming of ordered government, coinciding with an enlightenment in the attitude of the favored white toward his obligations respecting his more backward brothers, brought hope of real progress. The day of cheap exploitation was over. One result of war has been to increase a feeling of national consciousness. It may be some time before such feelings can be developed into real self-government, for many of the islands are still little developed, without even such elementary essentials as interior roads. But the way now is open, and enlightened administrators are already helping the Melanesian along it.

In February, 1947, a South Seas conference was held in Canberra, the federal capital of Australia, to prepare a constitution for a Native Welfare Commission, whose object is to study and recommend measures for the development of the economic and social life of the inhabitants of the Coral Sea islands and all the South Seas. Representatives of Britain, the United States, Australia, New Zealand, France, and the Netherlands attended and set up a research council to carry on the work. The Native Welfare Commission will concern itself, among other things, with trade, finance, public works, housing, education, agriculture, and social welfare.

All this is a long cry from the days of the blackbirder: yet there are plenty of men alive today in Queensland and elsewhere who remember blackbirding. Twentieth-century progress has been fast, though as yet the Coral Sea knows no New Jerusalem, and Queiros's cathedral remains unbuilt on the

shores of his Great Bay. The Spanish discoveries in the Solomons now produce copra, which keeps a great soap-making
combine busily at work. The gold fields of New Guinea, all
but ruined by the Japanese, already have begun to yield again.
The ores of New Caledonia, the phosphate rock of Ocean
Island and Nauru, the timber riches of Vanikoro, the great
copra plantations, and the trochus beds, the pearl banks, the
fisheries of Torres Straits and the many islands—all these give
abundantly of their wealth once more.

Queiros was right, after all. Extravagant in his language he
may have been, but in his vision of great lands free and enlightened peoples might rise to live in amity and with faith, he
pointed the way along which the Melanesians and all the
peoples of the vast Pacific might travel. Much of the pioneering has been done. The temporary setback of a global war may
serve as a steppingstone upon the way, for its ordeal brought
spiritual gains and strengthening. For the first time, the enlightened white and the exploited black were equally imperiled,
and they rose to the challenge like men.

Yet there may be further challenges. There is no historical
precedent to bolster the illusion that a people as capable,
militaristic, and proud as the Japanese will be permanently
kept down by their first major defeat. Nothing is more certain
than that they will rise again; and there are other Pacific
Powers. There may well be further tests of the white man, in
the Coral Sea. The member nations of the South Seas Commission now hold infinite ability to mold these scattered territories into the "Great Land" which, more than three centuries ago, Pedro Fernandez Queiros dreamed they might become. The chance is theirs: they may not have it long.

EPILOGUE

In the distance, the blue mountains of Misima and the hills of Sudest stood like moored clouds upon the sharp horizon. The rollers of the Coral Sea thundered upon the outside beaches of the islets of Bramble Haven; through Jomard Passage the blue sea swept in strength. Along the beach, just above high-water mark, an industrious skink kept sharp lookout for sand hoppers and other marine minutiae which the incoming waves might bring within its reach, ready to dash from its crevice in the coral and seize a meal. In the woods behind the glossy skink, little geckos hurried on their soft pads in quest of insects. Out in the lagoon, the triangular fin of a lazy shark showed for a moment, breaking the green water greasily, with languor, as if the big-mouthed scavenger already felt the full heat of day and detested all effort. In the woods, pigeons flew, undisturbed by the drone of bombers' engines or the furious whine of dogfights in the sky. A shapeless, splintered piece of wood tossed fretfully in the light surf which broke on the coral rocks of Duperré; careful examination would show that it had once been part of a Japanese ramp. In the swamp, the tail of a metal airplane protruded incongruously, the once-red markings faded almost quite away, and vines and creepers all but covering it. The bleached bones lying half hidden nearby were not Melanesian.

The grass hut of the fishermen still stood in its clearing, now almost overgrown. Inside, an ancient radio stood unused in a corner, where the occupants had listened to broadcasts in pidgin English or in Motuan. Instead of *tabus* to warn off intruders, a note was pinned to the rough table.

"Away in Moresby for reestablishment training," it said.

In the lagoon and beneath the warm sea along the beaches, the industrious polyp continued his ageless work, away from those places where the rust of wrecks had polluted the surrounding waters. The minute marine animal continued weaving his fantastic designs in blues and greens and lovely whites, as if he had never been disturbed.

BIBLIOGRAPHY

LIST OF BOOKS CONSULTED

VOYAGES (*LISTED CHRONOLOGICALLY*)

1521: *The First Voyage Round the World, by Magellan,* edited by Lord
   Stanley of Alderley for the Hakluyt Society, London, 1874.

Early Sixteenth Century: *Discoveries of a World,* by Antonio Galvao, a
   reprint of Richard Hakluyt's translation of 1601, Hakluyt Society,
   London, 1862.

Early Sixteenth Century: *Early Voyages to Terra Australis,* edited by R. H.
   Major (and supplement, *On the Discovery of Australia by the Portuguese*), Hakluyt Society, London, 1859.

1568: *Discovery of the Solomon Islands, by Alvaro de Mendaña de Neyra
   in 1568,* in *The Discovery of the Solomon Islands,* 2 vols., edited by
   Lord Amherst of Hackney, Hakluyt Society, London, 1901.

1595–1606: *The Voyages of Pedro Fernandez de Queiros,* 2 vols., edited by
   Sir Clements Markham, Hakluyt Society, London, 1904.

1615–1617: *East and West Indian Mirror* (containing the *Australian Navigations Discovered by Jacob le Maire*), edited by J. A. J. de Villiers,
   Hakluyt Society, London, 1906.

1642–1644: *Abel Janszoon Tasman's Journal of His Discovery of Van
   Diemen's Land and New Zealand in 1642, with Documents Relating
   to His Exploration of Australia in 1644, in Which Are Added His
   Life and Labours,* with an English translation, J. G. Heeres, Amsterdam, 1899.

1690–1700: *New Voyage Round the World,* by William Dampier, 4 vols.,
   London, 1729. Also Dampier's *Voyages,* 2 vols., edited by John Mase-
   field, London, 1906.

1721–1722: *Tweejarige Reize Rondom de Wereld,* by Jacob Roggeveen,
   Dordrecht, 1728.

1764–1766: *A Voyage Round the World in H.M.S. Dolphin, etc., by an
   Officer on Board the Said Ship,* London, 1767. Also in Hawkesworth.

1766–1768: "An Account of a Voyage Round the World, etc., by Samuel Wallis, Captain, Royal Navy." In Hawkesworth's *Voyages and Discoveries in the Southern Hemisphere, etc.*, London, 1773.

1766–1769: *Voyage autour du Monde*, by L. A. de Bougainville, Neuchatel, 1772.

1768–1771: *A Journal of a Voyage Round the World*, by James Cook, R.N., London, 1771. Also in Hawkesworth.

1768–1771: *Journal of the Rt. Hon. Sir Joseph Banks During Captain Cook's First Voyage*, edited by Sir Joseph Hooker, London, 1896.

1769–1772: *Nouveau Voyage à la Mer du Sud, etc.*, Crozet, Paris, 1783 (Contains also M. de Surville).

1785–1788: *Voyage de La Pérouse autour du Monde*, Paris, 1797; London, 1798.

1787–1789: *A Voyage to the South Sea, etc.*, by William Bligh, London, 1792.

1790–1791: *Voyage of H.M.S. Pandora, etc.*, Edward Edwards and George Hamilton, London, 1915.

1796–1798: *A Missionary Voyage to the South Pacific Ocean . . . in the Ship Duff, etc.*, by James Wilson, London, 1799.

1800–1804: *A Voyage to Terra Australis*, by Matthew Flinders, Captain, R.N., London, 1814.

1895: *The Cruise of H.M.S. Challenger*, by W. J. Spry, R.N., F.R.G.S., London, 1895.

COLLECTIONS OF VOYAGES

A Chronological History of the Discoveries in the South Sea, or Pacific Ocean, 5 vols., by James Burney, London, 1803–1817.

An Account of Discoveries Made in the South Pacifick Ocean previous to 1764, by Alexander Dalrymple, London, 1767. Also by the same author: *An Historical Collection of the Several Voyages and Discoveries in the South Pacific Ocean*, 2 vols., London, 1770–1771.

Principal Navigations, by Richard Hakluyt, London, 1589.

Voyages and Discoveries in the Southern Hemisphere, by J. Hawkesworth, London, 1773.

Terra Australis Cognita, by John Callander, Edinburgh, 1766–1768.

A History of Geographical Discovery and Exploration, J. N. L. Baker, London, 1931.

THE NATIVE NAVIGATORS

"An Introduction to Polynesian Anthropology," by Te Rangi Hiroa (Peter H. Buck), Bishop Museum Bulletin 187, Honolulu, 1945.

Argonauts of the Western Pacific, by Bronislaw Malinowski, Routledge, Ltd., London, 1932.

Vikings of the Sunrise, by Te Rangi Hiroa (Peter H. Buck), New York, 1938.

"The Canoes of Polynesia, Fiji, and Micronesia," by James Hornell; also "Canoes of Oceania," by A. C. Haddon and James Hornell, Bishop Museum, Honolulu, Special Pub. 27, 1936.

The Raft Book, by Harold Gatty, New York, 1943.

BLACKBIRDING AND EARLY ADVENTURERS

Sailing the World's Edge, by Thomas Dunbabin, London, 1931.

Slavers of the South Seas, by Thomas Dunbabin, Sydney, 1935.

Bully Hayes, South Seas Pirate, by Basil Lubbock, London, 1931.

Bully Hayes, etc., by A. T. Saunders, Perth, Australia, 1932.

The South Sea Islanders and the Queensland Labour Trade, A Record of Voyages and Experiences in the Western Pacific from 1875 to 1891, by William T. Wawn, Master Mariner, London, 1893.

Deportation of South Sea Islanders, No. 399 of 1871.

Adventures on the Western Coast of South America, and the Interior of California: including a Narrative of Incidents at the Kingsmill Islands, New Ireland, New Britain, New Guinea, and other Islands in the Pacific Ocean, etc., 2 vols., by John Coulter, M.D., London, 1847.

"Government Gazette," Queensland, August 28, 1875.

"South Sea Papers" (British), London, 1873.

BIOGRAPHIES

Life of Captain Matthew Flinders, Royal Navy, by Ernest Scott, Sydney, 1914.

The Life of Ferdinand Magellan, by F. H. H. Guillemard, London, 1890.
William Dampier, by C. Wilkinson, London, 1929.
Captain James Cook, by Arthur Kitson, London, 1907.
Captain James Cook, by Surgeon Rear Admiral J. R. Muir, London, 1939.
Captain James Cook, by Maurice Thierry, London.
The Life of Francis Drake, by A. E. W. Mason, London, 1941.
Dictionary of National Biography, New York.

GENERAL

Official Year Book of the Commonwealth of Australia.
The Exploration of the Pacific, by J. C. Beaglehole, London, 1934.
Cook and the Opening of the Pacific, by J. A. Williamson, London, 1946.
The Background of Eastern Sea Power, by F. B. Eldridge, Melbourne, 1945.
Naval Tracts, by Sir William Monson, London, 1703.
A Short History of the World's Shipping Industry, by C. Ernest Fayle, London, 1933.
South Pacific Ocean Directory, by A. G. Findlay, 5th edition, London, 1884.
Pacific Islands Pilot, vol. i, with supplements, Hydrographic Department, Admiralty.
Pacific Islands Year Book, edited and compiled by R. W. Robson, Sydney, 1944; also in condensed form as *Pacific Islands Handbook,* New York, 1945.
The Making of Australasia, by Thomas Dunbabin, London, 1922.
The Discovery of Australia, by G. Arnold Wood, London, 1922.
The Dawn of Modern Geography, by C. R. Beazley, London, 1897–1906.
A History of Geographical Discovery in the Seventeenth and Eighteenth Centuries, by Edward Heawood, Cambridge, 1912.
Historical Records of Australia, 33 vols., Sydney, 1914–1925.
Murihiku, a History of the South Island of New Zealand, by Robert McNab, Wellington, 1909.
Charting a Continent, by Geoffrey C. Ingleton, Sydney, 1944.
Sir Joseph Banks, His Relations with Australia, by George MacKaness, Sydney, 1936.
The Early History of Tasmania, by R. W. Giblin, London, 1928.
Discoveries and Surveys in New Guinea, by J. Moresby, London, 1876.

The Mutiny and Piratical Seizure of H.M.S. Bounty, by Sir John Barrow, London, 1831; reprinted 1914, 1928, 1935, 1936.

Pinkerton's Voyages, vol. vii, which includes Kaempfer's "History of Japan."

The Portuguese Pioneers, by Edgar Prestage, London, 1930.

The Quest of Spices, by S. E. Howe, London, 1948.

Pacific Horizons, Christopher Lloyd, London, 1947.

WAR

"United States Navy: Report Covering Combat Operations up to March 1, 1944," by Admiral E. J. King, U.S.N., United States Navy Department, 1944.

"Ocean Front: the Story of the War in the Pacific 1941–44," Ministry of Information, London, 1945.

Ramparts of the Pacific, by H. Abend, New York, 1942.

"Among Those Present, the Official Story of the Pacific Islands at War," H. M. Stationery Office, London, 1946.

"Pacific Victory, a Short History of Australia's Part in the War Against Japan," by H. Buggy, Department of Information, Canberra, 1946.

"Post-War Defence of Australia," Melbourne Research Group, Melbourne, 1946.

Development and Welfare in the Western Pacific, by Hogbin and Wedgewood, Melbourne, 1946.

PUBLICATIONS

The Mariner's Mirror, the quarterly journal of the British Society for Nautical Research, Cambridge University Press, London.

The American Neptune, a quarterly journal of Maritime History, The American Neptune, Inc., Salem, Mass.

The Royal Geographical Journal, London.

The Pacific Islands Monthly, Sydney.

Sydney *Bulletin*.

Sydney *Morning Herald*.

Bulletin of the Melbourne Research Group, Australian Institute of International Affairs.

"New South Wales Votes and Proceedings."

INDEX

A

Aborigines, Australian, 46, 100, 240
Abreu, Antonio de, 59–61
Acapulco, 92
Achen, 144
Achowlia, a Lascar, 183, 184
Admiralty sends Dampier to Coral Sea, 142
Admiralty Islands, 163
Agulhas current, 140
Aicken (or Aiken), James, 226
Airlines, in Coral Sea area, 267
Albuquerque, Affonso de, 59–61
Aldeburgh, 264
Alexander VI, Pope, 63
Almirante, the, missing in Coral Sea, 82
  with Mendaña, 79
  with Queiros, 99
Alvaro de Mendaña (*see* Mendaña)
American Civil War, 240, 241
American Revolution, 174
American ship, first, at Sydney, 228
Americans, in New Guinea, 13
  at Santo, 115
Anaa Island, 103
Aneityum Island, 39, 40
Anglo-French condominium at New Hebrides, 17
Anson, Lord, 43, 44, 152
Antarctica, 96
Aogashima, 55
Arab with de Abreu expedition, 60
Arab dhow, 48
Arab pilot, Ibn Majid, 56
Arab sailors, experts at sailing against the wind, 33
  at New Guinea, 56
Arabs in Indian Ocean, 56
Arafura Sea, 221
Argonauts of the Western Pacific, 51
Argus, Melbourne, 253
Aru Islands, 56, 60
Ashmore, commander of ship *Hibernia,* 7
Assistant, the, 187
Astoria, the, 279

Atollon, description of, 24
Atolls, 10
  description of, 24
Australasia, New Zealanders object to use of word, 10
Australia, aborigines of, 46, 100, 240
  and blackbirders, 237–254
  Captain Cook at, 169–172
  early maps of, 57
  early voyages to, 61, 62
  escapes from, 220–225
  Father of, 241
  founding of, 189
  known to Portuguese, 57
  narrowly missed, by Spaniards, 74
    by Torres, 112
  probably known to Portuguese, 65
  Queiros's theories about, 95, 96
  threatened invasion of, 276
  visited by Portuguese, 61, 62
  voyage to, in *Joseph Conrad,* 66–67
Australian black no seaman, 120
Australian cruisers in Coral Sea, 274–276
Australian prospectors, gold found in New Guinea by, 265, 266
Australian troops, in fighting in New Guinea, 282
  occupation of Rabaul and Kokopo by, 257
  sent to North Africa, 270
Australians, in New Guinea, 13
Australia Pilot, Vol. III, description of the Coral Sea in, 9, 10
"Austrialia del Espiritu Santo," 106
Azores, 63

B

Balboa, 59
Bali, 60
Balolo, a Fijian fish, 8
Bananas from Fiji Islands, 12
Banda, 60
Bank of New South Wales, 241
Banks, Sir Joseph, 65, 216

120°
140°
160°
20°
20°
40°
LUZON
PHILIPPINE ISLANDS
CHINA SEA
SAMAR
MINDANAO
MARIANAS ISLANDS
TINIAN
GUAM
M I C R O
CAROLINE ISLANDS
HALMAHERA
MOLUCCAS
BORNEO
EQUATOR
M E L A N E
CELEBES
CERAM
ADMIRALTY IS.
BISMARCK ARCH.
NEW GUINEA
SOLOMON IS.
JAVA
TIMOR
ARAFURA SEA
TORRES STR.
LOUISIADE ARCH.
Gulf of Carpentaria
GREAT BARRIER REEF
CORAL SEA
AUSTRALIA
NEW HOLLAND
TASMAN SEA
INDIAN OCEAN
BASS STR.
TASMANIA